98

How Far Do You Wanna Go?

The True Story of the Man Who Turned 16 Inner City Kids Into A Team of Champions

Ramon "Tru" Dixon and David Aromatorio

New Horizon Press   Far Hills, NJ

Requests for permission should be addressed to:
New Horizon Press
P.O. Box 669
Far Hills, NJ 07931

Dixon, Ramon "Tru" and Aromatorio, Dave
    How Far Do You Wanna Go?
    The True Story of the Man Who Turned 16 Inner City
    Kids Into a Team of Champions

Library of Congress Catalog Card Number: Pending

ISBN: 0-88282-155-5

Interior Layout: Howard Simpson

New Horizon Press

Manufactured in the U.S.A.

2001 2000 1999 1998 1997 / 5 4 3 2 1

Contents

Authors' Note

These are the actual experiences of Ramon "Tru" Dixon. The personalities, events, actions and conversations portrayed within the story have been reconstructed from his memory, interviews, personal papers and the memories of participants. In an effort to safeguard the privacy of certain individuals, we have changed their names and, in some cases, altered otherwise identifying characteristics and chronology. Events involving the characters happened as described; only minor details have been altered.

The Next Level players and the authors of *How Far Do You Wanna Go* wish to thank the Pittsburg Pirates players and management for their support.

Prologue

Causes have many faces.

They might appear as the bloodied bodies of babies in the Oklahoma City rubble. Sometimes, the faces are ripped and mangled with pieces of steel painted blood red from a bus blown up during rush hour in London. Possibly the emaciated shapes belong to hungry children in the United States or underdeveloped countries, begging. Most causes have passion behind them. All need champions to promote and sustain them.

Ramon "Tru" Dixon's cause drove him to attempt a walk from his hometown of Pittsburgh, Pennsylvania to New York City. He left Pittsburgh the day after Thanksgiving, November 27, 1995, a time when winter had not yet officially arrived but was charting a frigid course. There was no doubt that bitterly cold days lay ahead, that the weather would not be an ally.

Topography would be no friend, either. Western Pennsylvania, where the trip began is hilly. The rest of Pennsylvania and the small portion of his route in New York

State is mountainous.

However, Dixon's commitment to his goal pulled him up a seemingly endless number of steep inclines. Desire to make a difference made him brave freezing temperatures and push forward. Belief in his cause gave him strength to walk alone when his partner, Bart Hanks, got sick and had to pull out three days into the journey. As Tru trudged on, he sought help from others to make his dream become a reality.

Tru noticed the white Toyota truck pass him and then pass him again as he trudged along a country road in central Pennsylvania. Each time, the truck slowed and then started up again, until the driver finally pulled to a stop beside him. "Can I give you a lift, buddy?" the man said as he leaned across the cab and rolled down the slightly frosted window on the passenger side of the truck.

"Thanks, partner, but no, I'm just walking," replied Tru.

"My name is Joe. Listen, no disrespect intended, but I believe it would be in your best interest to get in the car, man. Seriously."

Tru's eyes caught the silver glint of a rifle mounted on the rear cab window in the stranger's truck. That was reason number one not to get into the cab. Reason two was the owner of the gun was white, and Tru was black.

He did not need a reason three.

"No, thanks, man. I really can't."

"Please just get in the truck so I can explain."

For some reason, looking at Joe's plain, honest face, Tru felt the truck driver was the kind of person you could believe in.

"What's up, man?" Tru asked. "What's the problem?"

"Well, I don't know exactly how to put this and I hope you don't take offense, but here it is," Joe said, fidgeting. "A couple of weeks ago a truck driver got killed around here. In fact, just right up this road. Seems a carload of colored kids followed him up to the rest stop and when he got out of his truck, they just shot him dead—in front of about thirty people."

"Why?"

"All they said was he had given them the finger or something. I guess they thought he was trying to cut them off. I don't know. It's just crazy. Anyway, folks around here ain't lookin' too friendly on your kind these days. I just thought if I could give you a lift to Mechanicsburg or somewhere it might save you from a problem you don't need."

"Oh, I see." Tru nodded, his face serious. "Thanks, man, but I really need to do this walk."

"Where are you goin' anyway?"

"Started in Pittsburgh and I'm headin' to New York City."

"Why the hell would anyone in their right mind do that, and in the winter to boot?"

"Well, I don't know about the right mind part, but I do know why I'm doin' it." Tru smiled. "Kids. Might just be the same kind of kids you described, only they are still savable. These kids were part of a Little League baseball team I coached this past summer, and I have a dream for them."

"That's cool, but what does walking all the way to New York have to do with it?" Joe pulled the truck back onto the road.

"This dream needs money. You know, we have become a society either waiting for someone else to solve our problems, or not believing they can be solved. Talking about problems gets politicians elected, gets officials more titles. But I want to get something done. We owe that to each other and the kids. They're so confused, man. Look at what they did to that truck driver. That happens every day in my neighborhood. We're losin' them, man. We can't keep blaming them for the way things are today and expect that if we tell them how they should act it will be enough. It wasn't enough when you or I were kids. What makes us think it will be enough for them today?"

"Okay, but how are you goin' to help them?"

I want to build a combination sports/academic complex for thousands of inner city kids headed for gangs and worse. If it takes me walkin' five hundred miles in the winter to find people to help, so be it."

"Is someone paying you to walk to New York, or what?" Joe said smiling.

"I knew that was coming," Tru said, shaking his head and smiling too. "I've sold my Jeep, pawned my jewelry, gotten rid of everything of value and moved back in with my mom to finance this trip. I'm trying to help kids who never got a break man, it's as simple as that. You gotta be able to lay yourself on the line if you want them to. There have been people, including the kids I'm on this walk for, that have laid it on the line for me. It's just time for me to ante up."

"Most of our kids around here are pretty respectful, their parents see to that," replied Joe from across the cab of his truck as they approached the borough of Greason. "Of course, this is a small town. It ain't near anywhere but everyone knows everyone. We kinda look out for each other. It ain't perfect, but. . . ."

"That's cool, but that's your place. It's just not like that in my city. There, a lot of kids get into gang life at ten, some have no homes, some are abandoned by their fathers, some by their mother. No disrespect, but I'm not on this walk for your kids. My kids need help badly and that's what really matters to me."

"Well, there probably ain't too many people that would do what you're doing, ah, what's your name?"

"It's Ramon Dixon but my friends call me "Tru.""

"I'd like to shake your hand if I wasn't driving. You're one of the good guys."

"You too, Joe," Tru replied. "I wish we could talk more, but I have to get back on the road." Joe protested but stopped the truck near the curb and turned off the engine.

"Are you sure you'll be okay?"

"Thanks for your concern, Joe, but I'll be all right," Tru said. As he opened the door and began to climb down, Joe handed him a twenty dollar bill.

"For the kids, Tru. I'm not sure you can succeed, but you have a good plan, be careful and hey, your 'hick' friend Joe will be prayin' for you."

"Thanks, man, for the prayers and money. You take care of your family now, hear." Tru replied as he waved goodbye.

Joe did not start the truck engine right away. He watched Tru as he shivered when the wind struck his face. Tru shouted through the window, "Does it ever get above zero around here this time of year?"

"Hell no!"

Tru laughed and a stream of cold smoke-like steam poured out of his mouth. It was not the first time he had encountered either freezing weather or skepticism and it was not the first time he had overcome them. He had not let that deter him in the past and he surely would not now. He was determined to go on. Harrisburg, the state capital fifteen miles to the northwest, was his next stop. His stride leaving the truck was stronger than ever. As he walked deeper into the barren countryside, he fell deeper into thought until he was consumed by memories of the place that began his journey and the events that had changed his life.

Chapter 1

Talk the Talk

Beads of sweat were accumulating on seventeen-year-old Ramon Dixon's upper lip as he blew on the dice in his hands.

"Seven, baby, sweet seven. Powww, talk to me now!" he urged the lifeless ivories as he threw them to the curb.

It seemed every August night was the same—hot and humid. Each of those nights, Ramon Dixon and his boys hung out on a street corner near his house shooting dice. Ramon's white tank top clung to his muscular, tawny body. Tonight was not his night: it was too damn humid.

"I can't roll in shit like this," he complained to one of his boys. "I need some wine, any damn way."

He stepped aside and leaned against a graffiti-covered wall. Looking down on empty Frankstown—no one ever said "road" when referring to the main drag of Homewood, one of Pittsburgh's eastern neighborhoods—Tru kicked his wine back. He peeled his shirt off in hopes some fine young ladies would be driving by looking for someone to talk to. His well-defined biceps shone from the combination of streetlight and sweat.

"Yo, little man, let me have the drink," said the big 'brother' standing next to him. When Ramon did not respond, he repeated, "Yo, little man, what the fuck's wrong wit' you? Can't your scrawny ass hear? I said give me your damn wine!"

Is this dude talking to me? Ramon wondered. *I guess his ass don't know who he's talkin' to. Shit, I ain't giving up my wine to nobody.*

"Nah, man, you can't have none of this wine," Ramon answered. Who did this dude think he was, some punkass dexter? Even way back at Sterrett Junior High, Ramon was "the shit." Not only was he smart—only the smart kids got to represent their school on Channel Four's *Junior High Quiz*— but he was cool. You don't want to have the reputation as being only smart, especially in junior high, because, after all, girls preferred cool to smart.

Ramon's chuckle turned into a full-blown laugh. "It looks like you had too much wine and beer already, man. Your fat ass don't need none of mine."

Though Ramon was with the in-crowd and had already gotten into some trouble hanging out with them. His single mother and grandmother, whom he respected more than anyone, had insisted on monitoring his schooling. "We're not having no more dropouts," they said again and again. It had been the junior high principal who persuaded Ramon it was in his best interest to transfer to Taylor Allderdice High School. Taylor Allderdice, although most locals never included the Taylor, was located in Squirrel Hill, a large mostly white city neighborhood to the west of

Homewood. Most of the students who attended the school came from the Greenfield, Hazelwood, and Shadyside neighborhoods, and the majority were the sons and daughters of steelworkers.

When he transferred to Allderdice, Ramon spent his first two years establishing his reputation. It was not easy. He'd had one in the inner city from which he'd come, but here tough steelworkers produced tough kids. Fistfights were the means of survival. Grades were not.

Meanwhile, though he hung around with schoolmates during the day, nights and weekends were spent in his own neighborhood with "the boys", many of whom had dropped out of school and gotten into other things—some legal, some not. He'd already gotten into trouble once, but luckily his clean records and sports activity saved him. By the time he was a junior, with the aid of good genes, weights and constant exercise, Ramon became a ripped, six-foot-one, two-hundred-ten pound dude who by those that usually looked for fights as someone not to mess with. His friends on the football team had finally talked him into playing. Since the Pittsburgh Public Schools required all athletes to maintain a 2.0 grade point average, Ramon, who had been tagged as smart without much effort at his previous schools, came to care about his grades even though caring wasn't often translated into attainment or study, which interfered with his after school social life. Despite this, Ramon made All-City as a tight end. At seventeen, he had left Allderdice when his grades fell and transferred to Wilkinsburg High. Where lax standards allowed him once again to play ball.

He grinned now, looking at his friend.

"What the hell you laughing at, Ray? You shootin' or

what, man?"

"Shut up before I kick your ass, man. Give me the damn dice." Ramon spoke with a hint of joking in his voice, but also with enough cockiness that said he might just do it.

The muggy night continued with all the usual shit-talking, mosquito-biting, and gnat-buzzing that only summer nights in Pittsburgh can bring.

Nobody really lives in *Pittsburgh*.

People live in neighborhoods, the living, breathing lifelines of the city. Pittsburgh gained its strength from the people that lived in the sturdy homes and the ties that bound all of its neighborhoods. Pride drove men from Brookline, Sheraden and Beltzhoover to pour their sweat into the steel mills that belched smoke. In every corner of the city, fairly paid workers from Carrick, Arlington and Garfield pulled double shifts supplying a growing nation with the steel for its skyscrapers and bridges, and to put food on their tables. In North Side, Lawrenceville and Oakland, the workers redoubled their efforts and smiled at noon when there was so much darkness in the sky it looked like midnight. They were grateful the mills were operating and people were working.

Scenes of young guys shooting dice were being played out all across the city's streets. Lightning bugs put on their fire show, chirping crickets drowned out noise from the J&L Steel Mill, car horns honked as drivers navigated the city's narrow roads, distant whistles of trains and barges sounded as they transported the products of Pittsburgh's labor across the country. And people sat out on their porches.

"Must be break-time," a voice said from the stillness as the mill's whistle called out in the night.

"I think Jimmy's on tonight, ain't he?" replied

another nameless voice in the darkness.

The crack of thunder interrupted them. A car pulled up next to the curb. The wind trailing the white Cadillac swept across Ramon's damp face as the car came to a stop. No one had ever heard of a drive-by shooting in those days, so Ramon and his boys were unalarmed.

"Are you Ramon Dixon?"

A bald, perspiring stranger strode up to the porch. "Are any of you boys Ramon Dixon? I was told he might be over here."

"Yeah, mister. I'm Ramon. Who wants to know?"

The man replied, "My name is Sam Braxton, son. I've seen you play football. You play pretty good, and I've got a proposition for you." He kept his eyes on Ramon's face, seeing he'd piqued interest. Sam Braxton continued, "I went to a university in Kentucky: Kentucky State University in Frankfurt. You probably have never heard of it, huh, son? Anyway, the point is, I still have some contacts down there. I think you can help their football team, if you're interested, that is. If you are, come to my house at nine tomorrow morning and I'll make a couple of phone calls, and we'll see what happens. What do you say, son?"

"My grades are okay, but they ain't good enough for college, mister," Ramon said.

"You let me worry about your high school grades. You just take care of business when you get to Frankfurt, all right?" Sam said.

Ramon stared at him. He had never really considered where his life would lead him.

"Okay, mister, I'll be there, but" Ramon slowly replied. Out of the darkness a police car siren cut off his words. The next morning, his future was decided. He would attend Kentucky State.

The first college football practice Ramon felt good in his team uniform. Among the other players on the squad he particularly noticed Kevin Coles. Coles was the biggest linebacker Ramon had ever seen. He was at least six-feet-five and a good two hundred and forty pounds. Worse, Kevin was the ugliest. His huge head stood above his teammates. It was the biggest blockhead Ramon had ever seen. You couldn't tell if the guy had a helmet on or not. His forehead seemed to stick out a good two inches farther than it should. Veins right in the middle showed the blood pulsating under his skin. One hour into that first practice, old bighead laid out a teammate with a ferocious hit that Ramon heard at the other end of the field.

"You just got dicked, boy," the crazed linebacker roared as he stood over his victim. "Don't never come into this 'hood again, cause I'm a true blue dick!"

The receiver lay motionless on the high summer grass. When he was finally helped to his feet, he went over to Head Coach Leroy Smith and traded eighty-eight, his offensive number, the one he had chosen because he liked Lynn Swann of the Pittsburgh Steelers, for a defensive back's number. Kevin's hit changed the receiver's life: he never again caught the ball for the Kentucky State Thoroughbreds.

The silence that had consumed the practice field while he lay unconscious was now replaced by murmuring.

"Who is that cat, man? Damn, that dude is bad. You see that shit, man?"

Some players remained silent. Some gave that laugh you give when you are scared out of your mind, but don't want it to show. Most of the team realized they had found a leader.

Looking on, Ramon was impressed and he was also energized. He wanted to see just how tough that bighead was. Later on at practice, Ramon got his chance. Ramon, catching a pass over the middle, knew a collision was coming. Instead of tensing his body to take the hit, he relaxed and tried to deliver it. The smack of two heads butting together was, in every sense of the word, violent.

"I can catch and take a hit, dude. I come through whatever 'hood I want," taunted Ramon as he jumped up and returned to the huddle.

Kevin the Blockhead smiled. "Nice hit, bro." He patted Ramon on his butt and went back to the defensive huddle.

Kevin and Ramon soon became friends. Actually they became soul mates. They somehow knew, from that first day on the football field, that they were about the same things. Later they discovered they came from the same Pittsburgh neighborhood.

The two young men came to think of themselves as true brothers. As roommates, for the first time in either of their lives, they were able to talk with all barriers dropped.

"You are a warrior, bro," Kevin always told Ramon. "You have the knowledge, man. Don't let nobody stop you. This world is a hard mother. *To survive it, you gotta be true to yourself.*"

"After I get out of this place, bro, I'm gonna be the shit," Ramon responded as if he saw his whole life unfolding in front of him. "Get me a 350 SL with some babe-els and live large, Kev, that's what's up."

The truths in their lives, what they believed in their

heart of hearts, could only be spoken of in the confines of their dormitory room. Inside that room, they shared almost everything. It was the only place they could be themselves, the only place where things were not said or done to get a predetermined response from some third party.

Outside, they played at being "pimp daddies." They would dress to the nines, walk the cool walk, talk the cool talk. After all, you never knew when there might be some fine young lady in need of attention.

When a third person entered their private world, they put into effect their rules of engagement. Never admit you were wrong, for that was a sign of weakness. Never show humility, for that showed you cared. Never work for something, for that showed you did not know how to take whatever you wanted.

One of the few things Kevin and Ramon did not bother with at Kentucky State was study time. Neither placed too much importance on his chosen curriculum, and by the end of their first semester, Ramon and Kevin were placed on academic probation. By the end of their third semesters, the two roommates had flunked out. They returned to Pittsburgh and told their friends they had quit because the coaches at Kentucky had shown favoritism.

"Would you sit behind some dude you knew you were better than?" they said to their friends. "Besides, Penn State was telling us they want both of us to come play up there. Hell, man, Joe Paterno and the Nittany Lions. I can see that. We'll probably take a year off, you know, just get ourselves together, work out. Gotta be ready when we go up there, you know what I'm sayin'."

Quitting was always easy to explain. When you came

from the ghetto people expected you to quit.

One year after they returned home, Kevin was shot and killed in a backyard argument over pit bull puppies.

With the death of his only close friend, part of Ramon also died. As a testimonial to Kevin and their true brother-hood, he added the name "Tru" to his given name: he promised himself to follow Kevin's advice—*always be true to yourself.*

Thoughts of suicide even entered his mind. These kinds of thoughts were only supposed to happen to other people, Tru thought, not to solid, good-looking men who have the ability to steal people's hearts. The thoughts were there, however. He could not deny them.

He started to go out on job interviews, but after each interview, his feelings of inadequacy only became stronger. He was beginning to realize he had nothing to offer that the business world wanted.

Each interviewer asked, "What is your degree in?"

Each time Tru sat there and, for an instant, he was not inside his body. It was like he was a spectator at an execution in slow-motion, where you could see the terror on the face of the victim.

"I have no degree," Tru always said. Then he always added, "But I can do this job if you would give me the chance."

The interviewer always replied, "Sorry. We need to see your credentials."

Tru's conviction and self-image grew weaker every time. His words grew more pathetic, his fears about his own inadequacy haunted him.

Night after night he sat watching the television blare meaningless babble. He looked endlessly through the yearbooks from Kentucky State. Nights now seemed just as bleak as they were years before when he had hung out on the corners in Homewood. The difference was in high school he could hide his insecurities by drinking wine and acting tough. Now his insecurities could not be hidden. In his mind he heard his old friends from college laughing at him as he looked at their graduation pictures. He knew he was smarter than some of them, but they had hit the books and he hadn't.

One night looking at the yearbook, he came across another student with the same last name. An idea hit him, an idea born of desperation. *Employers want a degree. I'll get a damn degree.* Tru was not sure what kind of student this Travis Dixon had been, but Tru was quite sure he had to have been better than Tru was, and he had a diploma.

The next morning he telephoned the registrar at Kentucky State and asked for a copy of Travis Dixon's transcripts and his degree. "They were lost in my recent move," Tru explained.

"You need to send a request for these items, Travis, along with a five dollar processing fee," the clerk on the other end of the line said. "After we receive those, please allow three or four weeks to receive the transcripts and degree copies."

It was an agonizing wait. When finally Tru received the documents, he went right to work. Using his self-taught but excellent computer skills, he produced more copies. They were almost as good as the originals. Tru had noticed that most employers just glanced at applicants' records anyways. He had some ammunition now, and for the first time since Kevin's death he had some hope.

Armed with the fictitious records, Tru began to apply

for the types of jobs that had a future.

"What's your degree in, Mr. Dixon?"

"Business administration, sir."

In December of 1985, Tru began formal training with United Computer Technologies. The training lasted six weeks and then he began his job with the research department in the Programming Division. He wasn't nervous. He had his foot in the door and he believed success lay on the other side. Tru now actually believed that he had graduated college with a degree in Business Administration.

Unknown to Tru, United Computer Technology had and has a policy of doing background checks on all employees. These checks are done with great detail and as expediently as possible. Until completed, the employee is considered to be on an interim basis. Each passing day, Tru believed, gave him time to establish himself as the best and most productive worker at the Pittsburgh office of the company. The background check on Tru, because of a large backlog, was not completed until nearly six months after his employment began.

One day as Tru sat at his desk working on a project, his boss threw some papers down in front of him. "Ray, tell me this is a mistake."

Bob O'Keefe was a longtime company man. He had risen to the position of Director of Corporate Programming by playing by the rules. When Bob had received the report on Tru, he was bewildered. He had never known employee checks to have mistakes, but how in the world could his highest producer be a liar? Nevertheless, he had to confront him.

Tru took a deep breath and said, "It's not a mistake, Bob."

"You're kidding me, right? Huh? Do you know what is going to happen to you, Ray? It's over. Shit, I don't believe this!" Bob's voice grew loud as his anger and disappointment grew. "Who the hell do you think you are, man? Holy shit, I thought I'd seen about everything. How the hell did you pull this off?"

Tru told him everything. He did not believe it would matter, since he was going to be fired whether he kept silent or spoke out. Had Tru thought for a second that it would have mattered, he probably would have lied again.

"I'm sorry, Bob," he finished. "I'll clean out my desk."

The other man grimaced. "Well, Ray, I'm sorry too. I guess there is not a whole lot more to say," Bob added more quietly now. "I wish there was something I could do for you."

Tru returned to his desk and began to remove his files and personal belongings, throwing them into an empty carton on the floor. He thought back to when he and Kevin had returned from flunking out of Kentucky State and the stories they had made up to save face with their friends. He wondered what he would tell to hide this new failure. Tru wasn't in self-denial. He realized a lot of things about himself that most people camouflaged. Tru wished he could change something, anything, although he knew if he had to do it all over again, he would have played the game the same way. Tru didn't wonder what that made him: he knew. A liar. A conniver. A person who couldn't be counted on to tell the truth. He winced. There couldn't be a lower place than where he was at that moment. He stood up and prepared to leave.

"Hold on, Ray," Bob said.

Bob was standing a few feet away, as if unable to leave. "I'm going to do something crazy," he said. "I can't believe I'm saying this. Let me make a couple of phone calls. I'll see if there's anything I can do."

"Bob, I don't know what to say." Tru looked at the other man, feeling choked up.

"Don't say thanks yet, Ray. I haven't done anything yet."

Tears began to form in Tru's eyes.

"No, Bob," Tru said quietly. "Thanks for trying, man." He knew if Bob succeeded, his days of hanging out were over. It was time to assume responsibility. Payback time.

In fact, Bob O'Keefe did succeed in preventing United from firing Tru. During the next few years, Ramon Tru Dixon became a star performer for the company. On July 11, 1988, he received a special achievement award for outstanding performance of duties and valuable contributions to the improvement and efficiency of the Department of Programming. In 1989 he received another award and was appointed an assistant programmer in the Pittsburgh office. Later that year he was given a bonus under a new performance management system that rewarded workers for contributions to the success of the company.

Tru had created several innovative programs for United Computer Technologies, including wage and hour summary sheets for employers to use and several wage transcription and computation programs. This time his computer skills served him well and for all the right reasons. Tru Dixon had become a contributing member of society and he was not about to lose ground. People had taken a chance on him and he had not let them down. He forged ahead.

It was during this period that he met a pretty, young woman who also worked at the company, and they married.

Now he fit the picture of a company man. The American Dream.

However, during the next two years, despite this picture perfect image, he felt somehow uneasy. Neither his job nor his marriage created the fulfillment for which he had so long searched.

By 1991 his wife, disillusioned by his discontent, left him. Tru quit his job. He knew giving up was wrong for him but he felt discouraged and depressed. He moved to a small apartment and was alone again.

This was a dark period in which he once again felt himself to be a personal and professional failure. He wondered when, if ever, he would find the right path.

Deciding that big companies were not for him, Tru began to form a small business of his own, Tru/Dix Inc., a computer consulting firm. He worked out of his cramped apartment. Nevertheless, people were well satisfied with the work he did. Soon Tru had little time for moroseness or pensiveness. His business consumed every waking hour.

Every night he was so tired he fell into a dreamless sleep, and every morning he got up to begin again. Only now he was his own boss and he felt, at least, some satisfaction in that role.

Chapter 2

Battleground

It was one of those summer days that make people find a reason to be outside. The sun shone like a spotlight inviting performers. Enormous billowing clouds floating across a sea of aquamarine gave refreshing shade. The wind occasionally and with precisely the right playful attitude blew through the green fullness of the oak and maple trees along the sidewalk. Streets came alive with Pittsburgh residents who had lived through a dark cold winter and now tried to soak in every ounce of sunlight, feel every caress of the wind and store in their minds' eyes every hue of the colors that surrounded them.

To Tru Dixon, who had for so long kept his mind riveted on his computer business, this was not simply a beautiful afternoon, but an event. Suddenly feeling liberated, he left work and got into his cherry red Jeep. He put the top down. Kenny G was blasting on his one-thousand-watt, six-disc CD changer, fourteen speaker system. He began driving with no destination in mind, absorbing the warmth and the scenery.

As he drove the feeling of freedom filled him.

Somehow he had shaken off the moodiness which had afflicted
him after leaving his job at United Computer and let go of his
sorrow about his divorce after two years of marriage. Today, he
was living again. And it felt great.

Part of the reason was he'd recently met someone
new, Tonya McCoy, a beautiful young woman with tawny skin
and black hair. She had a son and Tru loved kids. Lance had
just completed fifth grade. Lance did not do as well in school
as Tonya thought he could and should. Tru hoped he and the
boy would become friends. He planned to help Lance with his
homework during the next school year.

Also, Tru/Dix Inc., his new business, was becoming
more successful. His various clients employed him to use his
computer skills to set up and maintain their computer systems.
He also had a teaching component to his business and would
train workers how to run the new system. Occasionally, Tru
would write programs for various aspects of the businesses of
his clients. Tru's income had reached the level it was during
his years with United, and he realized, looking around on this
sunshine filled day, that his life was looking a lot better too.

However, it was hard for Tru to relax; his mind spun
in constant motion. As he drove past his old neighborhoods,
the sights and sounds brought back the past. He frowned as he
drove past the littered, grassless Ammons Park in the Hill
District and saw kids throwing baseballs mostly at and not to
each other. He remembered how he had used a fake address
after he left Allderdice High, so he could enroll at Wilkinsburg
High and play ball again.

" Let me run up past that damn high school's field,"

Tru murmured. The quickest way to get over to Wilkinsburg' s Turner Field from where he was in the Hill District (a large African-American neighborhood located next to downtown Pittsburgh) would be to go through East Liberty, Homewood, and the small easternmost neighborhood of East Hills. Tru headed in that direction.

Looking around at the decaying old neighborhood, he was startled.

Once, for the people living in these tightly packed wooden-frame homes, things here had been poor but passable, but in the 1980s, the back-to-work calls for the steelworkers had never come. As the mills closed, people lost their identities and way of life.

" Laid off? When do you think they'll hire you back?" was the question heard throughout these once smoke-filled streets. Most everyone's dad, grandpa, or, as in Tru's case, uncle, had worked in the steel mills.

" Probably before Christmas," his uncle said. " I figure we'll need to get inventory up for the spring, so it shouldn't be much longer than that" was the confident response. "We'll just have to tighten our belts a little. It'll be all right."

The back to work calls never came. The neighborhoods Tru had known disappeared. Environmental concerns became a priority. The quality of air in Pittsburgh was improving dramatically but, unfortunately, the quality of life was not. The closing of the steel mill meant that workers, who had once been able to adequately support their families, now fell into poverty.

No neighborhoods were more adversely affected than

East Liberty, Homewood, and East Hills, which lie adjacent to each other on the city's east side. These closely knit communities contained a majority of the young black population. In the mid-eighties, though it was first denied by city officials, a gang problem became evident. East Coast gangs were now emulating the West Coast's violent Crips and Bloods, as drug-dealing neighborhood gangs continued the West's violent feud and created a new problem for old and young.

These gangs were becoming the families most of the kids didn't have. Because of this, their allegiance was first to the gang. It was not only the parentless situation in the ghetto which prompted kids to join these groups. Many talented teenagers became gang members because the money they made from the sale of 'crack' and 'weed' was so easy that they didn't have time to waste going to school or playing ball games. In addition to dimming the kids' futures, these gangs also had dire effects on businesses in the neighborhoods.

Sears had been the center of East Liberty until the proprietors were forced to desert the Penn Avenue location because of the prevalence of shoplifting. When the first item each business must purchase is a set of iron bars to cover its windows, other business locations in other areas quickly become more popular. Now Larimer Avenue's buildings were deserted and splattered by messages from the Crips gang. Obscene words also splattered the fronts of the few businesses which remained open. No one was seen on these streets wearing the red colors of Peabody High School. Peabody, once one of the city's better schools, was now a war zone. In the winter, East Liberty became a firetrap, but these fires were not the tree and brush variety.

They were the apartment kind. Defective stoves cooked food by day, heated apartments and burned buildings by night. Firefighters did not respond to East Liberty calls as quickly as they might other places. By the end of the 1980's, East Liberty contained Pittsburgh's most brutal streets.

On them, drive-by shootings were a usual occurrence whenever a member of a gang flashed a sign at another or when some gang members felt they are being 'dissed' (disrespected) by another group. For instance, if a 'dis' happened in Wilkinsburg, a gang member would go out and shoot up. Homewood and the Homewood kids would reciprocate and do the same thing to the Wilkinsburg kids. Then the East Hills kids, who have an affiliation with the East Liberty and Garfield kids, would do drive-bys against the Larimer Avenue kids.

It all amounted to the dumbest, most unnecessary and senseless waste of life. When kids kill one another and this isn't unusual in these neighborhoods, lives are lost before they have begun. Many times an innocent person was caught in the cross-fire or a child was picked out at random for a sick initiation just because he or she was wearing a certain color. These children were being raised on a battlefield or a war zone in their own neighborhoods, unable to do simple things such as walking the streets or wearing the color of their choice without looking over their shoulders.

Homewood's best known street, Frankstown Road, had seen it all: active high-rise offices and now boarded up deserted buildings, children on swings in the park and kids killing kids, people washing shiny new cars and cars mutilated by bullets. Frankstown is the main drag through perhaps the city's roughest neighborhood. To the kids living here,

America, land of dreams and prosperity, meant nothing. To the adults, it was a fading memory. Homewood kids went to Westinghouse High School which they called The House. The tough gangs in Homewood set all the boundaries. If you lived on Susquehanna Street, you were not welcome on parts of Frankstown; if you lived near Hunter Park in Wilkinsburg, you watched your back when near Tioga Street. If you lived on Sterrett Street, you definitely didn't wander onto North Dallas Avenue if you didn't want to get stabbed or shot.

East Hills still had some decent residential and business sections. A main winding hilly road passed through them as well as directly in front of East Hills Elementary School. At the top of the hill there were forty acres of abandoned, desecrated land, the former East Hills Shopping Center. What was striking on the approach from either the Penn Hills or Wilkinsburg side, was the sense of emptiness. Buildings that once housed a Giant Eagle supermarket as well as numerous other clothing and specialty shops, were now barren. Only a liquor shop and a tire store shared this ghost town. The bright tan brick buildings that were once centers of activity now became dingy centers for graffiti. What had been shop windows were now dark holes with broken glass covered by plywood. It looked and felt like a battleground, because it had become one. For a stretch of one hundred yards or more, the pavement resembled an old country dirt road with varying sizes of broken-up concrete instead of dirt. Not many Pittsburghers traveled this road anymore—it was too dangerous. In fact, it was nearly a place that no longer existed, unless you happened to be a member of the East Hills Bloods.

Tru had always driven quickly by the area, never noticing the deprivation that had transformed his old neighborhood. Now he realized how different life was for him than for the people walking these streets.

As he came up East Hills Drive past the empty shopping center, he stopped the Jeep and got out to see the scene more closely. He lifted one muscular leg onto the roll bar and stared at the destruction.

"What a damn waste," he murmured, staring at the graffiti-covered walls. *Look at this. What the hell is wrong with these damn kids. What the hell is wrong with their parents, letting their kids do this? Damn, man.*

Now a contributing member of society, Tru became more and more angry as he noticed every broken piece of glass, the obscene writing sprayed on walls, the young dudes smoking or shooting up with their pants hanging down somewhere below their asses. He felt no part of all this. *If these damn people would only be responsible for themselves, none of this shit would happen. Hey, if they want to act like animals then they can live like them too—that's on them. Hell, we all struggle out here, but most people work for what they want. These damn people want shit handed to them and they hand out shit. They don't want to work. Nah, it's not about feeling sorry for any of these people. They can all kiss my behind.*

Tru climbed back into his Jeep to continue his drive.

He told himself he had no responsibility for what caused the destruction, but his conscience still bothered him. Had he been that blind for the nearly twenty years since he'd graduated from high school? Was he so caught up in his own life that he could not see the wasteland all around him?

Chapter 3

Games and Graffiti

As the Jeep approached Turner Field from the cobblestone road called Laketon, Tru felt depressed again. Looking straight ahead, he saw a bunch of kids playing baseball. He idled the car and felt a little better watching the boys, remembering the days when he'd played ball. Most of his baseball memories began on this field—the game now going on would take his depression away, he hoped. It would be a kick to check out some of the young bucks who were coming up, just to see if there was any talent here.

Tru pulled his Jeep behind the bleachers. Heads turned at the loud sounds of Kenny G announcing Tru's presence. Tru turned off the engine and thought he would watch a couple of innings from his Jeep, but then he saw that two of his old friends, Marcus Savin and DeWayne Perkins, were coaching the two teams. He couldn't pass up the opportunity to watch them.

Getting out of the Jeep, Tru approached the wooden bleachers behind the players' bench on the third base line. It saddened him to see only seven adults in attendance. He thought back to his youth and wondered whether his memories of packed bleachers were true or not. He moved to a spot farther down the left field line close to the players' bench and away from the other adults. "Come on, you rookies," he called out.

"What's up, bro?" A surprised Marcus Savin looked towards Tru and suddenly recognized him. "What in the hell brings you over here?"

"Nothin', man. I was just cruisin' and I thought it'd be fun to check out some of the local talent. When I saw it was you and DeWayne coachin' I had to kick it for a minute. You dudes still rivalin', huh? What's up with that, man?" Tru said grinning. "Which one is your kid, man?"

"He's at short. You know a Savin gotta be in the middle of the action," Marcus said with the pride a father is supposed to feel about his offspring. "Stick around, man. I'll check you out after we kick some butt. All right?"

"I'm not going anywhere, aren't you counting your chickens a little early now?" Tru said laughing a little. He couldn't help thinking about the sights he'd seen earlier. He figured that if a lot of the dads whose kids were on the other end of the spray paint cans could find more time to spend with their kids on fields like this, most of that graffiti wouldn't have happened.

"Yo, Marc, what's the inning and score, man?"

"Ah, I think it's the top of the third and we're up by four or five. Perk's squad is rebuilding this year—just like every other damn year," Marcus laughed as he headed back to the coaching box on the third base line. "We'll see if we can get you some more, man."

As the game continued, Tru started to hear the adults angrily calling out to the players and coaches. This was not a happy group of parents watching their kids play America's favorite pastime. These people were arguing viciously about everything from the length of time it had already taken to complete "three lousy innings" to the fact that "this damn coach" did not "know what the hell he was doing." Tru sat there trying to figure out what was wrong with them. *If they know this game so well, why aren't they out there?*, he thought. The only prerequisite for being a coach was a willingness to put in the time, and at least Marcus and DeWayne were willing to do that much.

In the bottom of the third, Perk's team was about to come up for their turn at the plate when one kid's leatherclad mom stood up and hollered, "Boy, you better run your ass on and off that field and stop your damn moping before I come over there and kick your little behind right there on the field."

Tru could tell by the boy's complete lack of a reaction that this was not the first time his mother had criticized and humiliated him publicly. Tru wondered if this woman had any idea what a negative message she was delivering to her son and about him to all the other eight-to-ten-year-olds who were on Turner Field that hot June day.

Tru kept telling himself to keep his damn mouth shut. He knew it was none of his business—but his naturally open manner urged him to speak out. Nevertheless, he kept quiet, watching and listening.

Every play, someone said something negative. Parents shouted insults. They complained about the silly rule that every kid had to play at least two innings and get one at-bat. They bitched about the once a week practices and loudly commented that it was no wonder kids didn't know what they were doing.

"You should think about swinging the bat once in a while," a man with grayish brown hair yelled. Never had Tru heard a nastier group.

Marc's team, the Angels, had big third and fourth innings and built a nine run lead. At the end of the fourth inning, Tru saw something he had never seen at a junior Little League game before.

"Would you look at this shit," an angry voice called as the umpire stepped away to the backstop and lit a cigarette.

Seeing the umpire, Tru felt as if he were back at the vacant, vandalized shopping center. He fidgeted and broke into a cold sweat. He needed to get out of there. It was only a matter of time before he said something to someone that he would surely regret. He would call Marcus later, he reasoned, as he started walking away.

"Steeerrrike three!" boomed Chuck, the umpire behind the plate.

Tru turned. "Thud" went the plastic helmet as the batter hurled it from his head to the dirt. Tears began to leak from the kid's eyes. "Clang" went his aluminum bat as it ricocheted off the chain link fence two feet away from the head of the on-deck hitter. "Thump" went the five-gallon water container as the nine-year-old kicked it with all the anger of fifty years on his face. Nothing was said by the umpire, coach, or the parents to redirect the frustration of the young player into positive action.

What the hell is going on here, Tru asked himself as he headed to the exit. He stopped and pondered what he'd seen. *What are these people trying to promote? Sportsmanship? Not when they let this kind of behavior go uncorrected. Teamwork? Couldn't be that when they let these kids rip each other and tell each other how rotten they are. Work ethic? Hardly. The few parents here want their kids to be superstars, but it's obvious they don't want to spend fifteen minutes working to teach them the game. Negativity? They damn sure cornered that market. No positive behavior is being displayed or reinforced.* Tru shook his head. This wasn't what games were supposed to be like. Parents should be here supporting each other and these kids.

All Tru could see was blame: kids blaming other kids and not listening to their coaches, parents blaming the coaches and bad-mouthing each other's kids, sometimes even their own, and coaches blaming parents for raising bad kids who didn't want to listen to anyone. It seemed obvious that none of the participants wanted to be there. Youth baseball was supposed to be fun but there was definitely no fun going on here—only confusion and anger and pain.

The baseball being played was equally as atrocious as the attitudes. The kids didn't know which base to throw to, how to bunt, how to field a ground ball, or how to slide. Fundamentally, they were inept because they were ignorant. Tru continued walking fast and almost bumped into someone.

"Tru, is that you?" Erica Savin stretched out her arms to give Tru an it's-been-too-long hug. "How you been?"

"Just great, baby!" Tru responded as he returned her hug, thankful to have his attention diverted from the field. "How are you doing?"

"Just fine, thanks. But what are you doing here?"

"I was just driving around and saw this game. I thought I'd check it out for a minute."

"So you've been watching Jim Leyland do some managing?" Erica laughed as she compared her husband to the manager of the Pittsburgh Pirates.

"Yeah, he's something, isn't he?" Tru laughed as Marcus's and Erica's eight-year-old daughter walked over.

"Here's my girl," Erica said. "Say hello to an old friend, Leah."

Tru smiled at the child. "Look at you! You're one

beautiful young lady." He turned to her mother as she said, "When will this game be over? Shoot, they play longer than the Pirates."

"It should be over soon. I think this is the last inning. Oh, they beat up on Perk's team."

Mercifully, the game ended a few minutes later. The score was 21-8 in favor of the Angels.

"We're taking the championship," Marcus said just loud enough for DeWayne to hear as he and his son Douglas, the shortstop, approached Tru and Erica.

"Wait until next year!" DeWayne Perkins shot back. "I might even have something for you later on this year, boy."

"Man, you two are continuously at each other!" Tru said with a smile as he extended his hand to each one of his two friends.

"Perk can't beat me, Tru. You should know that by now, baby!" Marcus boasted.

"Shut up, man. You got some brew in your trunk?" DeWayne replied.

"Nah, I'm watchin' the game coming up next. It's the Yankees and Indians. If the Indians can knock off the Yanks we'll be in first place by ourselves. Want to check it out, Tru?"

"Yeah, sure, but is this game going to be any better than the first one?"

"It should be. Both teams are pretty good and no one is rebuilding." Marcus laughed as he got in another dig at DeWayne.

"I don't mean the score," Tru explained. "I mean the scene. Will these parents be fussing like those at your game, man?"

"Shoot, that's just the way it is. None of these parents care about the game. Only if their little star is playing. That's what it's all about."

Tru broke in, "What's up with that ump lighting up the

cigarette, man? Why do you put up with all that?"

"Chuck? He's the best ump we've got. Kevin, the base ump, is real bad, man. He don't like to move. He's one we'd like to get rid of."

"You know how bad lighting-up looks, bro?"

"Yeah, I know, man. But what you gonna do? Nobody else wants to take all that grief for five dollars a game."

Marcus was right of course, Tru thought. Nobody wants to do much of anything these days, especially for too little money.

"Want a hot dog?" DeWayne asked as he started walking towards the concession stand.

"No thanks, this is too big!" Tru said, pointing at his stomach.

Tru and Marcus passed the next few minutes on the kind of small talk expected between friends who have not seen each other for some time.

Tru's attention drifted in and out of the conversation with his friend. He couldn't stop thinking of the baseball game he had just witnessed. What he had seen was a live version of the lifeless graffiti and trash he'd seen at the shopping complex. He wondered, other than the obvious reason that a person's child played on the team, why anyone would put themselves through the abuse of coaching these young kids and dealing with their obnoxious parents.

"Why do you do this shit, man?" he finally asked Marcus. "I know you have better things to do with your time."

"My boy plays. You think I'd be doin' all this if it weren't for him?"

"Yeah, I figured that. But there must be something more to it. Why not just teach him how to play and let some-one else take all the heat?"

Marcus grinned. "You want to help?"

"I'm not even goin' to answer that. I'm just curious. So what other reasons do you have?"

Marcus shook his head. "I don't know. I guess we all just do crazy things sometimes. Don't I recall you quittin' a decent job a while back? Now, to me, that's crazy, bro."

"I guess you're right, but you know this isn't even close to the same thing. I had to quit that job, man—there was no happiness there for me. But you don't need to subject yourself to all this."

Marcus ran his hand across his head. "I don't really know why I do it. I guess it's because someone has to. These kids got nothing to do when school is out. If they had no Little League, summer would just be a time to get into trouble. Their parents—those that have 'em—ain't about to watch them, I'll tell you that much. Most are hustling to put food on the table and dead tired the little they're home. Someone needs to spend time with these kids. I feel sorry for them. It ain't like when we were comin' up, Tru."

"I hear you. You should see how they've trashed the shopping center in East Hills!"

Marcus Savin didn't respond; he just shrugged.

Chapter 4

"Play Ball"

The game between the Little League Indians and the Yankees was about to start.

"Would anyone be interested in umpiring this game for us?" Bobby McGhee, coach of the Yankees, called to the adults seated in the bleachers. "Chuck had to go umpire another game over at Whitney Field, so we're one ump short."

"How much cash you talkin', bro?" a voice from the back of the bleachers asked as Tru and his buddy continued their conversation, paying no attention to the dilemma the two teams faced.

"Seven dollars."

"Man, that ain't no kinda money," the voice responded. "To put up with all that bullshit? You need to go look somewhere else, man."

Bobby McGhee took a walk over to the girls' softball game on the next field to see if he could recruit an umpire.

"Who does he think will umpire a game from over

there?" Marcus observed. "No parent gonna leave their daughter's game to come ump another game, not for seven dollars."

A tall woman next to Tru leaned over. "Man, he's desperate, that's all. Why don't you do it?"

Marcus laughed as Tru said, "You gotta be crazy. Me? I'm getting ready to get on up outta here any damn way. Man, I couldn't put up with them coaches and parents talking all that mess—hell no!"

Marcus looked at Tru. Despite knowing that Tru had quit his job, Marcus felt Tru was not someone to walk away from a real challenge, and it was obvious Tru felt Little League should not be played the way he had just witnessed. Besides, even though Tru had played college football, baseball was his real love, and Marcus thought Tru would do umpire if persuaded properly.

"Folks, if nobody umpires this game here, we're gonna have to send these kids on home," Bobby McGhee announced to the small crowd on his return from the lower field. "The kids will be terribly disappointed. Please, please will someone help us out?"

"Here's your man, Bob," Marcus Savin said as he pointed to Tru. "He was just tellin' me what a kick he thought it would be to straighten these kids—and you coaches—out!"

After a few minutes of protest, Tru knew he had been set up and protest was not going to get him out of it. He walked down the five bleacher steps deciding that if he was going to umpire it, the game would be very unlike any the Wilkinsburg Baseball Association had seen in quite some time.

"I'm not goin' for all this chaos, man," Tru said solemnly to the coach of the Yankees as they walked to the concession stand to get the extra set of equipment for Tru to wear. "We need to go over a new set of umpire's rules along with some new ground rules."

The coaches of the Yankees and Indians met at home plate to go over Turner Field's ground rules with Tru.

"Like I told you, man, I'm not goin' for any chaos. Y'all go too far arguin' any one of my calls and you're gone. No 'ifs, ands, or buts.' I'll tell ya when enough is enough but I'm tellin' you, don't test me, 'cause I'll run you. Any of your kids start poutin', arguin', or talkin' mess, I'll give them one warning and they're gone too. There are no friends when the game starts. Another thing: none of you will be standing at the backstop behind home plate. No need to try and get a better look at my ball and strike calls. So you can yell and jeer. We goin' to do this the right way."

There was an awkward silence. Finally Bobby said, "That's cool, Tru." The other coach nodded.

"Now I need to talk to both teams. I'll start with yours," he said to Bobby McGhee.

Tru walked over to the team bench. "Boys, I want you all to have some fun today. Beautiful day like this, you are supposed to have fun. Is there anybody here who does not like to play the game of baseball?" He paused. "Because if you do not enjoy this game, you should not be out here."

Tru looked into the eyes of the Little Leaguers and saw confusion. He could see from their raised eyebrows that they wondered why he was talking so slowly and deliberately and just what his point was.

Tru started to explain. "Now, there are some things I want you to be aware of before we begin the game. First, nobody will be permitted behind me at home plate. Second, anyone throwing equipment or losing their tempers will be given one warning and one warning only. If the problem occurs again, you will be ejected."

As Tru was about to continue, he noticed a couple of

the kids talking and laughing.

"Excuse me, gentlemen, but when I am talking I expect you to be listening. It is impossible to listen and talk at the same time, so I would appreciate it if you could hold off on your conversation for a few minutes. When you have something to say to me, I will be more than happy to listen to you and I expect the same treatment. Is that understood?"

There was a sudden silence. Looking around, Tru continued, "Third, if I hear any cussing, you will receive one warning followed by an immediate ejection if you repeat your mistake. Likewise, any pouting, sitting on a base or lying down on the field of play will result in ejection after one warning. Any questions?" He stared at each boy in turn.

Not only were there no questions, there was no blinking, talking, or looking away.

Tru went on. "Lastly, you will be immediately ejected with no warning, and I repeat, immediately ejected with no warning, for degrading—that means ripping on, or fighting— anyone from either your team or your opponents."

After a short pause to let it all sink in, Tru finished, "Now, gentlemen, is there anything which is unclear?"

Again, no one spoke. "Good. Then you're ready."

Walking away, Tru went over to the Indians' bench and gave the same speech. When he got the same astonished reaction, he turned to home plate and, with a smile, yelled, "Play ball!"

It didn't take long for Tru to be tested. In the second inning, after two consecutive errors by the shortstop and the second baseman, the Yankees' third baseman, L-Dawg, threw his glove to the ground in disgust.

"Time!" yelled Tru as he strode towards the third baseman. As Tru and Bobby McGhee reached the hot corner together. Tru spoke to L-Dawg. "Son, if you throw your mitt again while I am umpiring your game, I will eject you." L-Dawg stared silently at the new umpire. "Do we have an understanding?" The youngster began to walk away, giving only an affirmative shake of his head as a response.

Tru's voice rose. "Son, do we have an understanding?"

"Yeah, man," the boy said softly.

"I believe you meant to say *yes, sir*, is that correct?"

L-Dawg looked at the new umpire with great uncertainty and much hate in his eyes. Quickly he glanced at his coach who was shaking his head up and down. Looking back to the ump, the boy replied, "Yes, sir."

Tru called out somberly, "Okay, let's play ball." The moment had passed to his advantage, but Tru knew there was a storm waiting to burst in young L-Dawg.

Bobby McGhee remained with L-Dawg for a few minutes to try and calm his third baseman.

The very next play, a fly ball was hit to right field, which the right fielder misplayed into a double. The pitcher on the Yankees, Bobby's son, was frustrated because now the Indians were only six runs behind.

Bobby called out, "Don't worry about that boy. You just pitch, son. You know that boy can't catch anything, don't you? Don't let it bother you. That ain't your fault."

"Time!" Tru threw both his hands in the air. Peeling off his face mask, he called out, "Coach, we need to talk."

As he approached Bobby, he wondered just how best to handle the situation. Bobby was a good man and Tru believed he had the best interests of these kids at heart, but what Tru had just heard was the wrong way to serve those interests. Bobby might not have meant to embarrass one of his players, but in the end he humiliated him.

"Man, do you know what you just did to that kid?" There was no mistaking the seriousness of Tru's face.

"What you talkin' about, man?" a surprised and somewhat defensive Bobby McGhee responded.

"Whether or not that young man has any baseball skills is no reason to treat him like dirt in front of all these other kids, man."

"Man, I'm just trying to settle my own boy down, Tru. He's got to keep pitching, don't he? He can't be all upset about this kid who missed the ball. I'm just trying to get his head together, man. You should know that."

"Nah, man, that's not what this is about. You can do that by going out to the mound and sayin' something, the same thing if you want, in private, so the entire team doesn't hear it, man. Have a little concern for the young buck that is strugglin' out there in the field. Now he got everyone on his team, the other team, and most of the parents thinking that he's messed. No nine-year-old needs all that, man."

Another silence. Then Bobby took a deep breath and said, "All right, Tru. I'll talk with him when we get finished with the inning, all right?"

"Do that," Tru responded even though he knew the damage was already done. "Play ball!" he called, hopeful the game would proceed with no more incidents.

However, it didn't take long to test the new umpire again.

In the fourth inning the Yankees came up to bat. Antwan Sumner, the left fielder, grounded out to the shortstop. As he went back to the Yankees' dugout and Tru got ready to call the next pitch, an uproar broke out in the Yankees' dugout. Tru looked over and saw Antwan Sumner and L-Dawg squared off with bats in their hands. The faces of both kids were filled with violence. Bobby McGhee stepped between the two youngsters as they were about to swing at each other's heads. Tru ran over and grabbed

L-Dawg, and before any real damage was done, the boys were disarmed.

"What's the matter with you two?" Bobby screamed. "You are on the same team. Y'all better get your heads back into this game, right now!"

Tru said quietly, "Coach, both of these boys are gone. Ejected."

Bobby whirled to face Tru. "Man, you can't throw out my two best players! Come on now. They'll be all right!"

"No way, Bob. They are both out of this game."

"Ah, come on, man! I'm tellin' ya, Tru, they'll be all right. We can't afford to blow this game. We are tied for first place, man," Bobby pleaded.

"So what, man?" Tru said. "You just don't understand. I have absolutely no concern who wins or loses, who is in first place or who is in last place. My concern is with these kids and what they are learning. What message are you sending these kids? Good sportsmanship? Teamwork? Come on, man. They are gone and if I hear another word, you can go with them!"

Silence and shock came over Turner Field as the game continued minus two all-stars and plus one very disturbed coach. Bobby's team ultimately won the game in a blowout. As the two teams met to shake hands after the game, Tru tried to figure the quickest way to make his exit. As he was walking over to the concession stand to return his equipment, Lamont Dawson of the Indians and Bobby McGhee of the Yankees cornered him.

"Would you ump on a regular basis, man?" Lamont asked the stunned umpire.

"You're kidding," Tru said, dumfounded.

"Nah, man, that's what the kids—and coaches for that matter—need," Bobby added, sincerely.

"I don't think so, fellas. Shoot, I thought you were coming over here to get a piece of my butt. Thanks, but no. I'd probably be too hard on these kids, man. I get a little too serious about this stuff. Y'all don't need that."

"That's exactly what we do need. Please ump for us, man. Give me your phone number so I can give it to Chuck. He's the head of the umpires and will call you. Say all right, Tru," pleaded Lamont.

Tru stood there hesitating. He didn't have much leisure time and he had his new girlfriend, Tonya. On top of that he was a bachelor, not a parent. Where were the parents of these kids? He looked back at them and the nearly empty bleachers and sighed. That was just the point. They were nowhere. He took out a pencil and pad from his pocket and wrote down his telephone number.

Later that night, as Tru was relaxing at home with Tonya in front of the television, Chuck, the head umpire, called.

"Next Wednesday, Dodgers and Reds, six o'clock at Turner Field, Tru," the man on the other end of the line said.

"Hold on a minute, man. I didn't even say I was goin' to do all that."

"From what the coaches tell me you were very eager to do more games."

"Yeah, I suppose they would say that," Tru said laughing. He sighed. "All right, man, I'll be there."

Tonya looked at him after he hung up. "Those kids really got to you, huh?"

Tru nodded. "Guess they did all right."

Chapter 5

Clouds

There is rarely a cloudless day in Pittsburgh and June 14, 1994 was no exception. Tru looked up at the sky. He liked the puffy clouds because they provided relief from the sometimes brutally hot summer sun. Tru relaxed in the shade for five minutes while he waited for his second Little League game to start.

"Tru, can me and Manny go over to that other field to see who's gonna be playin' over there?" Lance McCoy asked. "We'll be all right and we'll be back in time to see you umpire."

"Yeah, we won't miss any little kids grittin' on you," Manny laughed.

Tru had brought Tonya's son Lance and Lance's best friend and neighbor Manny to the game to try and get them interested in baseball. "Man, you two should be out there playin' some ball. What's wrong with you anyhow?" Tru kidded. "Yeah, go ahead. Get out of here."

As the two boys walked away, Tru watched them and wondered just where his own life was and where it was headed. He and his girlfriend Tonya were thinking of moving in permanently together and here he was with two kids—one of them hers, neither of them his—getting ready to umpire a game involving about twenty-four other kids. He really needed to pay more attention to his business and not other people's kids, he told himself. After the game tonight, he'd call Chuck and tell him this stuff took too much damn time, and that would be it.

Around five-fifteen, the Dodgers and Reds began to arrive at Turner Field for their six o'clock game. Some arrived on bicycles, some on foot, and a few others came in cars with their parents.

Tru needed this time before the game to assemble his gear and rid his stomach of any butterflies. Why he was so nervous was a little confusing to him. He had no real interest in who won or lost. He did not know anyone playing on either team. He hadn't been nervous for his first game, so why this one? It was plain foolishness.

Despite his self-admonishments, the closer it came to game time, the more nervous Tru became and the more foolish he felt. Then it hit him. This game involved something his first time behind the plate did not. Anticipation. He was sure word had gotten around the league after the Yankees-Indian game about his strict style, and he was sure there would be repercussions.

A large heavyset men walked up and extended his hand to Tru. "You must be Ramon. I'm Tom Carter, coach of the Reds. Didn't you go to Kentucky State?"

"Yes, sir, right on both accounts," Tru said with a faint smile.

"We heard about your last game with the Yankees. I'm looking forward to seeing you work," Tom said as he scanned the field counting the players.

Tru took a deep breath. "I hope you say that after the game."

"I'm sure I will. Hey, Bart, come over here. We can be friends before we get to spankin' that butt," Tom called to his opponent for the evening, Bart Hanks, the tall thin coach of the Dodgers.

Bart wore a jacket and pants with the blue and white colors of his team, which matched those of the Los Angeles Dodgers. Tru was impressed. He thought it was appropriate for the coaches to be in full uniform, and Bart's outfit was the closest Tru had seen any of the coaches come to that. Bart had presence, Tru thought, almost like his late friend Kevin Coles. Tru liked Bart's style. He could tell that this man cared very much about what was going on at the baseball diamond.

"Bart, this is Ramon Dixon. Tru, to his friends. He'll be umpiring our game today and the rest of the season," Tom said easily.

"How you doin', Tru? Nice to meet you," Bart said, extending his hand.

Tru connected immediately with the lanky man. "Pretty good, thanks. I hope you don't believe all the stories you heard about my umpiring."

"Hey, I hope all the stories are true. We need some structure around here. We need new blood to shake this association up a little. Well, I better go get these kids ready before they start throwin' baseballs at each other instead of trying to whip their opponents."

As the coaches walked back to their teams, Tru watched their boys begin to warm up. His feelings of doubt began to surface again, only this time with more force. He had the prickly feeling he always got when he began to sweat from nervousness. *Hey, I'll be resigning from any future officiating duties this evening, so I ought to relax and try to settle down and enjoy this one,* he told himself. He didn't get much opportunity.

The "ripping" began during the pre-game warmups. Kids from each bench ridiculed whoever made an error. No one was hustling. If the ball was not hit directly at them, or if they missed it, they looked away. Even if it was hit practically into their hands, they slowly retrieved the ball with an attitude and then threw it with a sluggish motion. This was meant to show how little they cared about everything.

Tru's sense of pride was offended. This was the same slop he'd witnessed at the first game. *Someone needs to start demanding some discipline and sportsmanship from these kids,* he thought this to himself, shaking his head.

Tru looked up to see an old acquaintance, Marvin Mitchell, who ran the Pittsburgh Inner City Youth Alliance, a youth center housed in the Belmont Elementary School in Penn Hills, walking towards him.

Marv and Tru had been friendly competitors during their high school years. Marv was a pretty decent football player for Oliver High School on the city's north side. Before that, they played against each other on various youth football teams.

"I've seen it all now," Marvin Mitchell said with a smile that said he was glad to see an old friend. "I heard you were umpiring, but I never would have believed it if I hadn't seen it for myself. How you doin', bro?"

"Oh, I'm just fine. It sure has been a little while, bro. Good to see you, man. What brings you over here anyway? I know you didn't come just to see me umpire."

"If that ain't reason enough, I don't know what is, but no. My little cousin plays for the Dodgers so I really came to check him out. What you been up to, man?"

"Nothin' much, man. Just tryin' to stay busy, that's all. How about you? How's the youth center goin' these days?"

"Pretty good. Tryin' to keep these kids straight. You know, come to think of it, there might be some things that might interest you at the center. Let's talk."

"Sure, but I have to get these kids ready to play this game now, so I can get out of here. Talk to you later, man."

"All right, Tru. And, my cousin's number is fourteen. Don't ring him up, all right?" Marvin said with a laugh.

"Is the boy afraid to swing the aluminum or what?" Tru smiled as he turned away. He figured that a cousin of Marvin Mitchell was probably going to have some athletic ability.

Tru gave his pre-game lecture to both teams. He noticed several young men who did not seem to want to hear about any rules of conduct that were about to be placed upon them. "Listen, guys, either you pay attention to what I'm saying or you leave the field," Tru warned them. They listened. Finally he was ready to utter the two most famous words in baseball. As a church bell down the street announced it was six o'clock, Tru called out, "Play ball!"

He glanced around and saw Marv standing near. "Excuse me, Marv," he had to say to his friend, "but nobody can stand behind me while I'm umpiring. I'm gonna have to ask you to move."

"What's the matter, Tru, don't you want anyone to see when you miss one? I thought we were better than that," Marvin Mitchell said good-naturedly as he walked back to the bleachers and took his seat.

The game was going relatively smoothly when Tru heard two parents sitting in foul territory under a big oak tree along the right field line yelling jibes to the players and umpire. Turning in that direction, he saw the man lift a paper-covered bottle to his lips. Tru assumed they were drinking "forties." The hefty man and woman bad-mouthed just about everything that went on in the game. Every call by the umpires was questioned, every decision by the coaches was doubted and every error by one of the kids was the subject of taunting.

Thankfully, Tru did not know which boy the drunks were there to support, as if a kid needed support like that. He doubted, any of the boys, even if questioned, would tell him. Not wanting to further embarrass the kid they belonged to, Tru waited until between innings. Then he sauntered over, "There's to be no more drinking at these games," he said.

Tru's short reputation as an umpire must have preceded him. They said nothing and hung their heads kind of shame-faced. Relieved, Tru walked back to the plate and returned his attention to the game.

The distance from the crouching catcher to the wooden backstop was no more than three feet, barely enough room for Tru to stand. Apparently, neither team had really agile athletes. Both catchers struggled mightily to hold on to the pitches. Since they had such a short distance to retrieve the baseball, their ineffectiveness rarely hurt their team, other than to give the runner an easy stolen base. Seldom did the ball find its way to the backstop, however, without first hitting an unprotected body part of the plate umpire. Despite Tru's words of instruction and encouragement to the catchers, he still took a bruising.

The game ended with Bart Hanks's Dodgers winning with a score of fifteen to six. After the game, both coaches walked over to Tru.

"We want to thank you for the way you ran the game," Bart said.

"Damn right," Tom echoed.

Tru felt good. It was an up feeling to do something well and be appreciated by those you did it for. Nevertheless, he had made up his mind: tonight he would call in his resignation.

Tru went to collect Manny and Lance. "You boys up for a cone?" he asked with a smile, knowing the answer. Now that he and Tonya were moving in together, he wanted to get to know Lance better on an informal basis. Maybe he could get inside both boys' heads a little and see what made these two guys tick.

They followed Tru as he returned the umpiring gear to the concession stand.

"Can we go to the Dairy Queen over on Centre Avenue?" the boys asked in unison. "They got the phattest blizzards anywhere."

Tru nodded "yes" as they walked from the field.

Before the trio reached the exit, they were stopped by Marvin Mitchell.

"Hey, Tru, can you hold up a second? I got something I want to ask you."

"What's up, Mitch?"

"You know, you were asking earlier about the youth center. Well, I was thinking maybe the two young men with you would like to get involved playing some basketball. We have leagues starting up in September and we're taking applications now."

"What do you think, boys?" Tru asked challengingly. "You got enough game to try and play in the league Mitch runs?"

"My game is pretty good," Lance said, smiling as he looked at Manny for reinforcement. Manny just stood there, silently.

"You just think about it, boys," Marv said. "Just let me know in the next month or so. By the way, Tru, I know you are into computers. Would you be interested in setting up some systems for the center? I think we are going to be getting a grant for educational purposes through Ronald McDonald charities, but I don't know the first thing about computers. What do you think?"

"Give me a call, Mitch. Sounds pretty good. Right now I need to get these boys over to Dairy Queen before they have an ice cream deprivation attack."

On the twenty minute drive to Dairy Queen, Tru asked both Manny and Lance about playing basketball at the P.I.C.Y.A. in the fall. He was surprised to find out that neither boy had ever participated in organized athletic competition. Their lack of excitement told Tru that neither kid thought they were very good at sports. *It is safer for a kid who can't play not to play,* Tru surmised. Then the kid could talk about how good he was, and nobody could challenge him.

It bothered Tru that the boys, especially Lance, did not play any sports. He felt there were so many benefits from competition. It was not only about winning and losing: it was about learning responsibility, determination, sportsmanship, and cooperation. These were values that were imperative for a young person to have if he or she were ever going to be successful. He knew Lance had not done as well in school as he could have and thought some of the things he could learn from sports might help him do better in the classroom.

At Dairy Queen the boys slowly sipped their Oreo cookie Blizzards as if they were the last ones in existence. "It's better to eat slowly because we get headaches if we eat fast," Lance explained.

Tru nodded but he thought they took slow to an unbelievable level. Eventually Tru said, "We've got to get on our way, guys. Finish your treats in the Jeep. But if any ice cream is spilled on the leather interior, there will be some serious butt kicked."

When they arrived back at Edgerton Avenue, the boys jumped out of the Jeep. They picked up their bikes and Lance said, "We're just going to ride up to Lamar's house."

Tru reminded them to stay within the neighborhood boundary that had been set for them, but he doubted they'd heard him, since they flew off down the road.

When Tru went inside Tonya's small three-bedroom house, he wanted only to relax. He felt like unwinding in front of the television for a few minutes before he called Chuck, the head of the umpires, to resign.

As the theme song from Jeopardy hypnotized Tru, now sitting on the black leather easy-chair, he began thinking about Lance. He saw so much of himself as an adolescent in that kid.

Like himself at that age, Lance had no real discipline. He was not a bad kid, however like most eleven-year-olds, he had no goals and little concept of the future. *Hell,* Tru told himself, *the future to an eleven-year-old is the next half-hour.*

Tru felt that Lance's real problem was that he had no expectations placed on him, at least no expectations for which he was being held accountable. That much was crystal-clear to him, and if it was obvious to him, Tonya must surely see it also. Why then didn't she hold Lance accountable?

When Tru thought of the time and energy that it would take to turn Lance around, he was dumfounded. How could a single parent like Tonya possibly handle the problems of a kid like Lance who's apathetic, when she's working day and night to pay the monthly bills? He knew Tonya would do anything for, and cared more about, her kid than anything else in the world. Tru knew that she taught Lance all the right things and wanted the best for him. He also knew of other people, with worse living conditions, whose kids got excellent grades and were never in trouble. How, he wondered, could he help Tonya help Lance?

Waiting for Tonya to come home, Tru puzzled it out.

People need reasons for everything. The losers in our society must see themselves as robbed of success because they didn't get the right chance. They don't realize it isn't a matter of chance but drive, hard work and persistence. There isn't any-one to blame. The person they should blame most is themselves. And that kind of attitude, instead of the expectation of failure, has to be inculcated at a young age so that kids will focus on their future. Striving for success has to become their goal.

Tru knew he was definitely not able to do those things as a youngster and he doubted that most people, especially in his neighborhood, would have either.

How easy it is, Tru thought, *for others to criticize when a kid does not do what everyone knows he should.* In fact, Tru had also been one of the criticizers of the destruction of the shopping center in East Hills. He had labeled as rotten failures every kid that took part in painting the graffiti and trashing the buildings he saw. He had labeled their parents as well. Parents just like Tonya. He didn't know if he could do better, but he hoped she would let him try to help Lance out.

Chapter 6

Time and Time Again

A short while later Tru made the permanent move to Tonya's house and prepared to assume his new role. That night Lance returned home around eight o'clock. He walked through the living room and glanced at Tru without speaking. He had been told Tru would now be living with them, but Lance wasn't going to pretend he liked it. Tru wanted Lance to understand that he knew how he felt and understood.

"Hold up, man. You got a second?" Tru said.

"Yeah, sure. What do you want?" Lance knew he was either about to get a lecture, although he could not remember doing anything wrong, or he was going to have to listen to a speech with garbage about how they could be friends.

The ringing phone saved him. Lance shrugged his shoulders, pretending he was sorry that whatever it was Tru wanted to talk about would have to wait. He ducked out the front door.

Tru, feeling irritated that Lance had gotten away before he could speak to him, answered the phone.

"Tru, this is Marv. How you doing?"

"I'm just kickin' it. What's up, man?"

"If I caught you at a bad time, I'll call later." There was a pause, but Marv didn't answer and he continued. "But something came up. I mean, I still want to talk to you about the computers, but this is actually about something else altogether."

"Nah, it's all right. What's up?"

"I got this notice about a baseball tournament the city is putting together. They're calling it the Mayor's Cup."

"Since when was this mayor a baseball fan?"

"I hear you, man." Marv paused. "Anyway, they've scheduled it to coincide with the major league All-Star Game at the stadium this July. I guess they want the city to look good so they're trying to involve people in different events."

"Sounds like politics. As long as things look good, who gives a damn what they're really like. Don't tell me you want me to umpire some more of these games. I can tell you right now, I'm not. Fact is, I've been thinking of quitting."

"What for, man? You do such a good job with these kids."

"I haven't got time for this stuff. I'm a grown man, bro. I have to tend to my own business."

"You might want to reconsider after you hear what I'm about to say. I was looking for you to coach a team."

The word coach made Tru perk up but a million things raced through his mind in the few short seconds it took him to mouth his answer.

"I don't think so."

"Tru, you'd be perfect. You give these kids a lot of discipline and you don't play games with them. They need that and you know it."

Tru knew the kids needed discipline. He also knew no

one else was volunteering, but that was not going to be enough to sway him. It was one thing to umpire two games a week, but quite another to coach. To do it right would mean practice every day. He knew he would not be the type of coach who only showed up to play the game.

"I haven't got the time for all that, man. I appreciate you thinking I would be good for the kids, but I just don't have the time. I have my little business goin' and you know how much time that takes."

"Will you just think about it? This tournament is only open to city residents and we need to get a team in from the east. The Hill will be represented as well as Northside and Beltzhoover. Every other neighborhood will have a team. What will it look like if the eastern part of the city can't even put one together?"

"Can't you get a parent to coach?"

Marv laughed bitterly. "Well, you've seen the attendance at games. The few that come want to chew the kids out, but they don't want to coach them."

"Where would you get the kids for the team?"

"I don't know. Maybe we could get kids who didn't make the all-star teams."

That got Tru's attention. He did not believe Little League should be about winning and losing. The fact that he could use kids who were green meant he might be able to get Lance and Manny involved.

Tru relented. "It would be nice to give these kids a chance to be a part of something like that."

"There's more, man. The championship game is going to be played at Three Rivers Stadium before the major leaguers home run hitting contest. Plus, all the kids and coaches will get tickets to the home run hitting contest and serve as a backdrop to the unveiling of the statue."

The statue? He and the boys would get to be at the
unveiling of the statue of Roberto Clemente? Clemente was
his hero. Actually, he was every kid in Pittsburgh's hero
when Tru was growing up.

How many summer nights had he sat on his porch
listening to Bob Prince, the voice of the Pittsburgh Pirates,
describe one of Roberto's rifle throws from right field as
he threw out yet another foolish runner. Roberto was a
man's man. His athletic ability was superb but his heroism
went much deeper. Roberto had died in a plane crash in
1973 on New Year's Eve, while trying to deliver supplies
to earthquake victims in Nicaragua.

"That would be pretty nice, man. I'd sure like to see that
statue get unveiled," Tru said, his kid-like sports adoration
shining through even though he was now an adult.

"Then you'll do it?"

Tru was about to say yes when visions of fifteen kids
who'd never played before running helter skelter around on
the field, while their parents screamed at him about a play
came crashing into his mind. "I don't think so, man."

"These kids will get to march in the All-Star Parade
and meet the major league mascots. They'll be part of something they'll remember for the rest of their lives, Tru. You
know they need a hero, so think how bad it would be for
these kids to miss out on an opportunity like this, man. They
miss out on too many other things."

Marv was right of course and Tru had to admit it. Not
only did the kids of the eastern part of the city—Homewood,
East Hills and East Liberty—always miss out on things
other kids in Pittsburgh take for granted, their entire neighborhoods did.

Officials do not run the City of Pittsburgh Marathon
through East Hills. The Thrift Drug Classic, a bicycle race

attracting elite bikers worldwide, has never taken a route through the streets of Homewood. If you live in East Liberty, you need to drive thirty miles to enjoy the Mellon Jazz Festival. The only thing these neighborhoods do host are drugs, gangs, and killings.

Tru sighed. "All right, I'll think about it, man. Let me give you a call back. By the way, when does this thing get started?"

"Your first game would be in about three weeks. It's a single elimination and there will be thirty-two teams in the tournament."

"Three weeks! You gotta be kiddin' me!"

"Sorry, man, but I just got news of this myself. Don't worry, we can throw a team together pretty quick. Just don't take too long thinking it over, all right? I need to know pretty quick."

"I'll give you a call back within the next couple of days."

"Thanks, man. Don't worry about it. It'll be a nice experience."

"Yeah, right," Tru said. "All right, Marv. I'll be talkin' to you."

The phone had not reached its resting place when Tru began to consider the situation. The first stumbling block was simple. Did he want to be bothered? It was one thing to take a little heat for a close call from a parent, but it would be quite another to hear how every parent's little baby should be the star of the team. He had heard the remarks parents made to the coaches' faces and behind their backs. Tru was not quite sure he could be diplomatic enough to handle that type of criticism.

Question after question came to his mind. Did he have the time? His business required him to put in long hours (although it was somewhat under his control when those hours would be). There was always the chance of an emergency if a client's system went down, Tru had to get there and quickly. He couldn't coach unless he felt sure his business would not suffer.

Would he honestly be committed to coaching this team the right way? He knew it was easy for people to imagine how a good boss should act, but it was quite another thing to be the boss and realize the more demanding on workers you are, the more demanding on yourself you have to be. To ask for commitment, he knew he would have to be able to make a serious commitment of time and energy, since these kids were desperate for guidance and supervision.

As he debated inwardly he felt drawn to the task. Despite the drawbacks, he felt this could be his opportunity to put into practice what he thought was missing from the teams he saw while umpiring, a chance to teach kids who might be headed in the wrong direction a little something about responsibility, sportsmanship, and pride. To Tru these ideals were what made Little League an important developmental tool for youngsters. This was his chance to make a difference. He shook his head: it was time to put up or shut up. His bluff had been called.

Now he began to figure out *how* he was going to make coaching the kids a part of his life, instead of wondering about whether or not he should commit. He decided that although work would have to come first, addressing an emergency from one of his clients would be another way to teach the kids about responsibility. Next Tru wondered if he could do anything about the lack of parental support. The fact that he did not have a son playing on the team removed one possible line of criticism from disgruntled parents. Of course, they would learn in short order his relationship with

Lance. *No matter,* thought Tru.

He decided that he was going to take the challenge. He would call Marv in the next day or two.

Lance came down from his room around nine o'clock and was on his way to the kitchen when Tru stopped him.

"What do you think about playing on a baseball team I might coach that would play in a tournament against teams from all over the city?"

Lance hemmed and hawed. "I don't know. I guess that would be all right," he said with all the enthusiasm he would have if a teacher had asked him how he would like to read seventy pages of history for homework.

Lance's answer made Tru glad he had not called Marvin Mitchell back immediately. It forced him to consider something he had not thought of, the quality Lance and, he suspected, most of the neighborhood's seemingly hopeless kids, had in abundance. Apathy. Tru had thought any kid would jump at the chance to play baseball. When he was twelve, Tru reasoned, he did not need prompting to play ball.

No sooner had the disappointment of Lance's response registered, than Tru was already wondering why adults always thought their pasts were no different from the experiences of young people today. He realized he was looking at the opportunity he was offering the kids from the skewed perspective of a thirty-four-year-old adult, who knew well the struggles of life, not of an eleven-year-old who wondered if practice would cut into his playing video games or hanging out with his friends. Tru tried to spark Lance's interest.

"We get to march in the All-Star parade, sit at the unveiling of the statue for Roberto Clemente, and watch the major leaguers at the home run derby the day before the All-Star Game," he said, trying to build some excitement.

"That wouldn't be bad," Lance said, beginning to give

a hesitant smile. "Can Manny play?"

"Sure he can. We'll be doing plenty of practicing the next two weeks. You boys have a lot to learn about the game of baseball."

"How much is a lot?" Lance asked with his eyebrows scrunched together.

Again, Tru was disappointed with Lance's question and attitude. He heard the message. How much will I have to do? Would it be worth it? Why do we have to practice? This was not the time, Tru thought, to give a lecture to a basically disinterested eleven-year-old.

"It won't be that bad, man. You'll have time to do all your important stuff," he said with a trace of sarcasm. "Like playing Sega or ridin' those bikes or hanging out on some mean street watching punks do crime. Don't worry. Anyway, all of the mascots of the different major league teams will be marching in the parade with us."

That was what reeled Lance in. Not the fact that he would be able to compete against kids from all over the city. Not that he would witness the unveiling of the statue of the most beloved man in Pittsburgh's sport history. Not even the fact that he would get to watch Ken Griffey, big Frank Thomas, or Barry Bonds, and see how many shots the Pirate players could hit over the blue outfield walls of Three Rivers Stadium. It was just the simple fact that Lance thought it would be fun to walk in a parade with a bunch of guys dressed up like parrots and orioles.

Maybe there isn't such a difference between us, after all, Tru thought. He laughed to himself as he imagined talking to the mascot he would most like to meet during All-Star week—the San Diego Chicken!

Chapter 7

Play What?

Now Marvin Miller and Tru had to come up with fifteen or sixteen baseball players. "I know two already, Manny and Lance, but like a lot of kids around here they've never played baseball before and have to learn the game. We can't expect them to play right away. Where will we get the other thirteen?" Tru asked.

"Let me give Bart Hanks a call," Marv said. "He'll probably be able to give us some leads. He's coaching the all-star team in Wilkinsburg and there must be some kids who didn't make the team."

"Well, better hurry. We don't have much time."

That Sunday afternoon Tru, Marv and Bart Hanks met at Tru's house to discuss the future team.

"You know any kids that wanna play?" Marv asked Bart.

"Yeah, but they're all on my team and we're playing in the tournament over in Bloomfield starting next week," Bart said defensively.

"No, Bart. We don't want any of the kids who made the All-Star Team. We aren't about steppin' on anyone's toes," Tru explained, knowing what a sensitive issue this could be. "We're just lookin' for some other kids who want to play some ball and have a little fun. That's it, man."

"Oh, that's different. Yeah, sure. There are some names that come to mind. Darryl Weston for one. He has a lot of talent but he is raw...it looks like he's never been coached. But the boy is big! I mean, he's like six foot two and eleven years old. Let's see...there's Marcus Haines too. He is a good little infielder but quiet as anything, just like his dad, Ron. I've seen the kid play though and he's smart. He's always where he's supposed to be...steady. Then there's Todd Hill. That kid got more natural talent in his pinky than most kids ever have. But I hear he's a little tough to coach...misses practice...stuff like that. Let's see," he continued, "There's Antonio Williams and Joe Foster...they're cousins, I think...Joe is a good little outfielder but he don't hit much. Antonio can play about any-where but that's his big problem...he's always playin'. The kid never gets serious. Stan Coles' another, but I hear he ain't too reliable. Chris Williams...he's an infielder, I think, but his problem is he don't show up too often for practice...Most of these kids got some serious baggage, Tru! Maybe you should talk to all the other coaches and see if they can help you get others. I'm sure they will as long as you're not takin' any of the kids from the All-Star Team."

"Bart, you'll think I'm crazy, but I think those kids with the baggage are the kind I want," Tru said as he jotted down the names, "You've been a big help! You take care, now, and good luck!"

As Tru started to walk Bart out to his car, Bart thought of another kid.

"Yo, Tru, hold up! Listen, I'll tell ya who y'all should get! He's the best player in Wilkinsburg...Jerrett Thompson."

"Well, if he's the best player in Wilkinsburg," Tru asked logically, "Why isn't he on the All-Star Team?"

"That boy's a head case, man. He might not be worth the trouble. From what I hear, he likes to fight...with any-one...players, coaches, umpires, I guess it don't matter to that boy. He has an attitude with a capital A, know what I'm sayin'? I think someone said he's in a gang...and if he ain't, he probably will be..."

"He can't be all that bad!" Tru said trying to convince himself. He was willing to take a chance...after all that's what the team he envisioned was about.

"Okay, but I need to share something with you. His dad himself told me he's been kicked outta something like three schools already for fighting! The boy can play, though, that's for sure!"

After talking with the other coaches in Wilkinsburg and some friends of Marvin Mitchell in Homewood, East Liberty, Penn Hills, and East Hills, they had a list of fifteen names.

Richie Smith, Alonzo Payne, and Andre Jones were from Homewood. Robbie Elliott and Byron Knight were from Penn Hills. Robbie was supposed to be a fireballer...with no control...but talented, Byron was another infielder with promise. His coach said he did not make the All-Star Team because he was only ten years old.

Together with Lance and Manny, they would form the team.

Once the word on all the events they were to participate in began to circulate, other kids called.

The bumpiest impediment was they only had two and
a half weeks before their first and, Tru said, "maybe our last"
game. To add to the problem of their inexperience, they had no
field to practice on. To play or practice on any city-owned
baseball field required a permit. Usually, you had to request
that permit months in advance. The only park near enough and
big enough was Mellon Park on Fifth Avenue.

However, the next trouble spot became, when would
they be able to use the field? Tru drove by Mellon Park every
day at all hours of the day, and the only time he noticed it
empty was early in the morning. Moreover, that time slot
would cause the least amount of interference in his daily routine. He would still be able to visit all his clients during the day
and also teach the computer class he'd been offered at the
Community College of Allegheny County in the evening. It all
sounded good, but Tru knew getting kids to the field at eight
o' clock in the morning would not be easy.

Somehow Marv got them a temporary permit to
practice on the field during the early morning. "At least it
will weed out those that really don't want to play," Tru told
Marv. And they settled on that hour for practice time.

On the first day Tru scheduled the kids to report, the
thermometer was expected to climb above ninety degrees.
Even with the early starting time, the humidity was oppressive.
The park felt like a sauna and Tru' s skin prickled with sweat.
Tru was glad they would be finished before the weather
became unbearable.

The kids began getting to Mellon Park around 7:45.
Grumbling from the few parents who brought them was heard

immediately. "It's a ridiculous time to have baseball practice," one complained, and another said to Tru, "And I don't appreciate being put in such a position." Tru understood the apathetic attitude of those who lived just above the poverty line, so he took the criticism very diplomatically. He explained to the parents, "This is only for about a week. There's no other available time. I want to thank the parents who've come for their support, because I know there are many others who haven't your commitment." Despite the compliment, the grumbling continued.

Only one parent, actually a grandparent, did not complain. "How you doin' , Coach?" a bald-headed man sauntered up to Tru and said. "My name is Bud Harvey. This is my grandson, Brendon Banks." Bud extended his hand to greet Tru. "I'm glad to get him here any time."

"I'm not too bad, sir, how ' bout you?" Tru responded, feeling an immediate connection with the older man. Not ten minutes into their conversation, Tru convinced Bud to become his assistant.

"There's no pay, the hours stink, and most of the kids don't know how to play. Welcome aboard!" Tru laughed as he shook Bud's hand again and turned towards the kids.

"Everyone gather around," Tru called in a business-like manner. "I see we're not all here yet, so I guess we're goin' to have to delay the start of practice a few minutes. I am very pleased those of you who are here made the effort to be on time. That's one thing you will find I feel is very important. You must, and I stress must, always be on time for practice. Does everyone understand?"

The kids sat there silent and expressionless. Tru

studied them. Some were glancing over at the tennis courts that bordered Fifth Avenue where early morning tennis players trying to escape the later heat began volleying with each other. Others were distracted by a family of squirrels searching the sparse grass for their breakfast. Some were just spacing out. Few paid attention to what Tru was saying.

Feeling irritated, his voice rose several notches. "We do not have enough time to waste any. So I'm sorry that we have to wait for some of the others. In the meantime, why don't you get a ball, find a partner, and loosen up."

As the ten boys began to partner up and throw, Tru bit his lip pensively. The boys had seemed awfully disinterested during his short talk. It was not that they did not listen. It was that they did not hear. He knew that would not be the last time he had to address the problems of their attitudes and punctuality. Maybe repetition would help; he was going to have to keep stressing how important it was to be on time.

Tru looked over at Marvin Mitchell who was sitting in a wooden chair and looking every bit the part of a general manager in the major leagues. He wore a white short sleeve shirt with tan slacks and a wide-brimmed straw cowboy hat that partially hid his dark sunglasses. His briefcase was at his side. Tru rolled his eyes and nodded to him, trying to communicate his irritation. Marv looked away seeming to pay no attention.

By eighty thirty-two, all fifteen players had arrived. "All right, fellas," Tru said in an exasperated voice, "come on over here and park it on the grass. We need to get a few things straight." He watched the players straggle over to the maple tree where he was standing. His agitation at their attitudes grew. "Any time this side of noon would be fine, gentlemen."

His sarcastic remark changed nothing. The boys

continued to saunter slowly in Tru' s direction. Perhaps they could not read the underlying message of RUN!!!! in his words. He glanced back at Marvin Mitchell who was now wearing a big smile under those dark sunglasses, and Tru shook his head.

"Okay, gentlemen. Have a seat and relax. We need to talk about some of the things that will be expected of you. First of all, no matter what position you play, be here from now on at the designated starting time. I have to know who I can count on. For instance, practice might be arranged to get our infield work done first. If that's the order and you are late and the shortstop, it throws the entire practice off schedule. That is not acceptable." He pointed to each member of the team and spoke very slowly. "No one here is more important than the team. Is that understood?"

Tru waited for responses but only a few heads nodded yes. What was more disturbing was the apathetic looks on the faces of almost all the kids. Some rolled their eyes and tried to make the kids next to them laugh so they would get yelled at. Tru knew then the only reason the majority of the kids were playing was to participate in the major league All-Star Game, so he would have to use that as a prod.

"If you want to play as all-stars, the next thing I expect from you young men is *hustle*." He stared at them. "We may not be an all-star team but we will definitely be an all-hustle team. I'm not going to watch any of you *walk* onto the base-ball field. I'm not goin' for that, so we need to get that straight right now." His voice grew in intensity as he tried to intimidate the youngsters into listening. "The only thing you should never be beaten at is your dedication and your determination and your desire. Those three D's will make you a winner.

Whenever I call you over to me for any reason, I better see you run. Understood?"

Two looks stared back at Tru after this speech. One was a tired look, when the jaw just kind of hangs there and no muscle is actively keeping the lower lip near the upper. Gravity controls the face completely. The other was a peeved look, where the eyebrows and forehead scrunch together as if to ask, *Is this asshole talking to me?* Tru knew he had better start with some baseball activity before he lost them altogether.

He took a deep breath. "I'm gonna give y' all the benefit of the doubt and attribute this lousy attitude I see here to this being our first practice and occurring so early in the morning," he said, but agitation grew in his heart. Tru fought the urge that wanted to start shaking them but he wasn't about to resort to violence. Persistence was the key here. He continued calmly but loud enough to be heard as the team dispersed, "Find a partner. One of you line up on the third base line and the other in the infield: I want everyone throwing in the same direction so no one will get a ball upside his head. You must concentrate when you throw. I don't want to waste time chasing balls, because any time you spend chasing balls is time not spent improving your baseball skills. Remember, we only have a few weeks before our first game. Get busy, boys!"

Tru wondered if the words that came out of his mouth were in a foreign language they didn't understand. They must have been, he thought, after he scrutinized their first plays. Some of the kids were throwing across other pairs of kids, some were on the first base line, some behind home plate. Accidents waiting to happen. Rubbing a hand across his forehead, Tru strode towards his team and physically put the boys in the proper positions. Now, at least, he had cut down the chance of major injuries.

When Tru looked again at Marv, comfortably sipping on a soda pop and reading the newspaper, he felt irritated. He moved towards the director of the youth center and leaned over.

"I hope you're thinking about a new coach or a trade for some players," Tru kidded.

"What are you talking about, man? Looks like you got yourself a team there."

"Yeah? Well, that's your opinion, man. I'm about to start screamin' at these kids," he said as his joking manner became more serious.

"Hey, just be yourself, Tru. If you think these kids need to be hollered at, just do it."

Tru turned back to the field. He tried to pick out a player who had the beginnings of good throwing mechanics, who could possibly be turned into a pitcher. What he saw depressed him even more. Coach Bud was trying to help but they were arguing with him and balls were flying everywhere. Not only was there no one who looked like a potential pitcher, but there were only a few kids who could actually catch a ball. Manny and Lance were not among that select group.

That day ended mercifully.

The second day was the same only there were more missed balls, less hustling, and more kids didn't show, including Chris Williams, one of the best athletes.

The third day saw the shortest practice yet. Immediately at the end of practice, the boys scattered. Quickly.

Antonio Williams and Joe Foster hopped in Antonio

Williams, Senior's car for the short drive to Turner Elementary School in Wilkinsburg. Summer school began at noon and they barely had enough time to get there from Mellon Park.

"What you think of Coach Tru?" the usually happy go-lucky Antonio asked his cousin Joe as they exited his dad's blue Chevy Nova. Neither boy said a word to Antonio's father. In fact, they never acknowledged him. Their lack of manners did not bother Antonio Senior. He was pretty sharp about kids. He paid attention to their gossip, but kept his mouth closed unlike at games. Joe just looked at his cousin and rolled his eyes. "He's stupid, man. If he yells at us again I'm gonna tell him to suck my..."

Joe would have said the word, if it was not for the elbow Antonio gave him, when they saw Miss Boston, their teacher for the two hour session of summer school.

She was from 'the old school', Antonio's dad liked to say. Antonio wondered if there was electricity back then.

"Her face ain't bad, but is she ever big!" Antonio said "If it wasn't for her huge boobs, you would not be able to tell her and George Foreman apart."

Worse, she always wore those awful pink and mint green, flowery dresses. Antonio called them her army tents because they looked like they were camouflaged.

What was most intimidating to the boy, however, about the large, African-American woman was the fact that she did not hesitate to snatch any young man by the earlobes if he ever got out of line in front of her. What Joe was about to say in front of her would definitely have been considered out of line.

The boys took their usual positions in the last two seats in the row by the windows of the hardwood floored classroom. Everyone in the room wanted those two seats, but Joe and Antonio claimed them the first day of class and would have "kicked anyone's ass" had they dared take them.

To them, Miss Boston was speaking some mindless garble, her "big butt" facing the class, when a loud beeper sound filled the classroom. "What was that!" she said, turning quickly.

Antonio was unable to get to his beeper before it went off the second time.

Miss Boston made a beeline to the side of Antonio's desk. Twisting his right ear firmly, she said in her deep bass voice, "Hand it over, Mister Williams!"

"No!" a grimacing Tony said painfully, "It's mine!"

"Not any longer, young man!" she said determinedly. "Class, have any of you seen the sign next to the metal detec- tors...It plainly says all beepers, walkmans, and cellular phones will be confiscated until a parent or guardian comes to school with you!"

Miss Boston lifted Tony up from his desk, still holding his ear with her right hand. With her left hand, she pulled his over-sized Chicago White Sox jersey over his head, revealing not only the beeper fastened around his waist, but his sagging, long, black shorts. With amazing grace, she snatched the beeper from around him and plopped him back in his chair, humiliated and furious.

"Give it back to him ya fat bitch!" Joe said as he grabbed for the beeper when Miss Boston relaxed slightly. "Go Tone!!" he yelled to his cousin, as he ran to the door and out to the hall.

Before she knew what had happened, they were both out in the street. As they ran away from the school, they gave her the finger.

The act thrust them further down a path both of them

were thinking about walking. Neither Antonio nor Joe had officially joined the gang up in East Hills...yet. But they were already being enticed with street life and membership in a gang.

That gang was the Bloods. They nearly always wore red. Chicago White Sox jerseys were acceptable but red plaid, long-sleeved wool logger shirts were the official uniform. No matter the time of year. That was Joe's dress this hot July day.

Neither boy's parents were home to get the urgent phone calls from Miss Boston. By the time they got home and went to bed that evening, both Joe and Antonio had forgotten about the incident. After all, it was not like that was the first time something like that had happened.

The next morning, Antonio's dad was home, as was Joe's mom. When they heard the news from Miss Boston, they both hit the roof...and their kids. Both Joe and Antonio were ordered to stay home from practice that morning.

When Tru arrived that day he was annoyed at how practice was proceeding. Not only were Joe and Antonio missing, so were Chris Williams and Stan Coles.

Tru thought he knew why Joe and Antonio weren't there. The problem of running on the baseball field had been addressed. The boys' solution was to quit.

For a while he thought he should do the same. To hell with the All-Star Game...and to the statue unveiling...and to the San Diego Chicken.

Nevertheless, he stayed. When Tru returned home to Tonya later that afternoon, Manny and Lance were off on their bikes before he even got out of the jeep. *They're real upset that kids are missing!* he thought to himself sarcastically.

He was surprised to find Tonya home at one o'clock in the afternoon. "Why are you home this time of day?" he said dejectedly.

"I wanted to see you so I told my supervisor I was sick!" she said. "Tru, what's wrong, what's eatin' at you, anyways?"

"Half the damn team wasn't at practice today! That's what! I wonder why these kids say they want to play baseball, anyways? I know a lot of their parents just want to get them out of the house but..."

"Why don't you just quit, then?" she interrupted. "I don't know why you want to babysit fifteen little potential gang members...or however many you have. Tell them 'yo shove it' !!"

Tru turned away.

"Did any of the kids...or their parents call?" he asked.

Tonya just laughed and shook her head. "You're hopeless!" she said. "So I guess you'd better accept the problems, 'cause it's my opinion you don't want to quit." Tru sighed. "You're right again as usual," Tru said. She came over and hugged him.

Tru phoned all the kids who were not at practice the next morning.

One of them, Janet Williams had no idea where her son Chris was. She thought he went to practice.

Jim Coles, Stan Coles's father, was equally surprised.

Jerrett Thompson's father, Jim, said that he had dropped Jerrett off on the corner of Penn and Fifth at eight fifteen, right at the entrance to Mellon Park. He saw Tru down on the field. "I don't know what Jerrett did or where he went, but I'll find out and he'll be at practice tomorrow."

Antonio Williams, Senior talked to Tru about Antonio Junior and Joe Foster. They weren't making decent enough grades. "So, me and Joe's mom told them both they were done...no more baseball!" he finished.

"Were they upset?" Tru asked hoping to find a little meaning to the events of the summer.

"Sorry, Coach. They just didn't seem to care."

"You know what, Mr. Williams," Tru said as a thought came to him, "That may be just what they want! These practices aren't easy. They probably want to stay home! They've got video games in their room?"

"Yeah...why?"

"Don't you see?" Tru said with more energy, "Sending these kids to their room...grounding them...isn't punishment like it was when you and me were kids!"

"I never thought of it that way, Tru!" Mr. Williams voice rose in excitement. "You know, you're damn right!"

"We thought by getting them games they'd feel like other kids their age, you know the ones who have everything, not like ours."

"Bring the boys over tomorrow morning...all right Mr. Williams? If you can't get them there, let me know, and I'll come over and get them. We're bein' taken for fools, man!"

"I'll get them there, tomorrow, Coach Tru...don't you worry..."

At the next morning practice Antonio and Joe were there. So were Jerrett Thompson, along with Chris Williams and Stan Coles.

As Tru continued to evaluate his team, he thought of The Bad News Bears. But, hell, that was only fiction. This was live and in living color.

One morning, Tru couldn't be silent any longer. "Hold up, everyone. Hold the baseballs. Everyone step lively over here," Tru called to the kids. His annoyance grew as he watched them saunter toward the first base foul territory where he and Marv were standing. His patience had run out. He made sure all of the boys on the team, as well as the tennis players and squirrels, heard the next part. "Dammit, *RUN*!!! when I call you," he yelled.

It was as if an invisible huge paddle came down and swatted the boys on their butts at the same time. For the first time, Tru saw his future team move swiftly instead of do a slow walk.

He wasn't half through. "And what's up with this catching fellas?" he went on in disbelief. "My grandma could catch better than that, and she died five years ago! That's not gonna cut it, fellas. You've got to concentrate." His voice continued its decibel climb as sweat began to pour from his inflamed face. "Boys, if I have to tell any one of you once more to hustle while you're on this field, the whole team is going to run sprints as punishment."

"Man, that ain't fair," an angry voice whined. Tru was not even sure who said it.

"Is that right? We must have a coach among us!" Tru said as he jogged away from his team while grabbing control for the first time. "Okay, Mr. Coach, get your team over here to home plate. Being the great coach that you are, you must have heard of the rabbit run?"

Tru waited as the confused team walked over to the

home plate area.

"If any of the rest of you haven't heard of it, let me explain. You are goin' to start jogging around the bases in single file, right behind the man in front of you, as close as you can get without touching him. When I yell "go", the man at the front of the line sprints as fast as he can all the way around the bases until he reaches the back of the line. Keep doin' that until all of you have had the chance to be the rabbit. Sound okay to you, Coach? Well then, let's go. Start the jog." As he boys started their run, Tru added, "By the way, fellas, if any of you do not run as fast as you can, we'll all do it over again!"

A groan went up. From the pitching mound, Tru barked, "go" every fifteen seconds as his team circled him. There was no talking in the ranks or attempts to try to get the next person to laugh. The boys were not exactly sure what was going on, but no one, not even the unidentified coach, felt up to testing this crazy man to see what other form of punishment he could come up with. After the team completed fifteen minutes of nonstop running, Tru called them into the increasingly hot sun.

"Listen, don't ever talk back to any of the coaches like you did earlier to Coach Bud. When we want your opinion, we'll ask for it. Now, let me tell you why I think what we just did was fair. What would you think if you hustled your butt off to make a play and maybe saved some runs from being scored, only to see the runs come across the plate because one of your teammates did not see the need to hustle? Do you think that's fair?"

Tru could tell that made sense to the kids. For the first time, they were sitting up. Looks of disdain were being replaced by inclined heads as if they were listening. No longer were their eyes wandering all over Mellon Park: they were focused on him.

Now we're getting somewhere, he thought. "This missing the baseball has to cease, y' all. Concentrate. I know a lot of you boys haven't caught a ball before but all of you can do it if you keep your mind on the play. From now on, every time you miss a ball at practice, you will do three push-ups. As you do your first push-up, I want you to yell the word *Dedication!* on your way up. The second push-up, you will yell *Determination!* and on the last one, *Desire!*"

"You mean we do push-ups every time we drop the ball?" a moon-faced Antonio asked in disbelief. "Most of us don't catch any of them."

"Yessir. Every time. No exception. Understand me, fellas. I do not intend to waste my time watching you play a sloppy game. It isn't gonna be like that. I realize some of you may think this is bullcrap and if any of you want to quit after today's practice, I'll understand. No hard feelings. But that's the way it's gotta be if you stay. Now, are there any questions?"

Tru then instructed the boys, "Go back where you were and begin throwing again. Only this time with your concentration caps on." As they walked back to their positions, two of the young men, Darryl Weston and Brendon Banks, Coach Bud's grandson, yelled "run!" simultaneously. Tru smiled.

A few days passed. Every day, practice was at the same time, and each new day the boys had to be told fewer times about running on the field. The same two kids who called on the team to run, Darryl Weston and Brendon Banks, seemed to be emerging as pretty decent players and more importantly, to Tru, as team leaders.

Some of the others like Manny and Lance struggled. Their baseball skills were not very good, but considering this was the first time they had played the game, they were not that bad either. Still, Manny and Lance were the worst, they had to do more "triple D push-ups," as the boys began to call them, than any of the other players.

The last week, the boys practiced at Mellon Park every morning and some late evenings. On the day before they were to play their game, Marv announced who their opponent would be.

"Tomorrow night at six, you guys will be playing a team from Morningside," he announced to the anxious Little Leaguers. "The game is here at Mellon Park."

Enthusiasm struck immediately. The kids wanted to play right at that moment. They broke up into partners to warm up. Tru could see and hear the difference between these ready-to-go players and the laconic group which had first come to practice. They pretended to tag out Morningside runners each time they caught the ball. Most of the catches were accompanied by that sweet popping sound baseballs make when they are caught in the pocket just right.

Tru's reaction was quieter. Though the boys finally wanted to play, Tru was worried about the gossip that the Mornigside team was made up of whites who had the reputation of being more than a little prejudiced.

In fact, he knew it was more than gossip having experienced that prejudice himself. It happened when he was ten years old and had been riding his bicycle on a summer day, very similar to this one, near Highland Park and the Pittsburgh Zoo. He was looking for a shortcut home and ended up in the heart of Morningside. A group of boys from the school called out as they pursued him, "Get that nigger!" He had not really been exposed to much bigotry until he heard those words of hate directed at him and saw the group of white boys jump on their bikes and take off after him. "Let's kick his ass," someone had yelled. He'd pumped his legs as fast and as hard as he could and raced down Morningside Avenue until he finally saw a familiar street, Highland Avenue. He whirled his bike into it, knowing that in a matter of minutes he would reach East Liberty and safety—no white kid in their right mind would chase a black kid into East Liberty shouting the words he had been called. The boys pulled off their chase as they yelled that if he ever came back into Morningside he would be "a dead nigger for sure." Ramon didn't stop pedaling until he reached his home.

Now, twenty years later, his team would get a chance to play theirs. For all he knew and imagined, the coach for the Little League team they would play the next day could be one of the boys who had led the chase...

Tru's team had their best practice that muggy summer morning. The boys rarely dropped any easy throws, and their level of concentration had improved. During batting practice, the boys who were shagging balls in the outfield waiting for their turns to hit were diving to catch anything near them. Camaraderie, something the handful of parents watching practice had never seen before, was on display. The entire team did three push-ups with any team member who missed a ball. They were actually starting to believe they had a chance to win.

"Coach Tru, do we still look like 'The Bad News Bears' ?" Jerrett Thompson, the starting shortstop, asked.

"Nah, man. Y'all couldn't play with them boys.

They're out of your league."

Suddenly, the swish of the park's water sprinklers dampened the air. The entire team reacted the same way. Simultaneously, they threw their gloves in the air, screamed unintelligible chants of joy, and ran directly into the water shooting twenty feet into the windless, sticky air.

Tru watched with a wide smile that stretched across his face as they all laughed, hollered, and ran around like crazed animals. Some acted like they were showering, some stretched out on the wet grass and pretended to be swimming, and others just tried to drink in as much of the gushing spray as they could. Whether they won or lost tomorrow, Tru knew this experience was worth all the headaches. There was joy in the boys' hearts and on their faces.

The morning before the game the team met at Mellon at the usual time. It was not for another hard, hot practice but to get their uniforms. They were hyped. Soon Marvin Mitchell drove up. In his car's trunk was a big cardboard box overflowing with uniforms. He and Tru had used their own savings, begged and borrowed to get them. As Marv approached carrying the box, eager kids began to cheer. Not a formal melodic chant, but spontaneous clapping and hollering. The three men—Marvin Mitchell, Tru and Coach Bud—felt good. They clapped each other on the back. Anyone who happened to be at the park walking their dog, or stopped at the traffic light on the corner, could see something very special was going on at Mellon Park.

"You owe us three D's, Coach Mitchell," Darryl Weston said as he looked at an invisible watch on his wrist. "You're late!"

After seeing none of his excuses were being bought by

the youngsters, Mitchell said, "Boys, I guarantee you one thing. I've never been more pleased to do three push-ups. How about helping me with the words because I sometimes forget them."

"Dedication! Determination! Desire!" yelled fifteen very excited boys, two extremely proud coaches, and a general manager in unison to an empty Mellon Park.

Their uniforms weren't fancy but, by the looks on the boys' faces, you would have thought they'd been given the official uniform of the Pittsburgh Pirates instead of blue T-shirts, white pants, and blue stirrups. On the backs the white lettering "P.I.C.Y.A." meant to the boys "OUR TEAM."

No one even saw the purple clouds come charging into the Pittsburgh sky from the west. By noon, there was a torrential downpour. At one o'clock, fifteen crestfallen boys heard the game being canceled.

Tru and Marv explained to them that they could get just as excited two days after, when the game had been rescheduled. But the boys would have none of it. There was no doubt in any of their minds however, if the game had been played that day, they would have beaten Morningside. They could not get past the bad luck they felt had followed them all their lives.

"Come on now, fellas," Tru said to the heartbroken team. "Keep your heads up! So we get them two days from now. That's no big deal. One thing you must understand is that in life there are no guarantees. Disappointment is always just around the corner. Champions know their victory is just delayed. Champions rise above disappointment."

Through his tears, Manny said, "But we wanted to play today!"

Chapter 8

Reach Out
or Throw Away
The Key

The next day was not a good one for the team. First the storm continued, so they could not practice in the morning, the only time the field wasn't being used. Then when the weather cleared around three in the afternoon, Tru received a disturbing phone call from Roy Jones, Todd Hill's father.

"Tru, I hate to have to tell you this, but Todd was picked up by the Pittsburgh Police and arrested. He was taken to Shuman Center, a juvenile detainment facility in Highland Park, and charged with assault."

"What in the hell happened?" Tru asked.

"He and a group of kids found a way to leave Reizenstein Middle School during summer class hours and get over to Frick Park. I don't know exactly what happened there, but a fight broke out. The three kids involved were taken to Shuman."

"Are they going to be held there?" Tru asked, concerned.

"Yeah, about ten days, after which they'll be placed on

house arrest. If we're lucky," Todd's father said dejectedly.

"But Todd's a good kid," Tru objected.

"He's hanging out with the wrong crowd," his father sighed.

"Has he ever been in trouble before?" Tru asked.

"Never! He likes playin' ball with you so much, Tru." The father pleaded, "Maybe you can talk to him. He says he didn't start the fight. I don't know what to do, Tru. I know he thinks a lot of you—that's all he talks about. What the hell's wrong with these kids today, man? I tell him there's shit out there, and he just don't want to listen!"

"Hang in there, Roy," Tru said, keeping his voice calm. "He isn't a bad kid. You and I both know that. I know how hard this must be for you, but this might be the best thing that ever happened to him. If he isn't ready to listen now, he might never be. I'll tell you though, if I talk to him I'm not hearing that bullshit about how it wasn't his fault. He should've been in school. If you want, I'll tell him that. Unfortunately, I can't see him today because we have practice. I will first thing tomorrow."

"Thanks, Tru," Roy said weakly.

Todd was a very talented eleven-year-old. He was also a very likable kid. Tru saw much of himself in the young man from East Hills. He had considered dropping him from the squad because he was absent so much, but something about the boy had made Tru want to keep him.

Perhaps it was the similarity he saw in Todd to another pre-teenager. A kid who was confused, lacked confidence, and had a habit of being late and not where he was supposed to be and picked the wrong crowd to hang out with. That kid's name was Ramon Dixon.

Tru pondered what to do next. He knew he could not sacrifice the well-being of the team and their fragile commitments to baseball for the poor decision made by Todd. Yet, he did not want to turn his back on the young man at a time when, more than anything else, Todd needed strength and support.

Not blind support, however. Tru would not let himself fall victim to letting Todd find an excuse to explain his improper behavior. Racism or poverty was too often the excuse of choice. No, Tru would not be a part of deflecting blame from its real source in order to escape justice.

If there was one message Tru was stressing to the kids, it was to take personal responsibility for one's actions. This was the cornerstone of the philosophy in which he believed and promoted every day he was in their presence. It was why he frowned when teams argued with umpires. It was unacceptable, to Tru's way of thinking, for any member of a team to rip on or laugh at kids or adults on a team they were competing against. For him to express a different philosophy with Todd would ruin his credibility with the kids and more importantly, with the man he saw everyday in the mirror.

Tru decided that he had to tell the news to the boys before anyone else did. They needed to discuss it and settle one issue. Should they take Todd back on the team? In the beginning, Tru had told them that there would be some kids who would be difficult to keep on the team. There had been several kids who were marginal participants and Tru had to decide whether it was or wasn't in the team's best interest to allow them to play. Usually these were kids who skipped a lot of practices, had poor grades and belittled the others.

But Todd was different. Though he skipped too many practices, Tru felt he would become a team player. In fact, as time went on, Tru was discarding his early belief in pulling kids off the team. He was beginning to feel most kids could be saved with the right training and help. In his heart he felt Todd Hill was one of those kids.

Calling the kids to set up a night practice, Tru arranged alternate rides for the kids he usually took with him. He wanted to drive alone so he could think more about just how he was going to break the news to them. Tru arrived at the field around six so he was there when Ron's van pulled up and unloaded kids and equipment. Most of the rest of the team arrived about a half hour later. Coach Bud arrived with Brendon and a few of the kids Tru had asked him to drive. Shortly thereafter, two parents, Rob Haines and Tracie Elliott, brought their sons and one or two others. Bud Harvey usually came only minutes before practice due to his work schedule. Today Tru had asked Bud to leave work early and he had.

No one, not even Lance, was aware of what Tru had on his mind. He decided to hold the news until after the practice. He wanted the kids to concentrate on the challenge they were going to have facing Morningside.

The kids went through their normal routine and then they approached the bench.

Tru watched as the kids walked over to the bench area. Usually after practice there was not much chatter. Today they were much more vocal and excited than usual because of the next day's game. As he observed them, Tru's thoughts turned to Todd Hill. When the boys didn't ask for Todd, Tru was glad. He knew they were probably thinking their teammate had let them down being absent again. They probably didn't want to upset Tru by reminding him. Tru grimaced.

Tru spoke briefly about the game plan. However, he had more than the practice on his mind. He turned his post practice lecture to the topic that had been worrying him all day.

"Todd Hill was picked up yesterday by the Pittsburgh Police," he informed the kids. "Somehow or other, he and a group of kids left Reizenstein at lunch and went to Frick Park. I don't know the whole story but I guess there was a big fight and he was one of the guys who got picked up. Todd was arrested for assault and has to spend ten days at Shuman. I will be goin' over there to see him tomorrow morning, and I want to know how you guys feel about me invitin' him back on the team when he gets out. If you do, I'm gonna tell him that he'll be able to practice with us but not play ball this year. I'll also tell him that's not important—what is important is that he starts makin' better decisions about his life. I think we can help him to do that. He misses one more practice and he's done, I promise you and will promise him that! He gets in trouble again or skips school, he's gone, no questions asked. He needs to hang out with some good kids—not that you're what I'd call good kids—" Tru was glad to see some smiles on their faces. "So what y'all think? Raise your hand if you think that it'd be okay for Todd to come back."

It was unanimous.

The next morning Tru left the house early. Walking into Shuman Center brought back memories. Memories of when he was a teenager and knew everything. He recalled his mother's words of advice, "Boy, if you don't stop running around with them hoodlums, you are going to wind up in jail, or worse yet, dead!"

He remembered other words more harsh which finally effected a change in his behavior. "If I ever see you in my

courtroom one more time, Ramon, you better believe your
new address will be cell block number seven—for several
years!"

How sad, he thought, that it took the words of a judge,
someone who had no real interest in which path he chose, to
make him realize what a jerk he had been acting like. It was
sad that it was not the words of his mother, who struggled by
herself to raise three children, that were responsible for the
transformation.

While waiting in the visitors' room to see Todd, Tru
noticed how young the children now incarcerated at Shuman
were. They were mere babies. A bunch of twelve and thir-
teen-year-olds who people thought were too young to be out
after dark, who in reality would probably shoot someone
wearing the wrong color or rob in broad daylight.

"Thanks for coming," Todd Hill said as he was escorted
into the small visitors' room wearing the colors and uniform of
the jail for young delinquents. Tru sat down at a table in the
small room to which he'd been led.

"Don't thank me. Thank your mom and dad. I'm here
'cause you're in the program. They called 'cause they love
you." Tru's response caught Todd by surprise. "By the way,
you look great in handcuffs and prison orange."

Todd knew that his coach was a man who cared deeply
about his well-being, but his aggressive style confused Todd.
He was expecting and hoping for some support and sympathy.

"Let me give you a little dose of reality, my man," Tru
said instead. "The world doesn't care about you. It don't give a
fuck if you fail or succeed, only if you can make it some money
or if it can make some money off you! The only people that

truly care 'bout you is your family. You sold them out for a couple of *street nigas*. Nigas that encourage you to disrespect your parents. You listen to them 'cause they're your boys! The same boys who don't house you, who don't feed you, who don't help you with your homework!" Tru leaned in a little closer to Todd and looked him right in the eye. "The same boys who aren't visitin' you here. Right?"

Todd did not respond. He just stared with glassy eyes at his mentor. He knew Tru was aware that no one but his family had come to visit. He did not want to speak.

Tru continued, although more annoyed. "I just asked you a question, Todd, and I expect an answer."

"What was the question?" Todd spoke dejectedly.

"You know the damn question!" Tru attacked, leaning forward in the boy's face.

"No. No one's been here except you, my mom and dad."

Tru settled back. He ran his hand through his braids as he said, "And you sold your parents out for them. That's what disturbs me. You have parents who actually care about you. It isn't like a lot of these kids in here whose parents couldn't give a damn. You don't know how lucky you are, boy. Do you?"

Todd shrank down in his chair, his head in his hands as they rested on his knees. He had no response.

Tru stood up and said, "All this 'cause you think you know what's best for you, which isn't comin' in at night at a decent time and goin' to school all day. Shit like that cramps your style, takes away your freedom, huh?" He looked at the boy for a long time. "What freedom have you got now, Todd?"

Tru left, praying his words had done some good.

A few hours later, Todd's father called Tru, who was back home again. "I don't know what you said to him, but he'd like you to go to the hearing."

"Will do," Tru said, "I only hope it will accomplish something."

At four that afternoon Tru listened as the judge addressed Todd and his two accomplices.

"I find the three defendants delinquent of robbery and aggravated assault. Let me tell you something, boys. To me, it's appalling that our streets are not safe at night. For you three so-called tough guys to mug someone in broad daylight in the park is a disgrace! There's an old saying I like. 'If you are not part of the solution, you are part of the problem.' You three have now been convicted of felonies. That means you have no more rope. Because this is your first offense, I will accept the recommendation from the probation and community services offices. Ten days of house arrest followed by one year probation. But understand one thing—and be very clear about it—if I ever see you in my courtroom again, you will go to jail! Do you understand me?"

They all responded, "Yes, sir!"

Tru didn't know it then, but Todd took to heart the judge's words.

Chapter 9

Win or Lose

The next morning the sun was shining. The huge enthusiasm the boys had shown the day the game had been scheduled was not matched today, but their spirits were still up. Soon the Morningside team began arriving at Mellon Park. Car after car let out Little Leaguers, their families, and a seemingly endless caravan of supporters.

Tru was impressed. Morningside supported their kids, and that was the way it should be. There must have been twenty adults along with another fifteen to twenty kids to cheer their team. Tru looked behind the bench of his own team. There were maybe seven adults and four or five kids. He felt disappointed.

In a short while it was time to play ball. Morningside won the flip of the coin and chose to be the home team. In the stands he heard some rumblings of trouble, "We'll get the gorillas."

In the bottom of the first, Morningside's shortstop jumped on P.I.C.Y.A.'s pitcher Brendon Banks and began beating him up. "It's not looking too good," Tru murmured, running out to talk to his pitcher. He saw the nervousness on Brendon's face. Tru tried to reassure him, but he knew they would be fortunate to get out of the inning giving up less than five runs. In fact, it was three. When the third out was made, Tru and Coach Bud walked towards their team coming off the field.

Tru spoke first. "You're only three runs down, gentlemen, and it's only the first inning. No big thing! We have the whole game in front of us. Let's start swinging the bats like we know how. Brendon, all you need to do is relax and throw strikes. Just have some fun. That's the only thing I want all of you to do: have some fun. This game isn't over yet. We can still win. Now let's go!"

The next four innings produced some of the best baseball the parents from Wilkinsburg and the eastern neighborhoods that made up the P.I.C.Y.A. had ever seen. For the first time, P.I.C.Y.A. teammates helped each other. They yelled out which base to throw to so everyone would know what to do with the ball before it was even hit, so no one would throw to the wrong base. They supported each other as never before. Through the fifth inning the Morningside Bulldogs got no more runs. Excitement rose. The game went to the sixth and last inning with P.I.C.Y.A. still trailing by the score of three to nothing.

"Listen up, everyone," Tru said as the boys gathered around him. "This is it, y'all. It's now or never. Brendon pitched a heck of a game till now and it sure would be nice to get him some runs and win this game. When you bat this inning, don't think about the score. All I want you to do is get yourself on base. It doesn't matter how. Just do your best at bat and don't worry about anything else. Now get your hands in here and when I count to three, I want you all to yell,

'WIN!' All right. One! Two! Three!" The sound was deafening as emotions rose to a fever pitch.

Joe Foster, the number two P.I.C.Y.A. hitter, led off with a solid single to right. Rich Smith, the center fielder, was up next. He drew a walk on a three-two pitch after fouling off several near strikeout pitches. More catcalls rose from the Moringside stands.

It was one of those times at bat that can turn games around. Darryl Weston, by far the biggest eleven-year-old on the field, was up next. He lined a one-strike pitch into the left center field gap. Both Joe and Rich were off with the crack of Darryl's bat. The noise from the bench of P.I.C.Y.A. when they crossed the plate was resounding. Cheers and claps rose from the handful of supporters. Big Darryl ended up at third base. There were no outs.

After a conference between Morningside's coach and pitcher, the young hurler was able to strike out the next batter. The same noise that was uncontrolled only minutes before on the side of P.I.C.Y.A. erupted, only now it sounded like fireworks were blasting in the sky. It came from those on the other bench.

Robbie Elliot was the next hitter. The Bulldog infield again pulled up to the edge of the infield grass to cut down the tying run at the plate. The count was two balls and two strikes. Robbie swung at the next pitch. He hit the ball toward the shortstop. It was not hit with a lot of authority, but it could not be said it was hit softly either. There was no hesitation by Big Darryl. He broke for the plate. The shortstop came up with the ball cleanly and fired to the plate. It was a close play, one that caused a rather lengthy argument, but the umpire called, "Safe." The game was tied at three-all.

Alertly, Robbie had taken second base on the argument. The boys in the plain blue shirts had a runner on second with one out and the momentum was back on their side.

The next hitter, Marcus Haines, popped up to the second baseman. Now there were two outs and a runner on second. Tru's team was one hit away from the lead, or one out away from trying to keep the tie in the bottom of the sixth.

Usually, in baseball, there is a direct relationship between how hard the ball is hit and the chances of something good happening for the hitter. Antonio Williams's single to right was not one of those times. He hit the ball too hard.

As Robbie was digging around third, Tru circled his left arm and pointed towards home plate with his right hand. He stared at Robbie and pumped his arm vigorously hoping that would somehow translate into more speed in Robbie's legs. As he watched the ball bounce on a big hop directly to the right fielder, he knew their only chance to score the run was a wild throw. He signaled Robbie to run faster. The ball thrown by the left-handed right fielder streaked toward the plate as if it had been shot from a cannon. Robbie had no chance.

Tru gathered his team around before they took the field for the bottom of the sixth. He saw the disappointment in the boys' eyes.

"Come on now, fellas. That was a great comeback. Let's hold them here so we can win this thing in extra innings in the seventh," he said, but the boys looked spent. He knew they were going to lose as they slowly made their way onto the field.

The first Morningside batter hit a hard ground ball to the first baseman, Robbie Elliott. It went through his legs untouched. Their next batter hit a comebacker to Brendon Banks on the mound. Shortstop Jerrett Thompson broke for the bag at second to start the double play.

One of the toughest plays to execute in baseball occurs when a pitcher has to throw the ball to second base with no fielder there. He has to time precisely when the shortstop will arrive so that the shortstop and the ball meet at second base at exactly the same time. The shortstop takes the throw, steps on the bag, and fires to first base to complete the double play.

Brendon made a perfect throw to Jerrett who was standing about six feet to the third base side of second. However, at the crucial moment, Jerrett was standing on second base watching helplessly as the ball sailed past him into center field.

Fortunately, the runner had slid into second and was unable to go to third base on the overthrow. They could still get out of this, Tru thought as he called time and went to the mound to try to settle his shaken players.

"Listen up, y'all. We can do this! Brendon, keep the ball down so we can get an easy grounder for a double play. Remember, you infielders, you can step on any base and throw to first for the double play. Robbie, remember if you get the grounder and step on first, be sure and yell 'tag' when you throw the ball to second. All right, fellas, pick your heads up. Let's go!"

Brendon kept the ball down when the next hitter came up, just as Tru had told him, but he fell behind in the count two balls and no strikes. His third pitch was low also, but the hitter swung. He hit a grounder. The ball had eyes on it. It was hit just far enough from the shortstop and third baseman that neither could get it and it rolled slowly into left field. P.I.C.Y.A.'s Andre Jones got there and he knew the only chance he had to get the winning run at the plate was to charge the ball and come up throwing as hard as he could.

It was just not meant to be. The ball found its way under Andre's glove, and the Bulldog's winning run, without a throw, trotted across the plate into his teammates' hugs and high fives.

Morningside would be moving on to the second round of the Mayor's Cup and P.I.C.Y.A. would be watching the rest of the tournament. It did not seem like much consolation. Their season had lasted one game.

The boys did not take the loss well. It is mandatory for Little League teams to shake hands at the end of every contest. P.I.C.Y.A. wanted no part of that particular tradition. The hurt was too great, the emotion too strong.

"As bad as this feels right now, y'all," Tru said quietly to his sobbing players, "Don't put your heads down. Because in the game of life you are always in danger of losing. You are going to have to learn how to dig deep to look within yourself and find that energy to fight like a warrior; but not with your hands, with your minds. Because in the game of life you're going to have to be a warrior everyday. As you get older you are going to be in situations that may prompt you to quit school, sell drugs or use drugs, join a gang, or commit suicide because you feel that's your only way out. We hope you get older you get smarter and become leaders and not quitters. As for today, I couldn't be more proud of you. Everybody here gave his best effort to help us win today. *Everybody*! Even those of you who didn't play much. You helped everyone else by your spirit and your attitude. You all should be proud of yourselves. Winning the game would have been great, but becoming a winner is better and y'all showed me today that you are winners—that's what matters, not the score. Now, let's go and shake Morningside's hands. Those kids played their hearts out, just like you did. Some of the spectators need to be disciplined, but the boys deserve to be congratulated, just like you. It's tough becoming a man sometimes. Line up."

After the talk, the P.I.C.Y.A. boys slowly gathered their equipment and went over to shake the hands of Morningside's team. As they did, two parents approached

Tru. Tracy Elliot and Ron Haines said simultaneously, "That was one heck of a game, Tru. Are you goin' to do this next year?"

"Whew, I don't even want to think about that right now. I really don't know."

"We all want you to. Those kids played better today than we've ever seen them play. Shoot, we thought we were at the wrong field or something. Thanks for all the effort you put in with them, Tru. They really enjoyed themselves," Tracy said.

Their sincerity was apparent. They were not grateful just because he kept their kids occupied but because he'd helped them grow as players and people. "Well, thanks a lot. Y'all got some pretty good kids. It was my pleasure."

"Is the all-star stuff over?" Ron asked quietly.

"You know, I really don't know right now. We got caught up in the practices and things. I haven't checked the schedule, but I'll call y'all later this week. I think it is, but I'll let you know for sure."

"All right then. Let us know as soon as you can because these kids will be drivin' us crazy until you do. They'll probably want to practice tomorrow. What do you think?"

"Just tell them they're off till further notice. And thanks for gettin' your boys out here every day. You should be commended for that."

Bart Hanks stepped up behind the parents.

"Tru, that was a tough one. I'll tell you what, though. Those boys of yours looked real good."

"Thanks, man."

"I heard the others askin' you about next year. Are you plannin' on coaching?"

Tru did not hear any concern in the voice of the coach

of Wilkinsburg's all-star team, but he responded as if he had. "Nah, man. I don't want your job."

Bart Hanks was embarrassed. He knew his reaction when Tru and Marv approached him about forming this team had been defensive. "You think I'm worried about your coaching ability? Man, you must be crazy!" A smile appeared when he said, "If you are goin' to coach, though, I'd like my son to play on your team."

Tru grinned. "That's a high compliment."

Then Tru turned to watch his team grudgingly shaking the hands of the victors. He felt tears begin to well in his eyes but he held them back.

Images spun through his mind. To have seen the joy that was on the faces of his team when they made their come-back, even at the expense of feeling the pain that was in their hearts after they lost the game, would be something he would never forget.

Before the team dispersed, Tru called them over one last time. "I'll give you guys a call next couple of days to let you know if we have to meet again to do any more all-star stuff. Remember," he said with all the enthusiasm he could muster, "I want every one of you to pick your heads up. You've got nothing to be sad about. Don't ever let anyone tell you that you aren't winners. You are all stars! Be very proud of what you accomplished these last two weeks!"

As the boys dispersed to their various rides, Tru did not fight his own tears any longer.

Chapter 10

Centered

It had been two weeks since Todd's arrest. The hectic schedule Tru kept throughout the all-star activities had quieted. He was just getting used to the lack of pressure when the persistent program director of P.I.C.Y.A. called again. "Tru, would you be interested in not only setting up our computer system but maintaining it and, also, serving as the program director? I'm talking about joining the staff, man. I can pretty much guarantee you the funding will be there for at least one year."

"You're talkin' my language now, bro," Tru responded enthusiastically. Adding a new client that would require him to supervise middle school students on computers and see to it that they became computer literate fit in perfectly with his goals.

Without giving a definite yes, Tru was soon committed to this new project.

"The alliance receives most of its seed funding from the Ronald McDonald Children's Charities. Once the program is up and running, additional funding will be sought," Marv commented. It sounded good, but Tru was savvy enough to know seeding from outside wasn't a cut and dried certainty.

Marvin Mitchell found out quickly that Tru knew a great deal about computers. He was amazed that Tru had never received formal training.

During several meetings Marv and Tru discussed their ideas about bettering inner city kids' education. "When the Learning Center is operational," Marv said, "we can tie in the events to the kids' school goals."

"That will mean the Learning Center would be a supplement to the regular education the students are receiving in the Pittsburgh Public Schools."

Marv nodded. "If a boy is unable to maintain a C average in his schoolwork, that student won't be able to participate in the activities at the Center."

"So one will enforce the other," Tru said nodding.

They agreed that each student would be required to bring his interim report as well as report card to the Center whenever they were received at home.

"Yeah, being housed in Belmont Elementary School which is part of the public school system will give the staff at P.I.C.Y.A. inside information that makes their mission somewhat easier to accomplish. A student who has done poorly at school won't be able to tell the staff at P.I.C.Y.A. that he didn't receive an interim report from school because he did so well."

Tru laughed. "I remember trying to use that excuse."

"Me too," Marv agreed. "But these staff members know *all* students receive interim reports, regardless of whether they are doing well or poorly. They also will know the date when these reports are mailed home so there can be no excuse for students not bringing in their interims or report cards."

The ribbon-cutting ceremony at the Pittsburgh Inner City Youth Alliance for the After School Learning Center was attended by dignitaries from all across the city.

Within a few weeks, to Tru's surprise, Marv told him all the funding was in place. The centerpiece of the new program, the computer network, was located in a small vacant room adjacent to the library in the basement of the school. Marv had arranged for this space with the principal, Mr. Santer. He felt it was important to have a secluded spot conducive to learning for the middle and high school students who were to be part of the program.

The pair traveled to different computer stores. Once inside, Tru took over. He was in his element, but acted as if he needed every scrap of information. Later, he and Marv had some later laughs about acting like two computer illiterates. Nevertheless, because of Tru's later adroit bargaining and knowledge, the Center was able to purchase five IBM-compatible machines, two laser printers, over thirty different educational software titles, modems with built-in fax capabilities and access to the Internet, and still come in under budget.

The opening of the computer lab at the youth center was set to coincide with the opening of the Pittsburgh Public Schools. Tru's days would still be occupied with his normal clients, but his evenings would be split: he planned to spend two nights teaching his computer class at the community college and two nights supervising the program at the youth center.

On the first night, Tru set the ground rules for using the computers.

Meeting with some kids in the basement room, Tru told them seriously, "This is all business here. I will not tolerate any horseplay. If I find you playing around with this equipment, or misusing it in any way, you will be removed from the program. Improper language—like swearing or poor behavior, like ripping on another student—will also get you kicked out. If I see anyone playing computer games during study time, that's it—you're gone. We've started this program for you to improve your schoolwork, to learn how to use computers, and for you to have a little fun along the way. If any of you disagree, let me know right now so I can pull one of the kids on the waiting list in to take your place."

Many of the youngsters were not responsive or responsible. They'd never been serious about learning before, and all they knew of life was what the streets had already taught them.

Not giving up, Tru worked even harder with them. His days and evenings were again filled. He got up before five worked on the computer program. At 9:50 A.M. he left to catch the 10:10 bus downtown, parking his jeep in front of one of the kids' house. Having several teaching contracts with the community colleges, he fulfilled those by 9:00 P.M., ran across town, caught the bus back and picked up his car. The only time alone he had for reflection was in his Jeep as he began and ended the day. It was then he reflected on his new life.

For the first time in a very long time, Tru felt happy with his professional and personal life. His and Tonya's relationship was growing stronger. His business was prospering and he was continuing to put out the effort so it would continue to grow.

However, one aspect of his life not evolving well was his relationship with Tonya's son, Lance. It was not that it was bad. It was just that there was no real bond developing. Lance was not a tough kid to like but he was a tough kid to read. Neither he nor Tru knew how to proceed. Their talk was always superficial.

As the school year got into high gear, Tru tried to make it a point to try to tutor Lance at home and get him on the computers at the youth center. Tru thought it would be a good way to build a deeper rapport with the eleven-year-old as well as to help him with his studies. But Lance always had an excuse and they only met a few times, hardly enough to develop any type of meaningful interaction.

Tru usually stayed home in the mornings, as he ran his office from the upstairs bedroom. He rarely began making his rounds to his various clients until some time after noon. The phone calls from Lance's teachers started in the middle of September. They were usually the same. Lance was not motivated and didn't do much work.

Tru did not tell Tonya. He saw the calls as an opportunity to build his floundering relationship with the boy and to gain Lance's trust.

"Hey, Lance, you got a minute?" Tru surprised Lance as he walked through the door. He had made it a point to be there that day when Lance arrived because Tru had received a call from Lance's math teacher early in the morning.

Lance did not respond verbally but he did stop wherever he was going. Tru figured, this was his way of saying that he did have a minute.

"How's school goin', man?" Tru said with a smile.

"Fine," Lance said politely but firmly.

Tru leaned down. "Look, man, I got a call from your math teacher, Mr. Bell, today. He says you aren't doin' much homework. Is that true?" Tru asked in a non-confrontational way.

Again, there was no verbal response, just a shrug of the shoulder and a looking away which Tru knew meant the boy did not really care who had called.

Tru edged over to the spot at which Lance seemed to

be staring. "Look, man, if you're havin' trouble with some of the subjects, I can help you. But you need to ask; I can't read your mind," Tru said, trying to cut the tension.

Lance stiffened. "I really don't need any help. I do most of my homework at school, but sometimes I forget to turn it in, or I lose it," Lance said as he fidgeted, turning his head toward another spot, obviously wanting to be somewhere else.

At least Lance was giving him a response, Tru decided. "All right, Lance," Tru said, accepting defeat for the moment, "I just don't want you to fall behind this year. You're in middle school now and things are going to be a little tougher. If you ever need any help, just come and find me. Okay?"

"Okay," Lance replied in a noncommittal voice.

It was not that Tru believed what Lance had just told him, he was nowhere near that naive. He wanted to plant seeds for the future, not have a fight.

"You know how important your education is, don't you, Lance? Without it," Tru paused, "without it, you'll be on the streets. One day, you're goin' to look around at material things, and you're goin' to want them. But your bank is goin' to be severely limited if you don't get a degree. There will be little you can do. Do you understand what I'm tellin' you?"

"Yeah, I know, but none of my friends get picked on this way. They're out having a good time like kids should. Can I go over to Manny's house?"

Tru sighed. "Okay, but when you get home, I want to see you crack a book, all right? You must have some homework."

"I did all my homework at school."

"Should I call your math teacher and ask him?"

"Go ahead and call. I did my homework at school today."

Lance had called his bluff and Tru realized he had said

a dumb thing. It only served to further Lance's doubts about Tru. He was not Lance's dad. Although Tru had offered to help Lance with his homework everyday, Lance had only chosen to accept his help twice.

"What are you and Manny up to, man?"

"I don't know. Probably nothing," Lance said, quickly walking out the door.

Chapter 11

Just Hanging

Manny was standing at the open window upstairs watching Lance next door. There was no mistaking what his best friend Lance was doing when he reached into his house's mailbox, scanned its contents, then grabbed an envelope, balled it up, and tossed the crumpled paper onto Edgerton Avenue.

"Was that from your school, man?" Manny called down to Lance. He knew his friend had gotten into trouble a few days earlier at Reizenstein Middle School, and Lance had told him the teacher was going to send a letter home to his mother, Tonya.

Lance McCoy shot his usual answer back, "Don't say nothin', man, all right?"

Manny knew better than to tell because that would get his best friend punished and if Lance was put on punishment, well that was just about the same as Manny being punished, and he wasn't going for that.

"Are you coming here?" Manny called out.

"Sure."

"I'll be right down," Manny called.

Manny could never figure out why Lance kept getting into trouble at his school. Lance always said he was just cutting up, silly stuff like making noises in the back of the room while the teacher was talking. Lance said all the kids at the school did it and other kids would think he was some kind of nerd if he just sat there paying attention. But his friend asked himself why Lance would risk getting put on punishment all the time just to make some silly noises in the back of the room. That was the part Manny couldn't figure out. Of course, Manny also wondered why Lance kept getting the kind of grades that got him into hot water with his mom. He knew Lance was pretty smart, at least as smart as he was, and Manny had no trouble getting decent grades at Holy Rosary School.

Lance loped up the three stairs onto Manny's porch. The row houses on Edgerton Avenue were made of wood and had the gray green, splintered appearance of being forgotten. Some of the boards had huge holes in them and most of the windows, their glass shattered, were covered with cellophane so that when the wind blew the coverings would flap. But the porches were comfortable. Lance propped his feet up on the porch banister and slouched back into a chair. His friend soon plopped down in another.

"Mr. Ray was home, wasn't he?" Manny asked Lance, using the nickname they used for Tru. "Did he say anything?"

"He was on me about my grades and homework or something." Lance quickly changed the subject. "What do you wanna do?"

"I don't care." Manny paused and let the subject go. "Hey, did you see Emmitt run last week? Nobody can run like that dude, man. He's the best in the NFL."

"Marion Butts would run him over like I run your big behind over, fool," responded Lance.

"Marion Butts? He is butt ugly! Who'd San Diego ever beat anyway? You couldn't run my big behind over. I'd crush your bony butt."

"Your big fat overgrown doughnut-eatin' butt couldn't never catch me. With my runnin' skills? You must be crazy."

"You big-headed little freak. Man, I'd knock you. . . ." The boys were interrupted by the usual late day entertainment. Across the street, little four-year-old Billy was about to get in his 'Flintstonemobile' car for a little drive. It never failed. He was not big, strong, or agile enough to drive his car for more than five feet before it toppled over, leaving him sprawled on his side, crying his little eyes out.

"Watch him, man," Lance said with great anticipation. "Why does he keep doin' that?"

"Where you goin', Bam-Bam? To pick up Pebbles?" Manny called out to Billy.

"Oh shit, there he . . ." the boys said in unison.

SPLATTT!

The laughter that came from Manny was one of those that you can't hear. His entire body shook and he doubled over. Lance's laughter, on the other hand, came from the depths, if a scrawny eleven-year-old can have depth, of his belly. It was loud. Billy fell so that he couldn't open the door of his car. He was trapped. They boys watched, laughing more, as Billy lay helpless in his car until his mom came to his rescue. Not once did they ever consider helping the imprisoned toddler.

"Dang, that's funny, man. Let's go for a ride," Manny said as he picked up his old model Seneca with the fat seat and small tire in the back. "Go get your slow-butt little mountain bike and see if you can keep up."

Lance liked his "ride" because it was blue. He knew blue would not get him in trouble around his neighborhood, which was Crip territory, whereas other colors might get their rider attacked and the bike stolen. He picked the bike up off his dirt front yard, and off he and Manny went.

"Where do you wanna go?" Lance questioned Manny.

"I don't know."

Despite Lance's question, their route was usually the same, down Edgerton Avenue. Edgerton Avenue is a long street that parallels Frankstown and runs the entire east-west distance through Homewood. It was a fairly safe haven for the boys who were given boundaries they were not to cross. Boundaries that if crossed could lead them into a war zone where they might be hurt or worse. Despite or maybe because the danger intrigued them, usually they rode from Edgerton to Homewood Avenue to the little plaza on the corner of Homewood and Frankstown. If they were lucky, they wouldn't be attacked. Riding along, they might see some action there. As the sun went down they felt enough warmth to offset the crispness in the October air. Soon they began looking for excitement.

Gang members hung out as usual on the corners and that always confused Manny. He didn't ask them questions and they never asked him things like, *Why ain't you a Crip, little man?*

"Why do these dudes hang on the corner all the time?" Manny asked his biking partner, "How come they ain't never in front of their cribs?"

"Easier on business and you can see 'the Man' coming from all directions," Lance replied as if he knew all about it. "It gives them more directions to run when the police chase them."

That's what Lance and Manny were hoping to see, the

police chasing someone. Everyone knew the boys on the corner were selling drugs. Usually, the police would come through the neighborhood around five-thirty or six o'clock, but everyone knew that also. If you wanted to see any action, you had to be there a little early, maybe five o'clock, and hope the police tried to surprise the drug dealers.

No luck today. Manny and Lance rode around the little parking lot of the plaza and pretended to be stunt drivers as they wove their bikes between cars keeping as close to each other as possible. This did not look nearly as suspicious as it would if they had sat on the opposite corner and stared at the drug dealers. The dealers didn't like being watched, and it was kind of fun to be daredevils on bikes. After an uneventful half hour, except for a little wipeout Lance had as he tried a hook slide in the gravel where the parking lot ended, the boys figured it was time to continue on their rounds, which usually led them over to Homewood Park off Homewood Avenue.

"Would you ever sell drugs, Lance?"

"Nah, man, that's just stupid. All those guys gonna end up in jail or dead. Look what happened to Todd. Only good thing about these dudes is the money they make but I'll be making more than that once I get to be a mechanic. How 'bout you?"

"Nah, too risky for me. I can't run so good," Manny reasoned. Despite what he said, he was pretty athletic: after all, he was the nephew of one of the greatest basketball players to ever come out of Pittsburgh, the great Thomas 'June-bug' Howard. June-bug was all-everything in high school and he would have been one of the all-time greats in the NBA if the car he had been driving hadn't been in the path of a driver asleep at the wheel. Manny's Grandma Howard, with whom Manny lived, always said June-bug had more moves than the south had cotton. No, Manny's problem was not his genes, it was his weight. When you are four foot seven-and-a-half inches tall and weigh one hundred fifty-three pounds, you're just too heavy to move fast.

As they pedaled down to the park, Manny thought about Lance. Manny's concern was more than finding someone else to hang out with if Lance was put on punishment. He was worried about Lance's future. He sure wished Lance would do better at school. He did not want to see his best friend fall into the same tired life that a lot of the other kids on their street seemed destined for. Grandma Howard was always telling him how easy it was to get caught in that life even though most of the boys were pretty good kids. They had just fallen with the wrong crowd or didn't have much direction at home.

"Manny," Grandma often said, "learning is one of the best things you can ever do for yourself, and the only way to better yourself is to become a better self. Books are the only way to learn how. When you gain knowledge, you gain ammunition. When you have ammunition, nobody can hold you down. If you don't say yes to them books, one of these days you are going to run out of reasons to say no to them streets."

He wished so hard that he could find the right words to say to Lance something that would make his lifelong best friend do better at school. Somehow, every time he tried, the words never came out of his mouth the way they did from Grandma Howard's.

When the boys arrived at the park, old Miss Effi was there.

"How old do you think she is?" Manny asked Lance before the boys got too close to her. "About a hundred?"

"I don't know, man," said Lance. "Her dog's as old as dirt!"

The boys straddled their bikes as they sized up the situation. They silently debated whether to ride away while they had time or stay and see which Miss Effi was approaching them. Sometimes she would just start in on them for no reason at all. The other day they had been playing catch on the sidewalk and she started screaming at them like they were trying to hit her with the ball on purpose. Other days she was pretty cool and she'd ask them how they were doing in school and tell them they were getting so big and handsome, stuff like that.

"You two hooligans watch where you are riding them damn bikes!"

Today was obviously not going to be one of her good days. "If you come close to me, I'll call the damn police on both of you. Good for nothing, that's what you are. Just like everyone else in this damn neighborhood," she wailed. The boys noticed she didn't seem to really be talking to them. She had the glazed look in her eyes that they had seen on many occasions; the one the boys recognized as her being too drunk or high. She was dressed in her usual worn blue jeans and woven green sweater, which thankfully hid most of her skeleton body.

"This damn world is falling apart, boys. Don't nobody care about nothing. You boys ever get to selling them drugs, I'll call the police on you, and don't forget it. Miss Effi'll call the damn police on you. Miss Effi ain't scared of no damn body."

As always on the bad days, she ranted on and on, but the absolute worse part about it was right before they left. Miss Effi always wanted to kiss them. That meant getting close to her which meant . . . the smell. Man, did that old woman stink, especially on "the mad days" as Lance and Manny called them. They couldn't keep backing away from her because she would keep closing in until the only place for them to go was into the traffic on the street.

Then it happened.

SMACK. Right on Manny's cheek. Lance was calling on every last ounce of will to not burst out laughing as he momentarily forgot that he would be next.

"See ya, Miss Effi," Manny called out, barely able to hold his own laughter as he watched Miss Effi plant one on Lance's cheek.

"It was nice talking to you. You looked nice today," Lance managed to get out before the two boys could hold their laughter no longer.

The boys laughed at Miss Effi for a while, but they knew she wasn't really haha funny. Grandma Howard had told the boys that poor old Miss Effi was really a nice old lady when she was sober. She would do anything for anybody. Many times she had given money to people who were poor or brought food to the hungry. Grandma Howard had said Miss Effi had a lot of heartache in her life and had turned to drinking and drugs to kill some of the pain. She always told them to be nice to Miss Effi, even when she would start up on them for no real reason.

For some reason they obeyed that wish, but they also got away from Miss Effi as soon as they could. "Fool, this is where you wiped out yesterday," Manny said to Lance as they approached Snake Row, named for the windy path cut through the woods behind the park. "You want to turn around?"

"Hell, I never saw you try to take it as fast as I did, man. You're scared. Shoot, if you think you're so bad, let's race," Lance responded.

"I don't want to race, man; let's just do some hook slides over by the fountain," Manny said as he took off. "See who can get the closest without hitting it or wiping out."

To perform a hook slide properly required lots of

speed and courage. The boys thought they had plenty of both. According to the rules they'd set, it was important to fly directly at the cement fountain and be within at most five feet. If you broke the rules, your opponent got to call you a "pussy" as you saved yourself. Manny and Lance used to pretend they were like Mario Lemieux of the Penguins going full speed into the boards at the Civic Arena and sending the ice high over the glass as he stopped on a dime. They competed for twenty minutes. No champion could be declared, so the boys decided it was time to move on.

"Let's go over to East Liberty and see what's up there," Lance said.

East Liberty was not one of the adult-approved stops on their excursions. It was much too far from the safe confines of Edgerton Avenue. Manny and Lance both knew why they were not permitted to go there: blue was not an acceptable color in East Liberty. You could get jumped at any time if you wore a trace of blue. Of course, in Homewood the boys could jump someone wearing a little too much red.

"I don't want to go over there today, man," Manny said, riding back in the direction of Edgerton. "Let's go see what Lamar's doing."

"Are you scared, doughnut boy?"

"Shut up before I kick your skinny big-headed butt. I want to see if Lamar got his bike fixed yet."

To get to Lamar's house, the boys headed back to Edgerton through the somewhat isolated neighborhood of Hilltop. Even if you asked a postman where Hilltop was, he probably wouldn't know. Only if you lived there were you certain where it was. To get there demanded a little planning and sometimes a little courage, depending upon who was hanging out on the two nearby streets. Hilltop was still in blue country.

"If they're out, man, don't act scared," Manny lectured Lance as he thought back to the time last summer when he and Lance became very frightened on one of their trips into Hilltop. They had been walking through the neighborhood on their way to Lamar's house that day. Walking was always more risky than bikes. Then they saw some dudes hanging out on the corner. Lance made the fatal mistake of showing he was afraid; he walked faster. "Slow down," Manny had called in a loud whisper, but it was too late. As Lance passed the guys on the corner, one of them started after him. Manny caught up to his friend and whispered, "We're being followed." Anxious, both picked up the pace even more. When they made it to the other corner, the tormentor ran up on the boys and yelled, "BOOO!!!" and began to punch them. The punk stood there laughing. "POW, POW," he yelled after the scampering boys.

"Remember last summer?" Manny jibed now.

"Shut up, man," Lance said. "I don't want to talk about it."

The boys knew from their many trips to Lamar's house on Baxter Street that it was much wiser to approach from Brushton Avenue, which was directly behind the house. Baxter Street was Crips' territory and there was a greater chance of getting messed walking on Baxter rather than Brushton. Today they got through the territory safely.

"Where is this fool?" Manny wondered as he rapped on the door.

"Man, I don't know. Probably tryin' to fix another flat tire on that cheap bike of his," Lance replied with a laugh. "Let's get over to my uncle's crib and ride the go-cart."

Lance's uncle was always home. The boys liked going over there, because he would let them do pretty much anything they wanted as long as they did not bug him too much.

Along with the go-cart, they got to mess with the kids and the Rottweiler puppy. Saying "hi" to Lance's uncle who was outside and gossiped with them a few minutes before he disappeared inside the house, they took out the go-cart and pushed it into the alley behind the house. Pushing the cart up the little grade after riding it back and forth for a while, the boys noticed it was starting to get dark. They knew they had to be home soon or risk being put on punishment. Putting the cart back, they yelled goodbye and got back on their bikes.

As they began the ten-minute ride back down Edgerton Avenue, the cool summer-like day began to turn into a cold autumn night. Manny had on a baggy Pittsburgh Penguins T-shirt that dropped below the belt buckle of his black jean cutoffs and he was shivering. Both boys hopped off their bikes as soon as they reached their destination and ran to their next door houses with intentions of putting on some warmer clothing.

"Come over after you change," Lance said.

"Sure. I'll ask," Manny replied with no doubt that the evening was only just beginning.

Lance opened the door of the house wondering where Tru was. "I'm not about to go looking," he murmured and went upstairs to get his coat. Then he headed for the kitchen and took a Coke out of the refrigerator. He was sipping it at the counter when Manny came in.

"Hey, what's with the jacket, man," Manny said. "It ain't winter."

"I ain't got that layer of doughnut around my behind, you overgrown pumpkin," jibed Lance.

"Let's go down to the basement and do some WWF."

WWF was the boys' version of the World Wrestling Federation. In it Manny took on the toughest opponent, The Kid Taker, otherwise known as his best friend, Lance McCoy.

The matches would not be timed and had no particular rules, especially since no one was the referee.

In the basement they had hung a cardboard belt from the bare water pipes between the wooden joists in the cellar's ceiling. The belt had been meticulously painted by Manny who had a knack for art. The only object of the competition was to grab the belt. No holds were barred, and no moves were unacceptable. The belt was all that mattered. Lance's skills were more in the dexterity of his hands and speed of his lightning quick reflexes. He needed all his speed and guile to claim the belt from Killer Instinct, otherwise known as Manny. The champion could raise himself to reach the belt and hold it around his waist. There was nothing like it in the world, at least not on Edgerton Avenue.

The combatants agreed the music to begin the match would be from the rap group Bone. They put on the track called *It's an Everyday Thing*. It was time to get it on.

Kid Taker went for the legs and missed. Killer Instinct grabbed the early advantage. It was a perfect opportunity for Manny to throw the 'Sharpshooter' on his skinny pathetic behind. The Killer placed his knees in the middle of the Kid's back, so he could not move or breathe. Kid's head was directly under Killer's butt and to successfully perform the 'Sharpshooter,' Killer grabbed one leg of the fallen Taker. Once he had it, Manny placed his right foot between the legs of his increasingly helpless opponent and pulled Lance's leg up as hard as he could. Then Manny sat on Lance's back with all the force he could muster. An anguished scream came out of the Kid's panicked body as he searched for a way to get out of this deadly hold.

Eleven-year-olds seldom think there is a bad time to pass gas, but they do know when it is an extra good time. This moment was definitely one of those. Kid Taker could only hope his fart was sufficiently potent. His prayers were answered.

"Damn!!!" screeched Killer as he tried to hold onto the legs of the revitalized Kid Taker while pinching his nose shut with one hand. It was futile. He was overcome by the fumes and by the laughter. Killer felt his strength vanish as he faced his risen tormentor. "That stinks, man!"

Kid Taker was now on the offensive and he smelled blood. He juked the dazed Killer and made a mad leap for the prize. In his mind he could see the belt around his waist, he could hear the fans going crazy, victory and fame were to be his. Until...

Lance was ready to reach for the coveted belt when he felt his neck snap back. The force of the push drove Kid Taker into the cement block wall. After ricocheting off the wall, he fell into a heap on the cold cement floor. The beat of the music matched the beating of the pain that erupted in his left shoulder. Killer Instinct towered above his victim, a huge smile on his face. Killer's fists pumped vigorously. The battle was won.

Gracious champions are not common in the savage world of wrestling, but this day, the victor decided, would be different. After taking the treasured belt from its lofty position and holding it around his waist, Killer Instinct consoled his respected adversary.

"You all right, man?" Manny asked.

"That hurt, man," was Lance's pained response.

The boys, with no cameras rolling, no interviews to be done, no autographs to be signed, shook hands and hugged. They congratulated each other and spoke of what a tough opponent each had been. They related to each other about the key moments in their titanic struggle as they permitted their tired bodies a well-deserved rest.

Soon it was time for Manny to go home.

"Come over when you get home from school tomorrow," Manny said.

"What do you wanna do?"

"I don't know," Manny said frowning. "Let's just hang."

Chapter 12

Fall Encounter

Leaves on the maple trees were turning into jewel-colored autumn shades of burgundy and gold when the first report cards were issued by the school district of Pittsburgh.

Apparently, Lance had not taken Tru's lecture very seriously. Most of his grades showed that he was not achieving at a passing level. In math and reading, he was not achieving at all.

"I should have let them hold him back," Tonya sobbed. "Why is he doing this? I know Lance can get good grades. Why do these teachers wait so long to let you know what's happening? And why do I have to send him to a school where failing makes you a bro?"

Tru watched Tonya with concern. He had been thinking he was doing Lance a favor by not letting his mom know about the teachers' phone calls when he was home working. Tru thought he and Lance had an understanding that Lance would do all his homework and improve his grades. Here it was in black and white from most of his teachers: Math - E - needs to improve skills and the area of homework; Reading - E - needs to improve in the area of homework; Science - D - needs to improve in the area of homework. Lance had played him and Tru had bought into the boy's game.

"Let me speak to him, Tawn. Maybe he'll listen to me," Tru said. "As soon as I get home from the Center tonight, young buck and me will have a little talk."

It had slipped his mind that the students at P.I.C.Y.A. were also bringing their report cards to the Center that evening. Tru did not think it would be difficult to deal with their problems, because the policy had been set from the first day the computer center had opened. In order to participate in any of the activities at the Center, students had to maintain a C average when report cards came out.

However, at least one of them hadn't.

L.J.'s report card looked like Lance's. He received a D and an E in reading and math respectively, and the comments from his teachers indicated he was not doing his homework either. His grade point average worked out to approximately a D-minus average.

"What's up with these grades, man?" Tru asked, with more than a little anger in his voice. "This is terrible!"

"Man, those teachers ain't fair. I did all my work. That's wrong!"

Tru knew what was coming. He found it much easier to be himself with his students. He knew when they were telling him lies, and told them "to cut the crap." Whether they liked him or not, he was the teacher.

"You want me to believe that every single teacher in that building is out to get you? You must take me for some kind of fool!"

"Whatever, man." L.J. shrugged as he turned his back and walked away from Tru.

"Boy, don't you ever turn away from me when I'm talkin' to you!" Tru said as he came around, bent down and confronted the boy nose to nose. "Who do you think you're talkin' to, man? You think I'm playin' some kind of game? You think I'm here wastin' my time to collect some piddly-ass paycheck?"

"Probably so, just like most teachers," L.J. said as he tilted his head to the side, his eyebrows raised.

Was that what Lance saw? Someone just playing a game with him? Tru's heart sank. He had been exposed.

"Nah, man, this guy here ain't about all that. No hoops for you tonight, bro. You need to get busy with those books."

Tru left L.J. in the computer classroom with his assignments and went down the hall to the gym to see if there were any others trying to sneak their way into practice.

Most of the others had mediocre but passing grades and he let them continue. Suddenly Tru heard a ball echoing as it was bounced down the ramp leading to the main gym. He looked around and saw L.J.

"What did I tell you, man?" Tru asked with a surprised and irritated voice. "Aren't you supposed to be doing your work?"

"Marv said I could come over and hoop, man. Take a chill."

Tru fought the temptation to grab L.J. and spank his butt till he couldn't sit for a week. "Nah, man, I'm not about to take a damn chill. We're about to see what's up with all this. Where's Marv at?"

"I'm not his keeper. Maybe the library."

"Come on with me." Tru and L.J. began to walk over to the library in search of Marvin Mitchell. Tru did not believe that his decision could be questioned. There must have been some kind of misunderstanding. Marv probably didn't even know L.J. had been told to stay in the lab to work on extra assignments.

"Excuse me, Marv. L.J. here tells me that you told him he could go upstairs to practice."

"Yeah, I did," Marv said, excusing himself from a conversation he was having with another youngster. "His team's practice starts in a few minutes. Is there a problem?"

"Yes, there is. Did you know I told him that he had to complete some extra assignments because of his poor report card? He is not to play basketball until it is done. It may mean he'll miss practice tonight but that's the way it's gotta be."

Marvin sighed slightly and said, "Yeah, I know, but I gave him another assignment. He can finish it after practice."

The smile that came across L.J.'s face was more than Tru could handle. Not only had his authority been questioned, it had been stripped away in front of one of the students. Tru felt humiliated.

"This is your program, Marv." Maybe Tru had miscalculated his role at the youth center. "You call all the shots." Tru looked hard at Marv. Very deliberately he added, "You don't ever have to worry about me steppin' on anyone's toes again. I'm through." Tru turned to L.J. "Good luck with your basketball career."

Tru walked to an exit and strode outside. He would be damned if he'd set foot into Belmont Elementary School again as part of the staff of the Inner City Youth Alliance. Tru had always prided himself on being able to read situations and discern the motives of others as they related to him. But this time was different. He searched his mind for signs he might have missed forecasting that Marv would not stand by him. He could find none. Was he too caught up in everything else that was happening in his life? Were his heart and soul in the activity? Did he pay attention to details? These questions raced through his mind.

Mostly though, Tru was frustrated at himself for not seeing through the lie he was living. He had thought he was beyond being duped by the silly games of others. Obviously not.

On his short drive home from the youth center, Tru focused on his relationship with Lance. He realized the situation was not entirely Lance's fault. When school began, he had told both Lance and Tonya that he would be there to help the boy along with his studies. However, when Lance hadn't come to him, he'd told himself the boy didn't need help and had promptly turned to other things. He admitted all this to himself with a sigh of relief.

He envisioned the confrontation he was going to have with Lance later that evening. Tru knew that basically Lance only tolerated him out of respect for his mother. Although Tru had always tried to be fair with Lance, he sensed the distrust.

Tru knew this occasion could not take the same path the few previous talks they'd had. Lectures on what Lance should be doing were not effective. They would not have been effective on him when he was Lance's age. What had made him think they would be now? No, this talk had to be different. He would have to try a new method, involving discipline and inducing a new emotion, fear. Lance would have to understand after this evening that because Tru's relationship with Lance's mother was important, Tru would be assuming a new role. He wouldn't be Lance's father, but he would be acting like he was. And he figured Lance owed him for keeping Lance's teachers' criticism from his mother even though Tru now questioned that course of action.

Nevertheless, that was all over. Now Tru was going to promise Tonya he would see to it that Lance would get adequate, if not good, grades and that was exactly what Tru expected to happen.

He parked the car, got out, walked to the house and opened the front door slowly. As soon as Tonya saw him she knew something was wrong.

"What happened, baby?"

"Let's talk about it later. We have to talk about Lance first," he said patting her arm. Tru sat on the black sofa in the living room. He picked up the remote control and turned off the television.

"Where's Lance, babe?" he asked.

"I hate putting this on you. You aren't his dad," Tonya said uneasily.

Tru turned and looked Tonya directly in the eyes. "No, but I'm here."

"Maybe he's studying up in his room."

"No, he isn't studying, baby."

Tru told her about the phone calls from Lance's teachers which he'd hidden.

"But you know what, honey? All that doesn't really matter anymore," he said determinedly.

"We need to get this kid headin' in the right direction. I want to start working with him on his schoolwork."

"You would really?" Tonya looked so tired and dejected

Tru wished he could spend more time comforting her, but there was none to spare.

Tru nodded. "I've tried a few times, but not the way I should have. Lance knows it. He knows I've just been going through the motions with him. I was goin' to tell him he was ruining the relationship between you and I. Now what kind of thing is that to do to a young buck like that? I didn't want to help him—I wanted him to help me with you. That's messed up, Tonya. I'm sorry."

They hugged for several minutes. Then Tru stood back. "What time is it, hon?"

"About nine-thirty. Lance will probably be asleep."

"It doesn't matter," Tru said. "It's time."

Tru knocked on the bedroom door. He heard Lance mutter some unintelligible words. Tru opened the door and turned on the light. Lance sat up in his bed and looked at Tru. "What's wrong with you? Couldn't you tell I was asleep?" He turned his face to the wall.

Tru walked purposefully to the side of Lance's bed and sat down beside him.

"Look at me," Tru said slowly with a tired but firm voice that Lance had never heard before. Lance turned over towards him. "Don't take your eyes off me," Tru continued. "I want you to listen very carefully to what I'm about to say. Do you understand?"

"Yeah?" Lance mumbled half under his breath.

Tru paid the mumbling no mind.

"Yes, sir," Tru said gazing into Lance's eyes.

"Yes, sir," Lance repeated.

"By the end of the school year, there will be no D's or

E's on your report card. Do you understand?"

"I guess so."

"No. *Yes, sir.*"

"Yes, sir."

"It will be you and I working on your indolent attitude toward school."

"Yes, sir."

"You have a good night's sleep, Lance."

Tru knew Lance did not know the meaning of the word "indolent." As he turned off the bedroom light, he turned back to Lance and said, "Tomorrow I want you to tell me the meaning of the word indolent. Look it up in the dictionary."

"Sure," Lance murmured sleepily. "Yes, sir," he mumbled, barely legibly.

Returning to his office, Tru sat down in a comfortable chair to do some more thinking. He did not believe Lance fully understood the changes that were about to happen in his young life. Thoughts of how to help the boy to focus and concentrate went through Tru's mind. Finally he arose, tiredness overtaking him. As Tru walked towards Tonya's and his bedroom, he wondered if he fully understood the changes that were happening in his own life.

Chapter 13

What's
Indolent Mean?

Lance McCoy arrived home from school the next day with every intention of hooking up with his friend Manny and going through their daily activities. It was not that he had forgotten about the conversation he had the evening before with Tru, it was just that Lance didn't put much credence in it. Tru had told him since the beginning of school they would be doing homework and studying and they had spent only a few hours together. Why would this time be any different? The only thing that seemed the least bit unusual was Tru coming into his room to talk last night. *He has never done that before,* Lance thought, a bit uneasy for the first time.

Now Lance walked through the empty house to his room and tossed his backpack on the bed. He'd put the whole thing out of his mind. Manny had said he had homework to do, so Lance had time to kill. He decided to grab some chips and stuff to eat and watch television before going over to his friend's house. After he got the food and munched on it, Lance made himself comfortable on the couch. Minutes later he heard a car door shut and knew Tru was home. He didn't think twice about it.

Seeing Lance sitting in front of the television irritated Tru. It wasn't just that he wasn't studying. Perhaps it was the potato chips scattered all across the brown carpet. It appeared Lance had taken the bag, somehow crushed all the chips, then opened it and shaken the contents onto the floor.

Maybe Tru was irritated because of Lance's Air Jordans. It was not that they were strewn about the floor; in fact, they were still on his feet, dangling over the arm rest. Or maybe it was the laces. Not only were they untied, those laces had never felt what it was like to be tied. They were barely woven through the eyes of the shoe. There was not enough string coming from the last two eyes to tie the shoes, even had Lance wanted to.

Seeing a large expanse of skin above the waistline of Lance's pants also annoyed Tru. He knew if Lance were standing those pants would come no further up than the cheeks of his ass. Of course, to stand at all from the All-Pro Couch Potato position he was in would be no easy feat.

Tru went into the kitchen to get a Coke and thought perhaps he was just looking for trouble. He'd just had one of those days where nothing seemed to go right. Computers are not supposed to have minds of their own, but after today he had some doubts. It wouldn't be wise to go looking for a confrontation with Lance. The civil approach would be his tactic. Carrying his drink, Tru walked back to the couch.

"What's up, Lance? How's it goin' today?"

Lance was fixated on watching the Power Rangers. The sound was turned up as loud, Tru thought, as it went. The only response Tru heard was the crunching of another mouthful of potato chips. There was no eye contact, no shrug, no indication whatsoever his question had even been heard. Tru grew more irritated.

He tried to maintain his composure. Actually, he wanted to walk over to where Lance was sitting and grab the young boy by the collar and shake him.

Forcing himself to show restraint, Tru repeated his question, this time shouting over the television's deafening sound.

"I said, What's up, Lance? Don't you have any homework?"

"No, sir," Lance said without ever taking his eyes off the television. "I did it all in school."

Tru knew that was complete bullshit, but he smiled as he undid the black tie that hung around his neck. He had not intimidated the boy the night before. Though Tru had been going over last night's scene all day, Lance must have promptly tucked it in his subconscious. It was then Tru realized that Lance didn't give a damn about what Tru thought or said. It was going to take a lot more to change the boy's attitude.

"Did you look up that word like I asked?" Tru said as he looked around the living room. He continued his thought with a whisper only he could hear. "Can you give me a reason why not, boy?"

Again, without a shift of his head or any shifting of his body position, Lance answered, "Nah."

That was it.

Tru was pissed. "Boy, you better turn around and look at me when I'm talking to you, *especially* when I'm talking to you."

As Lance turned around, his face reflected anger. All

of the anger was directed at Tru. The man who'd come into his life and professed he cared while changing the things Lance was comfortable with. "You're not my dad," Lance hissed. He stared at Tru.

Tru walked over to the television and flipped it off. Then he approached Lance very slowly until he was no more than one foot away. Tru bent over until his large face nearly swallowed the young boy's, and said just above a whisper, "Do you understand me, boy?"

The toughness Lance was trying to exhibit suddenly disappeared. He began to cry. "Yes, sir," he managed to say through his tears.

Tru straightened up. He towered over Lance sobbing on the couch. In a soft voice he asked, "Why didn't you look the word up, man?"

Wiping the tears from his face, Lance responded, "I didn't know how to spell it."

Another excuse. Tru gave Lance credit for being a quick thinker, but he wasn't buying into his story this time. Tru was not doing this because of an ulterior motive. He wanted nothing from Lance. It wasn't to make Lance like him or respect him. Tru just wanted to help Lance to have a future.

The new alliance between them would have to be built on honesty. Whether it went both ways or not was not that important to Tru. He knew he could only do his part.

"That's crap, man, and you know it," Tru said firmly but with no hint of annoyance. "All you have to do is ask someone. Why didn't you ask me?"

Lance replied with a shrug of his shoulders.

"Listen," Tru continued. "Do you like school?"

"No, not really," Lance said matter-of-factly. "It's

boring. All we do is sit around and listen to the teacher yap."

As he ran his right hand down his throat, Tru's eyes looked up at the ceiling. He sighed and said, "You're gonna have to put all those feelings away, Lance. Whether you realize it or not, you need an education. There are too many kids around here on the streets at your age doing drugs and worse. Do you know how they're gonna end up?" Lance shook his head. "Maybe dead on those same streets. We have to get busy with this schoolwork, you and I, and it isn't gonna be the way it was before so you can forget about that. Every night, man. We're goin' to be workin' on that homework, every night."

Lance stared at Tru. He saw that Tru wasn't kidding. What surprised Lance was that he was not angry. There was something about Tru's attitude that reassured Lance.

"How about if I really don't have homework, Ray?" Lance asked with a hint of a smile.

Tru didn't smile back, not yet. "We can always get ahead. What do you think your teachers would do if Lance McCoy came to school and was ten pages ahead of the rest of his class?" Tru said grinning. "None of your teachers ever had a heart attack, have they? I wouldn't want to be responsible for killin' a teacher."

Until that occasion, whenever Lance or Tru would laugh at the other's joke it was because the person knew he was supposed to. This was the first time they shared a laugh that was genuine.

"Listen, man," Tru said with conviction. "This isn't goin' to be very easy on either of us. There are goin' to be times when you resent me, probably even hate me. I just want you to know I'm doin' this because I care a lot about you and your mother."

As Lance got up heading towards the kitchen, he said honestly, "It'll be all right, Ray. You want another Coke?"

"Thanks, man," Tru said as he nodded "yes." He fell back into the couch and let out a big sigh. He clasped his hands behind his neck and propped his feet on the glass-topped coffee table. For the first time he felt relaxed dealing with Lance.

When Lance returned with the soda, Tru asked, "Do you ever raise your hand in school, man?"

Lance's lips curled in a half smile as he shook his head from left to right.

"Oh, man, you're a case, huh? Why not, man? When I was your age, I always had my hand up, askin' questions, answerin' questions. I about drove my teachers nuts with questions," Tru reminisced. "My friends would be moanin' and groanin' when I'd ask all those questions. Then they'd moan and groan some more when they saw the A's and B's on my report card and compared it to theirs."

"Did you always do good in school?"

"Nah, man. I went through my hard-head period where I didn't think much about school. During ninth and tenth grade at Allderdice, I thought I knew it all and I didn't figure school was goin' to help me much. I know how school can be sometimes and I also know how your friends can be. I got into a little trouble hanging out with the wrong kids. Sports was what got me interested in school. I had to keep up my grades to play football and baseball. You ever think about playin' a sport at school?"

"Not really. It would take up too much time. Plus, Manny wouldn't be on the team. I want to be a mechanic, anyway."

"How about if I teach you and Manny how to play baseball? We can go to a park somewhere before we do our homework. I bet if you knew how to play, you'd have a lot of fun," Tru said, trying to get a response that showed a little enthusiasm.

"I guess that'd be okay," was the very unenthusiastic response.

Tru went on, despite Lance's attitude. "Let's do it. I'll figure out where our workouts will be and we'll start them as soon as I find a place. But homework will start tomorrow," Tru said as he began walking towards his second floor office. "I'll give you a last reprieve today." He turned back. "Have you ever been proud to show your report card to Manny?"

Lance just shrugged his shoulders.

"I don't know what that means, man. Does that mean once?"

"I don't know. Maybe once or twice," Lance said shyly.

Tru knew that it probably was more like zero, but he added confidently, "I guarantee you one thing. Whatever the number, it will be one more at the end of this school year. Then I'm goin' to ask you again if you like school."

Tru paused for a second and motioned for Lance to follow him. "Before you return to the boob tube, come up to my office. You've got a word to look up."

Chapter 14

Change, Change, Change

The Pittsburgh autumn quickly turned into winter. The bright colored leaves now turned brown and whirled their way to the ground. The once cool crisp air now held a bite. Gray cloud-filled days of rain or snow became the predictable forecast on the evening news.

As the weather outside became cold, the study sessions inside the three-bedroom house on Edgarton Avenue grew more heated. Tru learned firsthand that Lance's academic skills were not on a sixth grade level. In fact, most weren't on a third grade level. His handwriting was unreadable. He averaged four words per line on standard paper. He couldn't spell words of more than one syllable.

Lance's reading, Tru estimated, was so weak he doubted if he could get through a second grade primer. There was no way he could read or comprehend a text written for sixth graders.

The subject Lance had the most difficulty with was math. "The teacher always picks on me," he complained. Tru observed that Lance used the fingers of both hands to do simple addition and subtraction problems. He had no problem-solving skills.

Tru was irritated, not only at Lance for being lazy and having a non-caring attitude towards school, but with the school. In Tru's eyes the school system had failed his people once again. Though the Pittsburgh Public School System had its share of urban problems with troubled kids, the schools still had an excellent reputation. How could they permit this to happen to Lance? He had been passed along, promoted when he did not deserve it. Either because he was not a troublemaker, or perhaps because he was. Either way, Tru was not about to accept the situation. In the near future he planned to visit and keep on visiting each of Lance's teachers, as well as the principal.

However, it was hard finding the time. Tru's days were occupied servicing clients and two evenings were spent teaching his computer classes at the community college. Despite this, Tru allotted from two to four hours every evening to helping Lance with his homework. If there was none assigned, just as Tru had told Lance he would, the extra time was spent on Lance's writing, reading, and math skills.

It was not an easy schedule for an underachieving sixth grader, who had never spent two hours a month studying at home, to keep.

On numerous occasions Lance would complain of being ill. "Ray, I have a headache. Can we stop tonight?" Lance whined as he closed his math book around eight o'clock one evening. He looked over at Tru who was lying on Lance's bed with his head propped up. "We started at what—six? I'm tired."

"We didn't start until closer to seven, man. Don't be

tryin' to squeeze an extra hour in on me now!" Tru said, smiling. "Why don't you go splash some water on your face and get some Tylenol. I could use a little break, too."

"Can't we just quit, Ray?" Lance said as desperation in his voice surfaced. "I'm really tired. We could start earlier tomorrow, I promise. I just don't feel like doin' no more tonight!"

Tru was not going to let Lance off so easily. "I know this is hard on you, Lance," Tru said gently. "We're making progress. And it's going to help your grades. It has to. Don't stop now. Keep pushing yourself. We're going to see real results very soon, I promise you."

Lance made a lukewarm attempt to continue, but Tru could see neither his heart nor mind was in it. Twenty minutes later, they called it a night.

Walking up the stairs, Tru knew they had come to a crisis point. He had to find something additional to motivate Lance. Tru walked back down and into Lance's bedroom.

"Remember when I talked about teaching you and Manny how to play baseball as part of the deal with the studying?" Tru asked as he stopped in the doorway. Lance shook his head yes, and Tru continued, "I don't want you to think I've forgotten about that. I've been waiting for a call from the principal over at East Hills Elementary. I think we'll be able to use their gym; I'm just not sure when. If he doesn't call in the next couple of days, I'll stop over to see him. Okay?"

"Yeah, sure." It was plain that Lance really could not have cared less. The rolling of his eyes and the shifting of his head confirmed Tru's interpretation.

However, Tru chose not to comment on Lance's reaction. "Okay, as soon as I know, you'll know." Tru added evenly, "Oh, I almost forgot. I'm gonna stop by your school tomorrow to see some of your teachers and meet your principal."

"Why do you want to do that?" said a nervous Lance.

Tru did not tell Lance there had been new phone calls from some of his teachers—this time about Lance acting up in class. He hoped Lance had developed a little trust in him and would discuss the reason the teachers phoned. "Why," Tru inquired, "is there something I should know?"

"Nah, not really," Lance said as he closed his eyes and a moan escaped.

If you are not an employee of or student at Reizenstein Middle School and step inside, you must be escorted by security at all times. Periodically, metal detectors are brought in to eliminate disasters before they occur. Some call this a pro-active school, others call it a school with many problems. It depends on your perspective.

When the security officer dropped Tru off in front of Lance's third period math class with Mr. Bell, he hesitated before knocking. He was a little nervous about going into one of Lance's classes. His pause gave him a few seconds to look into the room through the large glass window in the wooden door.

What Tru saw going on in Mr. Bell's class was disturbing.

Four youngsters in the back of the room were paying no attention to the teacher as he wrote the day's lesson on the chalkboard. They appeared to be involved in a pencil battle. He looked closer and recognized the instigator—Lance. Lance was whispering to the other boy. A duel began. Concentrating on the battle, they couldn't keep their eyes on the teacher. They were obviously pros at this and had chosen two kids, a boy and a girl, as lookouts. They were glancing

around every five seconds to see if Mr. Bell had finished
writing on the board and giving the sign to the duelers. Tru
took the initiative and walked in quietly.

Mr. Bell asked, "Can I help you, sir?"

That's when Lance turned around and saw his worst
nightmare standing just inside the doorway staring directly at
him. He sank his skinny body low into the wooden desk.

Mr. Bell approached Tru and repeated his question.

Tru responded, "I'm very sorry to disrupt your class.
My name is Ramon Dixon."

Mr. Bell knew immediately who he was from the
many phone calls he had made to Lance's home. The teacher
reached out his hand and shook Tru's as Tru explained he
was there to see Lance McCoy.

"Do you think it would be a problem to see him in the
hall for a minute or two, Mr. Bell?" Tru asked loudly enough
for the entire class to hear. Tru stepped outside the room.

"Oooooooohhhhhhh!!!! You gonna get that behind
whooped now!" kids called out to Lance as they fought
cracking-up completely.

Lance did not see the humor. He was terrified. And
furious. He ran to the door, opened it into the concrete block
hallway outside the math room and stepped outside. Anger
was on his face. He not only hated Tru: he wanted him dead.

Tru walked over to Lance. "What were you doin'?"

When Lance lowered his head, Tru said loudly, "Boy,
you better pick your head up right now and look at me. I
expect an answer to that question immediately!"

As Lance raised his head, Tru could see his lower lip
quivering.

"Pencil fighting."

Tru leaned over and spoke softly. "I suppose this is the
junk you say Mr. Bell is always pickin' on you about, huh,

boy? That's just what you'd have told me this time too, if I hadn't been here to see for myself! Isn't that right, Lance?" Tru said, raising his voice.

Reading Lance like a book, Tru continued. "Oh, now I suppose you're angry, right? What's so bad is that the person you think you're angry with isn't the one you're really ticked at. You think you're angry with me? With Mr. Bell? Nah, wrong guys. The one you're really angry with is yourself—because you've been caught. That's all. So you can pull that tough-guy look off your face, 'cause I'm not goin' for it. You have nothing to be angry about. You're guilty and you got caught!"

Directing Lance back to the other side of the hall, they peered into Mr. Bell's room. Tru knew the students would be checking for Lance every few minutes and when they did, they would probably be joking about their classmate. He wasn't disappointed. When they saw Lance standing so meekly next to Tru, they pointed and snickered and laughed. They could not have reacted more perfectly for Tru to make his point.

"Who are your boys laughing *at* now, Lance?" he said. "Huh? Looks to me like their havin' a good time! How about you?"

Lance tried to save himself further embarrassment by burying his neck into his chest.

"Nah, nah! Pick your head up and check this out!" Tru demanded. "Who are your boys laughing at? Answer me!"

The embarrassed boy answered meekly, "Me."

"Why are you lookin' so sad? That's what you wanted, wasn't it? Well, you got it. You're the clown! Congratulations!"

Tru became quiet letting Lance think it out for a few minutes.

Then he looked at Lance. "When is it goin' to sink in, Lance?" Tru stopped. Then he repeated, "When?"

They stood motionless together, staring into the room.

"I think we'd better go back," Tru finally said.

He opened the door. Lance went to his seat, and Tru approached Mr. Bell in front of the class.

"I'm sorry for interrupting your class, Mr. Bell," Tru said loudly enough for all to hear. "Do you think it would be possible for Lance to sit in one of the empty seats in front?"

"Why sure!" the teacher said. "He can sit in the first row," Bell added, pointing to the vacant seat near his desk.

Lance could not think of an uglier punishment. It was bad enough to be shamed in front of his classmates, but to have to sit in the first row, first seat was the worst.

Lance slowly swayed from side to side, pants barely above his butt, as he slowly made his way to his new seat. "You better get rid of that walk, boy! And pull up those pants," Tru barked. The startled sixth graders sat up in their seats. When Lance sat down, Tru called to him again, "Don't you have something to say to Mr. Bell?"

"I'm sorry, Mr. Bell," Lance said in a singsong voice.

There was complete silence, maybe for the first time all year. One of those things so unbelievable to kids that it would be passed on for future generations of sixth graders.

Lance stared at Tru with a look that vowed revenge.

After leaving Mr. Bell's class, Tru made arrangements with Lance's other teachers to drop in whenever he could. Every one of them said he would be welcome to sit in on as many classes as he wanted, and whenever he wanted. "We really appreciate the support of parents and step parents," each one told him. Tru saw no reason to tell them he was not married to Lance's mother.

Tru left the school and walked slowly to the parking

lot. He paused as he looked at East Liberty's skyline before climbing into his Jeep. He thought of the study session with Lance coming up that evening. He sighed. Nothing with kids would ever be easy. Would he ever learn? He frowned slightly. Then he climbed into his Jeep and headed downtown to his next client.

No one was home when Tru finally reached Edgarton Avenue. He undid his light blue tie and tossed it onto the bed he and Tonya shared. Out of the corner of his eye, in the mirror on the dresser, Tru saw the flashing red light of the answering machine. He walked over and played the message. It was from one of the counselors at Lance's school.

After going downstairs to the kitchen and pouring a glass of Pinot Noir, his favorite red wine, he returned the call to the counselor whose name was Mrs. Dickinson.

"Thank you so much for calling promptly, Mr. Dixon," said the formal, high-pitched female voice.

"Oh, no problem. What can I do for you?" Tru replied politely. "Is there a new problem with Lance?" he added, with a trace of nervousness in his voice.

"No, it's not that, Mr. Dixon." She paused and gave a slight cough, then went on. "I heard from several teachers about your visit today. They were all very impressed with your concern and eager to work with you."

Tru thought he detected apprehension in her voice. "Please call me 'Tru'," he said. "What seems to be the problem?"

"Well," continued Mrs. Dickinson, "afterwards, I was looking through Lance's school records, and. . ." She paused and coughed. "Excuse me. Well, because you are not technically Lance's father or stepfather, we are not permitted to divulge any information to you or let you sit in on any of his classes."

Tru explained the situation to Mrs. Dickinson, and she sounded relieved. "Please stop by my office with Tonya. After she signs the necessary papers there will be no problem at all. And thank you for your support."

As they sat together in the early minutes of their evening study session, Tru noticed Lance was not offering any insight about the events at school that day. Lance acted so nonchalantly about the entire situation that Tru wondered if the boy had repressed the memory of being in trouble or just didn't care.

Less than an hour into a normal homework session, Lance began to rub his forehead. Tru knew what was coming.

"Ray, my head is hurting," Lance said coldly. "Can we stop?"

Tru had had about enough of this excuse. "Can't you come up with anything better than that, Lance? You use it here and, from what I hear, at school as well, all the time. C'mon now, an old pro like you oughta do better than that!"

At the desk where he was working, Lance rolled his eyes and stood up. After a minute of silence he said quietly, "I ain't gonna do any more work tonight. I don't care."

It was the "I don't care" that was the final straw. "Of course you don't care!" Tru said, his voice rising. "If you gave a damn, you wouldn't be in this spot—would you? What the hell am I doin' wastin' my time on you any way?"

"Why don't you quit then!" Lance said, matching Tru's anger.

"I don't care about stupid school," Lance went on. "It ain't gonna make any difference what you do anyhow, I'm still gonna fail out one day!"

Tru's attempt at motivating Lance had backfired miserably. Now there was anger on both sides, and it was flowing freely. There was no stopping it.

"You're just a sorry-ass little lazy punk, boy!" Tru said as he tossed the math book on the floor disgustedly. "You're right, Lance. You *will* fail out with that attitude. Go ahead, start flunking all your classes again. You think that makes you something special? You think that makes you a tough guy—some kind of rebel? You want to know what that makes you, Lance?" he said in a low voice as he walked toward the door. "A young, stupid nigger."

"You ain't my dad!" Lance hollered as he fell onto the bed. "I don't care about you and you don't care about me! I don't care what you think!" Lance's voice grew in disgust as he tossed a pillow at the wall. "I *quit*!"

Calmer now, Tru turned towards Lance lying on the bed. Lance did not know if he was going to get screamed at, ignored, or blasted.

"You're right, Lance. I'm not your dad. But if your father was here he would say the same things that I'm saying. No responsible father could ever ignore your behavior and allow you to fail. You're wrong though about me not caring. I do care about you. You might not be able to understand this but I don't care about you because you're Lance McCoy—I care because you're a young brother setting himself up for a sorry life he can't even imagine. A life so empty it'll make your head spin. Boy, you have no idea. You want to quit? I'll show you how easy it is to quit." Tru walked out.

Lance sat up in bed crying. He was not sure if he was crying because he was relieved, sad or angry. Ray had found out everything. He knew what was going on at Reizenstein and he saw through Lance's headaches at home. Lance felt confused. On the one hand he wanted to run away from home and on the other he wanted to run down the steps after Tru.

As Tru descended the ten steps to the living room,

Tonya looked at him with tears in her eyes.

"Why does there have to be all that screamin', Tru?"

"Tonya, you have to stop babying the boy," Tru said as if he were in a business meeting. "We could lose him. You can't keep bendin' for him while he keeps bullshittin' us and the school. He had just started doing a little better in school and now he's slipping back again. His teachers say he just doesn't care. We have to be completely serious!"

"I don't want to lose my baby," she cried. She buried her sobbing face into Tru's shoulder. "I just can't lose my baby boy."

"Then you have to quit giving in to him. Put him on punishment when he needs it. He just told me he wants to quit. He might mean only studying, but what he doesn't know is, if he quits, he'll quit anything that's hard. We have to fight this fight now, baby. It'll be too late when he's seventeen and out on these streets."

"I know," Tonya said. "It's just so hard."

"That's what he says," Tru embraced her for a moment and then sat down on the couch.

He waited. He did not want to go back up to Lance's room. He needed a sign from Lance that he was ready. It didn't have to be Lance crawling on his knees. It could be anything. It happened around nine-thirty.

Lance walked down the steps into the living room. Tru looked like he was just kickin' back, watching television as if he didn't have a care in the world. Inside, his thoughts were churning.

"Ray," Lance paused, "my headache feels a lot better if you feel like doin' any more homework," he said.

There was no reaction from Tru. Not a look, not a repositioning on the couch, not a sound. Lance went back to his room.

When he got back there, he picked up an English book, went back to his bed, and began studying punctuation. Another half hour passed. Lance really was tired this time. He was about to turn out the light when the door opened.

"You see how easy it is to quit something? Shoot, you just walk away. No sweat off my butt. Quittin' is the easiest thing you'll ever do, Lance," Tru said with resolve.

"Yes, sir," was the embarrassed response.

"I told you when we started this it wasn't goin' to be easy, didn't I?"

"Yes, sir."

"It still isn't. None of life is goin' to be easy. Who told you it was supposed to be? That isn't written anywhere that I know of. I told you that you would resent me, didn't I?"

"Yes, sir."

"You still will, Lance. I'm not perfect. I'm pretty sure you know that by now. Far as I know, there is only one perfect being and that's God. I've done things I'm not proud of and so have you. We can't erase the past. I can only try to live my life better tomorrow. If I don't try and live my life better, then I haven't learned anything. Understand what I'm saying?"

Tru sat down next to the boy. "You think Michael Jordan wants to go to work every day? You think the kids at your school who get good grades like to study? Look at Manny. He gets pretty good grades, doesn't he?"

Lance nodded his head but did not speak. This time, his silence was not a form of disrespect.

"You think Manny is a nerd?" Tru did not pause, he answered his own question. "Of course not. Do you think he is just smarter than you?" he asked raising his eyebrows. "I doubt it. What is it to be smart?"

Lance knew this time Tru was waiting for his answer. "I don't know. Smart people get good grades."

"And how do you think all these smart people get good grades?" Tru asked, trying to draw the boy out. "Are they smart because they get good grades, or do they get good grades because they're smart?"

"What do you mean?" Lance looked as though someone had asked him to describe photosynthesis in detail.

"Never mind." Tru smiled. "Look at Manny. What does he do that's different from you when it comes to books?"

Lance thought for a second. "I don't know. What?"

Tru felt it was important for Lance to figure this one out. "What was he doin' yesterday when I asked you where he was?"

"Studying," Lance said quietly.

"You know your friend better than anyone else, right?" Tru paused as Lance nodded. He asked seriously, "Tell me, does he love school?"

Lance's slight smile gave Tru the answer he already knew but more importantly, it gave Lance something to think about.

Sensing Lance was digesting their talk, Tru kicked his speech into high gear. "Whenever you think you don't have the energy to study, whenever you think you can't take it no more, whenever you think all is lost, remember this." He put his hand over Lance's heart and spoke softly. "You have to ask yourself this question over and over and over again. The question is 'How far do you wanna go?' Because there are going to be times when the only person around is you! No mother, no family, no friends, only you, Lance. That means you are going to have to dig deep, so deep within yourself that it is going to hurt at first because it is you. After the hurt, your body, soul and mind will answer that question...to the next level!" Tru cupped Lance's face with both hands. "Believe me when I tell you, there is no other level like the next level. To reach it and for it is the greatest feeling in the world. A feeling with one reward, knowing that whatever obstacles life presents you, you are mentally prepared to overcome them and go beyond." Tru watched Lance. He knew it was up to Lance to start believing in himself, but knowing someone else did just might make a difference. He put an arm around the boy and said, "Once you commit, you're going to be all right. Lance, you're going to do just fine."

Chapter 15

Working Out

After their rocky beginning, Tru and Lance began to study together more easily in the few weeks that followed. Lance even started asking questions. Their time together became more productive. Learning was happening. Then they hit a wall of complacency. It was as if the sessions ran out of gas.

Serendipitously, that's when the phone call from Dr. Frederick at East Hills Elementary came. "You can start baseball workouts immediately. Just remember, Tru," Dr. Frederick explained over the phone, "different groups use the gym every night and your permit begins at nine. You'll have to wait until then to get started."

"Oh, that's not a problem, ma'am," Tru said happily. "Even if we can get in there for a half hour or so that would be great. We'll take what we can get. I really appreciate it. Thanks very much!"

"We support anything that supports our kids, Tru. You are the one deserving of thanks," the principal said enthusiastically. "When you are ready to leave, let Ron the custodian know, and he'll take care of the cleanup on the late night shift."

Tru was psyched. He felt the workouts would serve many different purposes. First, they would give Lance and him a different atmosphere in which to develop their relationship further. Second, besides breaking the winter monotony, the workouts would provide an atmosphere based on fun rather than necessity. Third, there would be interaction based on shared camaraderie. Tru hoped this would be an opportunity for Lance to see a different side of the man who invaded his life, and for him to relate to Lance on a new basis.

Also, if he could get Lance to enjoy baseball and want to continue playing, that might give the boy another reason to keep up his grades. It had done exactly that for him, when he was about Lance's age.

His last reason was a bit selfish. Lately he had been feeling a void in his life. He came to realize it was coaching. He'd told himself he should not coach again for supremely logical reasons, but he could never get the idea out of his head.

Every time Tru thought about how angry he had gotten when so few parents showed up or some drunk parent embarrassed his or her kid, he would think of last summer and the looks on the faces of the boys when they received their uniforms. Each time he thought of the emotional practices, when he had to yell at the kids to get them to hustle, he remembered Darryl Weston and Brendon Banks screaming "RUN!" to the team.

For every negative, there were two positives. The biggest of which was Tru had the fever. Not only baseball fever, but kid fever. He wanted to make a difference in the lives of these kids by getting them on the right track before they got derailed.

The gymnasium at East Hills Elementary wasn't a showplace. It was a bandbox made of wood. There was no more than four feet of floor from the undersized hardwood court boundary to the peeling white wood wall. All of the basket backboards were wood with small red boxes painted where the ball should presumably be hit to ensure a basket. The modern age of plastic backboards had not reached East Hills. The facilities were on par with the setting. The boys had to change their clothes on the stage, which was cut out of the wall opposite the eight rows of wooden bleachers that ran the length of the floor. There was an ancient game clock, which no modern kid, or adult for that matter, could read. The numbers were black marks spaced evenly from eight, which was where the twelve would be on a normal wrist-watch, to one, which was where the eleven would be. There was only one hand on the clock and it was the second hand. An odd iron cage covered its rusty body. It was a clock that gave no information as to time remaining in a contest. The only way you knew that was when a buzzer sounded. The words, Home and Visitor, were scratched to the left and right of the face.

As Tru spoke with Ron the night custodian about practice and leaving time. As he spoke he saw Manny, Lance and Lamar changing into their baggy blue gym trunks on the stage.

A few minutes later he went over to the boys. "What do you boys think of this place?" Tru inquired, wondering if they had noticed, as he had, its decaying condition.

Manny looked at Lance and Lamar, then at Tru, whom he always called "Coach Ray," and said with a smile, "It's kinda small, ain't it?"

"Let's see how small you think it is after your butts run five laps around it," Tru laughed. "Let's go! Don't cut any corners—stay outside the boundary lines of the basketball court."

Manny did not complete one!

Lance and Lamar were barely able to keep running, they were laughing so hard. They lapped Manny barely three-quarters of the way around the outside edge of the floor.

"Yo, butterball," Lance roared to Manny as Lamar cracked-up even more, "is your butt that outta shape you can't even run one little lap? One lousy lap! I can't believe it!"

Tru said, "Come on boy, you can do it." He began to trot backwards like a stallion, trying to encourage the struggling youth.

Unfortunately, when running backwards it is impossible to see what is in front of you. Things like walls can present serious impediments to progress when they loom unseen.

"Ray! Watch . . . !" Lance shouted his warning two seconds too late. Tru's back hit the solidness of the wall, throwing him off balance. As he threw his right hand to help break his fall, he saw Manny's panic-stricken face.

"Ah, shit!" Tru shouted, unable to hide his pain and frustration. Manny was draped over him like a blanket.

Gasping for breath, Manny smiled, and with no intent to bring humor to the scene, said, "Coach Ray, you mind if I take a little break?"

Tru glanced at Lamar and Lance who, by their reactions,

Proud Coach Tru Dixon poses at the tailgate party in the Three Rivers Stadium parking lot, prior to the Championship Game against Brookline.

Coach Tru addressing players during a skull session.

Antonio "John Doe" Williams stops traffic in all directions while promoting his team.

Bring on the U.S. Olympic Team! (The banquet at Sandcastle)

The Next Level car wash to raise money for the team.

Once on the playing field, The Next Level stands up to be counted.

The Next Level players scrutinize their opposition.

Homewood Field.

Go Team, Go! (Three Rivers Stadium scoreboard)

Jim Thompson

Brendon Banks..."The Whiff"—Three Rivers Stadium Championship Game.

Tru Dixon

The site of the soon to be erected Next Level Sports / Academic Center.

The Next Level—the players and their coaches.

were in danger of pissing their pants. He looked back to the fallen Manny and fought off his own smile. "Butterball, if you don't get your round butt up off of me, you'll be hangin' from the rafters."

Manny lost it. He laughed hysterically. Sweat from his challenging one-half lap poured down his face.

"Does this mean practice is over?" Lance said with a straight face.

"No way! Not a chance," Tru said, unable to stop his own laughter.

After Lance and Lamar completed their five-lap run and Manny his one-half lap run, four-and-a-half lap walk, Tru sat the boys down at center court. He gave them a quick talk and explanation of what they would be doing at future workouts.

"Seriously," Tru said to Manny, "you gotta learn to push yourself more. This'll be the last time you walk four-and-a-half laps."

Manny was not offended or ashamed. Tru had said those words with love in his heart, not belittlement. Manny understood and Lance and Lamar no longer laughed either.

"All right then," Tru said, flipping a new white baseball underhanded to Manny. "Let's get warmed up. We have no time to waste!"

They put on their gloves and formed a triangle. They had excellent intentions, but as they began to throw no one could seem to catch the ball thrown by another.

Lamar was the worst. He kept peeling balls off his chest, as if he had no glove on. Each time, Tru cringed at the deep hollow sound created by the ball bouncing off Lamar. Tru waited for Lamar to start crying or complaining about his self-inflicted pain. He never did.

Tru realized quickly he was gutsy. From what Lance had told Tru, Lamar also thought himself to be quite the young ladies' man and schoolwork was not high on Lamar's priority list. If he did not keep up his grades, he would be unable to continue the practices. Tru knew the boy had lots of potential, but he was not extremely hopeful of Lamar's ability to formulate a goal and try and reach it. *Another decent kid with little discipline,* Tru frowned.

"Hold up, fellas," Tru called as he threw his hands up in the air. "Get your little butts over here! What's up with this catchin', y'all? I know you can catch a little better than that!" He paused and said, "Lamar, you got a glove on your hand for a reason, man. That's where the ball is supposed to land, not off your bird chest!"

The boys began laughing again. Lamar, too. Not that the other two boys were adroit; Manny and Lance had a lot of trouble catching also. In fact, Tru knew he would have to keep his cool because he was dangerously close to anger.

"Can we do better?" he asked after the boys had calmed down.

They all looked at each other and broke out into laughter again. Tru knew they were not taking the work-out seriously. It was, to the boys and perhaps even to himself, a little break from the inactivity that occurs in Pittsburgh winters.

"We aren't very good," Manny finally responded. "That ball hurts when it hits you, Coach Ray."

"What's the only way to stop the ball from hurtin' you then?" Tru asked after the laughter from Manny's answer quieted. They motioned with their gloves. Tru nodded his head and continued, "Yeah, that's right. You gotta catch the rock. The only way you can stop it hurtin' you is to catch it. The more you're afraid, the more you'll get hurt."

Tru had their attention now. "As far as I can tell, Lamar is still livin', right? Pain goes away, fellas. Any of you ever fall off your bikes?"

The boys grimaced at each other as Tru continued, "Y'all still ride though, don't you?"

The three boys nodded.

"If you visualize playing this game a certain way, that's the way you'll begin to play. Nobody has to know you aren't very good as long as you play with confidence." He paused and said slowly but firmly, "Nobody will know!"

Despite his words, Tru knew all the confidence in the world wouldn't suffice forever. Once the early stages of playing were over, higher goals must be reached for, and talent is the arbitrator. However, Tru also knew that lack of talent can be caused by lack of knowledge. In this case, ignorance of the proper techniques for catching and throwing.

The next two weeks of practice were spent solely on those fundamental skills. After their five laps and before practice Manny and Lance would play catch for almost half an hour. Lamar was showing up for practice only sporadically.

They had to learn everything: when to turn the thumb of the glove down while catching a ball, how to catch a ball thrown opposite of the glove-side of the body, and how to properly grip the baseball to throw it. The small and large things. Everything. They always ended up practice with a brief "skull" session.

A skull session occurred when the boys gathered in a vacant classroom to go over situations that were common, and not so common, in the game of baseball. Tru used the blackboard to draw a defense on a field and assigned each boy a position, always rotating them. He then told the boys where, if any, the base runners were. After everything was set, Tru predicted what the make-believe batter would do. He asked each boy to describe his responsibilities at each position. If they were incorrect, they dropped to the classroom floor and did three pushups. This gave the kids a chance, for the first time in most cases, to think about and explore the intricacies of the game. Tru always gave them an explanation of the whys and why-nots of each situation before the end of each skull session.

"Coach Tru," Lance asked on the cold drive over to East Hills School one night, "do you think it would be okay for you to stop coming to my school?"

It had been nearly two months since the scene in Mr. Bell's math class. Tru's weekly, sometimes biweekly, visits had been very productive. Lance had begun to talk in class, once even answering four questions in a row, three correctly, and turning to smile at Tru in the back of the class. Lance's teachers were very supportive of the arrangement and continuously told Tru how much Lance had improved.

"Now why would I want to do that?" Tru asked, eyebrows raised.

"I'm not gonna cut up in class anymore. I promise!" the skinny eleven-year-old said, looking directly at Tru through his wire-rimmed glasses.

Tru smiled to himself. He had finally heard self-respect emerging in Lance's voice. "I'll have to think about it, Lance. I know you've made progress, but I don't want to quit goin' there and have you start actin' like some old knucklehead again. Let's see how this next report card turns out, okay?"

"All right. That's good, 'cause I'm goin' to get pretty good grades this time." Lance smiled, shaking his head as he looked at the snow falling, highlighted by the streetlights. "Ah, Coach Tru, I almost forgot. Do you think it would be okay for Darryl to start coming to our practices?"

Tru knew Lance meant young Darryl Weston III whose father had died recently. Tru had known Darryl Weston, Junior quite well. "I've got no problem with Darryl coming to practice, Lance. Tell him I'd be thrilled."

The drive to East Hills continued in silence. There was none of the usual ripping that went on among the three. Tru's thoughts were on Darryl Junior, his friend, whom he had very fondly referred to as "Big Baaaby."

Darryl Weston, Junior's son Darryl III was a descendant of Pittsburgh's legendary sports heroes, the Weston family. The Westons had produced a long line of athletic and academic stars at Westinghouse High School. All-City and college All-Americans were part of the family football tree. Darryl Junior's father—Darryl Senior, never missed a game in which his son played—and had himself starred at Ohio State.

The fact that Darryl Junior had been such a good father made his untimely and tragic death two weeks before that much harder to understand. Tru had heard of the accident on the radio as he was driving to see a client. He remembered how badly he'd felt. Later he'd gone to see his friend's father.

Now, as he pulled into the lot at East Hills, he felt as though it was that dreadful night. He remembered hugging Darryl Senior, usually so upbeat, usually so happy, and then so heartbroken, so lost. Tru remembered how they'd cried together.

Lance and Manny looked at Tru's face and knew something was wrong. Getting out of the Jeep, they called back, "You okay, Coach?" Not realizing time had passed since he'd last spoken and with tears welling in his eyes, Tru said softly, "I'm fine. Yeah, you tell Darryl I'd love to have him with us."

The first practice to which Darryl came was a good one. Somehow kids seem to get past all the uneasiness that grownups feel. They acted like nothing bad had happened to Darryl's family. Perhaps they did not fully understand the impact of the trauma because many of them had, in a sense, already lost their own fathers. Darryl was welcomed into the small group not because he'd experienced a tragedy, but because he was their friend.

"It's a little different than last summer," Lance explained, not wanting Darryl to be surprised at the practice. "Coach Tru makes us run five laps around the gym first. Be sure to stay outside the lines 'cause he gets awful mad if you take a shortcut. You know how he is. And remember what happens if you mess up?"

"Yeah, I remember." Darryl smiled as he looked at his bigger than normal biceps. "A Three D push-up! Desire, Determination, and Dedication!"

"Yeah, but we never just do one set anymore," Manny added. "It's usually like five or somethin'—depends how sorry we were! And now we gotta keep our grades up, at least a C average!"

The practices fell into a nice routine. They would work out at least three, usually four, times weekly at between nine and nine forty-five in the evening. At each practice Tru added a new drill. Manny and Lance struggled with old as well as new skills, but they always had enthusiastic Darryl Weston there motivating them. Lamar rarely showed up any longer.

One of the most difficult drills was called "Speedball." This was a fielding drill. The fielder would face Tru from perhaps seven feet away, with knees bent and glove on the floor. Tru rolled a ball to either the fielder's left or right. If he saw him leaning one direction, Tru would purposefully roll in the opposite direction. As the ball was fielded, Tru rolled another one in the first direction.

Tru watched to see that the boys didn't cross over their own feet. On balls hit slightly to the left or right, the proper technique was to slide to the ball. Then Tru looked to see they were bending their knees, not their backs, and lastly, if they looked the ball into their gloves.

As ball number one was being fielded, another ball was rolled in the opposite direction that they would have to field in the same manner. Each set lasted approximately thirty seconds. For every ball missed, they were required to do a Three D push-up. Whoever fielded the most balls cleanly would not have to do an extra set of Three D's.

Darryl almost always won the drill, which was physically challenging and at the same time promoted proper technique. It also gave the boys the chance to motivate each other.

This drill helped Tru to realize just how special a kid Darryl Weston was, and what a natural born leader he would become. Even though it was obvious he was the most gifted athlete of the three, he never let on he knew. He always tried to inspire Lance and Manny to get more from themselves than they thought they could give. It was hard for Manny and Lance not to push themselves when they saw the energy Darryl put forth in each of his turns.

After the rigorous drill there was a quick warm-down which consisted of walking two laps and a short skull session.

As the practice and game began to mean more to them, they became more serious and studious.

On the ride home they were generally quiet. The boys mostly did homework. Usually each one studied on his own until Darryl asked Lance one night if he needed help. From then on, they always helped each other and did it without making the other person feel inadequate. Tru felt sometimes that he was not even in the car; it was as if he was just another one of their friends. He took it as a sign that their self-reliance and independence was growing.

Tru felt good about that.

Chapter 16

Crips vs. Bloods

The phone calls began shortly after Darryl Weston joined the practices.

The first one was from Glenn Harvey, who the boys called Coach Bud.

"Tru, I hear you and some kids are working out up at East Hills."

"Yeah, just me, Lance, Manny, and big Darryl Weston. It's no big thing. Just goin' over some fundamentals—breaking up the winter a little. See if any of these guys want to learn to play some ball before next summer, you know."

"You think I could bring Brendon up there? I'll help out if you need me. I'd sure like to see him stay active this winter," Bud said hopefully.

"Man, you don't have to ask! What's wrong with you?" Tru said with respect. "We'll be up there tomorrow night at nine. We can't get into the gym until then, and we'll be done at nine forty-five. Come on up, we'd be glad to have you both!"

Marcus Haines, a twelve-year-old now, phoned asking to come.

Then Stan Coles did. He had also played for Tru the previous summer.

Janet Williams and her son Chris.

Jim Thompson and his son Jerrett.

Joe Foster and Antonio Williams.

They wanted to bring other friends with them. Robbie Elliot asked if a youngster from Penn Hills, Byron Knight, could come also. Kids were coming from everywhere.

"So you gonna have a team or what?" Bart Hanks asked.

"Hey, Bart, what's up, man?" Tru said, recognizing the voice on the phone immediately. "Nah, we're just workin' out with some kids. No team."

"I'd like to have Johnnie work out with you if that's okay. You start at nine, right?"

Tru gulped. "Of course he's welcome, and yeah, it's nine."

"I'll try and get up there tomorrow, but we won't be able to make it by nine," Bart said and added kiddingly, "Can't you get a later starting time?"

"I'm workin' on that one, Bart!" Tru said. It was nice to hear from Bart Hanks. In their conversation, they reminisced about the past summer. Bart spoke with purpose and conviction. *Johnnie is a fortunate little brother to have a father like Bart,* Tru thought.

Within three weeks, the number of boys participating rose to ten, and by the end of February, twelve kids were attending practice nearly every night. Some of the kids had played the previous summer. Tru was glad to see a few more parents sitting in the bleachers and observing the practices.

One evening one of the parents who usually showed up, Janet Williams, approached Tru looking concerned. "Tru,

I don't know how to say this," she said as Coach Bud took the boys through their warmups. "I think Chris is going to stop coming to practice."

He saw the pained look on her face. Chris was one of the kids who really seemed to enjoy the practices and Janet had been religious about his attendance and punctuality. "What's the problem?" Tru asked. "Is he gettin' bored?"

"Oh no, it's not Chris," she continued as she rubbed her hand across her tight sandy brown hair tied just above her neck. "If he knew I was telling you he would probably kill me. I have some problems that I'm havin' a hard time solvin' in my head."

Now Tru was confused. Why would a parent sacrifice something her child obviously wanted to do and was good for him for selfish reasons? He tried to hide his disappointment and a trace of annoyance. "I don't understand."

"Tru, we're not from East Hills. We live in Wilkinsburg," she responded with resignation.

Now he felt foolish. "I'm sorry, Jan," he said, letting out a deep breath. "I thought you were looking for a reason to get Chris out of these sessions because you were tired of bringin' him. I apologize."

"Forget it, Tru." She diplomatically let him off the hook. "Anyway, that's not the real concern. Chris tells me kids at school are givin' him a hard time about comin' up to East Hills to practice. They say stuff like, why would he want to do all that if he's a for-real Wilkinsburg dude. What the hell's wrong with these kids, Tru?"

"I don't know, Jan, I really don't," he answered wearily. "But I do know they're looking for a place to belong, for people to belong to. I think that's why the kids enjoy comin' here. It's something else." Tru tried to put his feelings into words. "Have you ever seen a bunch of crabs caught in a basket? If one manages to climb out, the others reach their claws up to grab him back. Maybe the other kids are jealous."

"I think that's the reason," Janet slowly replied. "All Chris talks about is Coach Tru, Coach Bud, or these kids who come here. He ain't worried about none of the kids at these practices jumpin' him. He's just scared comin' up here. I try to tell him nothin' will happen, but he keeps saying that he shouldn't be here. And to tell the truth I'm afraid for him too, and I think he knows it."

"Are other kids having the same concerns?" Tru asked as he imagined the problem escalating.

"Yeah, some. I've only talked to two parents, Tracy and Ron. As you know, a lot of the kids here don't have active parents to talk to. Tracy and Ron are thinking just what we're thinkin'—you know, the place, the time, the way kids at school treat each other. Chris is afraid he might get 'jumped by his boys' if he doesn't stay away. Damn, I hate that phrase."

Tru and Janet walked to the bleachers where Ron Haines and Tracy Elliot were watching Coach Bud continue the boys' warmup.

Tru went over to talk to Tracy. She and her son Robbie were from Wilkinsburg. Janet had said they had the same concerns. Next Tru walked over to Ron. He and his son Marcus were from Homewood and Tru found out people from certain parts of Homewood were not welcome in East Hills.

After the discussions, Tru returned to the practice. Nothing else unusual occurred. He saw Bart Hanks and his son come in, but Tru was too busy batting to talk. While the boys worked on fielding grounders hit by Bud and took batting practice using old beat-up tennis balls, Tru coached as usual. But his mind was not thinking about the things his voice was talking about.

The problem of gang members and other kids at

school undermining these sessions could ruin the gains these kids were making, Tru reasoned, and something needed to be done. Somehow, he had to communicate to the kids and parents that if you run from problems you have to keep running. But if you confront them, the problem ends.

In Tru's book, to confront was the only way to solve.

The next evening, despite Tru's words, only six kids showed up. The parents had narrowed down to Ron Haines and one of the Elliots. After the practice was over he telephoned the absent kids and their parents or guardians. He explained, cajoled and explained some more.

Then he asked them all to at least show up for the practice the next night. At that practice, he motioned to them and explained to the boys in a loud voice, "I asked the adults to join us this evening, because something has come up that we all need to discuss."

The boys were used to Tru talking to them alone, but he'd never asked parents to join them before. The boys looked at each other and whispered as if they were trying to figure out what the adults had done, just like they would if a classmate was called to the principal's office over the intercom at school.

No one was sure what was going on but the adults approached the center of the floor. Not only did that further confuse the kids, it made them sit even closer together.

"Something has been called to my attention," Tru began as the adults struggled to sit comfortably on the hardwood. "I've been thinking about it most of practice and I think we need to discuss it. Some parents have expressed concern to me about the safety of their kids, not only coming to East Hills, but at their regular schools. We all know what it's like around here, the crazy world we live in. Some of the kids out there have no respect for themselves or anything else. With nothing better to do, they jump somebody for some stupid-ass—excuse me, but I get irritated just thinkin' about this—some ridiculous reason like—this." Tru paused briefly and lowered his sweat pants to a point just above his butt. Then he continued with a perfect impersonation of a twelve-year-old wanna-be-thug. "Yo, homey, I peeped you playin' some hardball up in East Hills. Wha's up wit dat, cuzz? You thinkin' you too good for Wilkinsburg? You a Blood or a Slob, baby?" Slob, in this instance, refers to a Crip, for a true gang-banger would never recognize the actual name of a rival gang. "Dat shit's gotta stop, man. Befo' we git to grittin'!"

Not only did this imitation make the kids crack up, it brought smiles to the faces of the adults. Even Janet Williams.

Tru went on. "Some of these kids are in gangs by the age of ten. Isn't that something to be proud of? Y'all know we can't hide from it though, right?" he said angrily. "We sure can't—unless we can afford to move out to Fox Chapel or some other suburb. But I know I can't and I doubt you can either."

He paused and shook his head negatively as he lowered his eyes, a look of depression and frustration on his face.

Slowly he raised his head. He looked first at Janet Williams, then Ron Haines, and finally Tracy Elliot. "But I'll be damned if I'm," he said defiantly as he pounded his chest, "gonna let some *punk* tell me where I can and cannot go. Nah, not me! I live in Homewood and I'll come up to East Hills, or anywhere else I want, any old time I want. And, you know what? We're gonna keep practicin' up here, maybe twice on Sundays!"

The kids smiled. Sitting up, clapping, and swapping fists in a form of a high-five, they nodded to each other confirming that each felt exactly the same way Tru did.

They were ready to walk out onto East Hills Drive and call out in the night each of their neighborhoods. East Liberty! Penn Hills! East Hills! Homewood! Wilkinsburg!

The few parents there were not as amused. They were deeply frightened for the safety of their kids, and they knew the realities of the world. "How can we force our children into fights for no other reason than to play baseball? They may get cut," Janet asked.

"Tru, you know it ain't that simple!" Ron Haines challenged. "C'mon now!"

"But it is that simple, Mr. Haines, Janet. How could it not be?"

"Suppose my kid gets jumped by a group of these punks and gets beaten bad or worse? What am I supposed to tell him then, Tru?" Ron asked. "I'm not a man who backs away from a fight, but I don't go looking for one either. And this is my kid. You want me to tell him to go get a gun? To get some of his friends and go get his ass back? What good does that do? What am I teachin' him then? Man, you can't beat these punks by goin' down to their level. You know that!"

"What are your choices, Ron? Quit? Hide? Run?" Tru said, pausing between each word. "What are you teachin' him then? I understand your concerns. All your concerns," he said as he scanned the parents' faces, stopping only on Janet Williams. "But you all know they can get hassled at school for no real reason anyhow. Could be for the shoes they're wearin', maybe their jacket. But my point is still, what you gonna do? How far you gonna let yourself get pushed? Again, I'll say, we can't afford to move to Fox Chapel. You think we wouldn't have problems there? You know better than that.

We live here. If we aren't ready to do what we can to

improve where we live, then we aren't really livin'. You see what I mean. I'll promise you nothin' gonna happen to you or your kids while you're in this building. I'll guarantee you that much! Y'all gotta do what you think is best for your kid—I'm not tryin' to tell you otherwise. All I'm sayin' is that I'm gonna keep comin' up here until there aren't any kids left!"

"Does that mean you'll be practicin' tomorrow night?" a deep voice asked from behind Tru.

"You better believe it." Tru turned and smiled as he acknowledged Bart Hanks. He walked over to his tall, wiry friend. "Yes, we'll be practicin' tomorrow at nine o'clock sharp. What can I do for you?"

"I'd like to get my boy here on the team," Bart replied, putting his arm around his son. "It isn't too late, I hope."

Almost everyone knew Bart Hanks. They had heard Bart was one of the main people in the Wilkinsburg Baseball Association. Those who knew him personally felt the same way Tru did. He was someone to respect. Bart had chosen tonight to bring his son. To have him speak out and support Tru, not only eased the minds of some parents, it raised the level of respect they felt for Tru.

"We really don't have a team, Bart. We're just keepin' a few kids busy this winter, havin' some fun, checkin' on their grades in school."

"Well, is it too late or not?" Bart asked.

"It's never too late, baby!" Tru said, hugging his friend.

Chapter 17

One Shoe On, One Shoe Off

At noon the next day, a storm began. By the time Tru was ready to go to the evening's practice, the rain had turned into thick ice. Then heavy snow fell. Tru scraped the mixture of crystallized rain and snow from his windshield for what seemed the millionth time. "It's permafrost," he muttered.

Jumping into the Jeep, he turned on the engine and immediately noticed the arrow on the temperature gauge was still pointing directly at the C. The Jeep couldn't seem to warm up either. He wondered if the bad weather would ever change. He wondered why, of all climates, he had to be born and live in Pittsburgh. Here it was the end of March and the blustery winter weather showed no sign of abating. Definitely the cold was not conducive to getting thirteen kids outside in order to start practicing baseball, as he had hoped to do this week.

Hearing the car chugging and coughing, Lance and Manny came running. Manny and Lance looked like they came right out of *Eskimo Weekly*. Manny's large purple hooded jacket covered every inch of his upper body from the elements. A bundled up Lance looked about the same. Tru laughed seeing them. Although Manny had seventy pounds on Lance, for the first time they were the same size.

It could not have been two seconds that the car door was open before it was shut again as the two Eskimo look-alikes quickly settled themselves into the not very warm Jeep.

"What's the matter with you two?" Tru kidded. "Y'all don't think it's cold, do you?"

Neither boy acknowledged Tru's jabbering. Warmth was on their minds as they bent over and tried to tuck their faces into their knees, forming some kind of protective ball. If he could have seen their faces, Tru would have known their eyes were shut and lips scrunched in frozen pain. Tru shook his head as he pulled away from the curb and headed for Darryl Weston's house to pick him up for the evening's practice.

During the pickups both boys were quiet. In a short sleeve shirt, Big Darryl strolled out his front door looking like it was the middle of August. The sight made Tru think back to what Grandma Howard had said a few days earlier when the boys were complaining about the weather. "If you let the sun determine if you'll have a good day, Pittsburgh ain't the place for you. Your sun needs to be burnin' *inside!*"

Tru went on to Wilkinsburg via Penn Avenue to pick up Chris Williams. The entire trip usually took about twenty minutes, but Tru always allowed an extra ten minutes when he had to bring Chris. He was the type of kid who was always late. Usually, Tru pulled up in front of his house on Pitt Street and honked the horn several times.

Without fail, Chris was always finishing dressing

when he came out of the door. What would it be today, they each wondered, zipping his jacket...tying his hood...or pulling on his gloves? Manny, Lance, Darryl, and Tru waited, each planning how they would rip on him when he got in the jeep. It made no sense to them, why he was always late. But that was just Chris.

This night, however, the door never opened and Chris never emerged. After nearly five minutes, Tru went to the door and knocked. Janet Williams soon came to the door and was puzzled that Tru was there to pick Chris up.

"Chris told me you called and said you were going to pick him up down at Burger Palace!" she said with no real concern in her voice, "Did you forget?"

"I must have," Tru stuttered trying to conceal his realization that Chris was up to something. "Sure, I just forgot, that's all!" he continued with more assurance in his voice.

Tru walked back to the car and told the other boys that Chris was sick and would not be coming to practice that night. They drove past Burger Palace, and, as expected, Tru did not see Chris Williams. He sighed and wondered where Chris was and who he was running with.

The next stop was Stan Coles. He lived about six blocks away from Chris, also in Wilkinsburg, on Princeton Street. Sometimes, depending on who else he had to bring, Coach Bud picked up the very quiet, light skinned twelve-year-old. Today, however, Bud was busy before practice and would not have time to go through his entire schedule of stops. Any talking that was going on in the Jeep usually stopped when Stan got in. It was not that the boys did not like Stan; they certainly did. They stopped talking out of respect for his shyness. They did not know why he was so shy. They just accepted it.

Stan was always prompt so that when he did not come out of his door immediately, Tru knew something was wrong. The knocks on Stan's door were fruitless. There was no one home.

Tru thought, hoped really, Stan was at church. His mother was constantly trying to get the young boy involved with religion. It was her attempt to surround Stan with the types of kids that would have a positive impact on him.

Tru, again, tried to mask his concern when he returned to the car. Apparently he was successful because none of the three boys appeared the least bit concerned.

As they walked into the gym at East Hills nearly ten minutes late, Tru saw the evening's practice was sparsely attended.

Jerrett Thompson and Robbie Elliott were also not present. Bart Hanks, who was supposed to come with his son, did not attend. As usual, few parents were there.

The practice itself was lifeless. The drills were done with low energy and Tru did not demand more. Everyone wanted to get out of there as soon as possible but the practice dragged on endlessly. Tru wondered if the clock on the ancient wall had stopped.

It was with great relief that Tru finally climbed behind the drivers seat to take the boys home. Finally arriving at Edgarton Avenue, he told Lance and Manny to get out and that he was going to run down to 7-11 to get some coffee.

They walked in the bitter cold back to their respective row houses as Tru pulled away from the curb. He felt like driving endlessly. Doubt was eating him alive. He drove back to the deserted East Hills Shopping Center and stopped the Jeep.

As he looked at the street where kids were destroying the buildings, he wished he had his own can of spray paint to spray them. Then he could tell all these damn kids and parents to go straight to hell. Nobody cared. Tru felt so tired he wanted to quit.

Instead Tru drove off. He had no destination in mind. The Jeep seemed to be driving itself until he found himself looking in the parking lot of the Burger Palace in Wilkinsburg. That's when he saw them.

The gang of choice in Wilkinsburg is referred to as L.A.W., it stands for Larimer Avenue - Wilkinsburg. It is perhaps the most notorious street gang in the Pittsburgh area. Fifteen kids, Tru estimated, all identically dressed in L.A. Raider hats and winter jackets, were sitting on parked cars and milling around the lot. It did not appear as though they had anywhere to go.

If it was not for the streetlight barely hitting their young faces, he would not have recognized the two boys that he knew. Their enormous L.A. winter jackets hid their body features and the hoods nearly covered their eleven-year-old faces.

Chris Williams and Stan Coles never saw Tru coming.

"What's up, homeboys?" Tru called out in his best imitation of gangster rap, "What set y'all niga's with?"

They looked at him and froze, never looking at each other. Slowly Tru walked away.

He drove off.

Later when Janet called him, Tru said, "The other kids told me they'd gone to get something and I couldn't wait."

During the next evening's trip to practice, Tru changed his routine. He left the house early, having arranged for Lance and Manny to go with Bud.

He drove straight to Chris Williams' house.

"Hi, Janet," he said stoically when she answered his knock on the door, "Can I come in?"

"Sure Tru," the usually laid back white woman said. As she opened the door wide she saw the concern on his face, "What's the matter?"

"Is Chris here?"

Chris Williams, a handsome youngster, descended the creaky old steps in the run-down Victorian home.

"Last night," Tru said quietly, "It wasn't that I couldn't wait for Chris. I never told him I'd go to the Burger Palace."

Janet sat stunned. Her gaze turned to Chris. Her eyebrows raised ever so slightly and the look of bewilderment came over her face. The look quickly turned to anger.

"So what?" Chris said belligerently as he slumped even further in the tan easy chair. The television blared to no one. The room seemed to grow darker. "I'm tired of practice! No one else wants to go neither! Who cares about a 2.0 grade point, anyway. It's stupid and boring!"

"You better get you're ass up to your room, boy!" Janet said threateningly, "Before I kick it all the way up there! Don't worry about going to practice any more boy...you're ass is off that team...matter of fact, you ain't gonna leave this damn house for two weeks..."

"Excuse me," Tru interrupted, "But before he goes upstairs, there is a little more I need to tell you. I'd like it if Chris were here to listen."

Tru told Janet everything. Her anger was replaced by fear.

As he walked by Tru, Chris gazed at him while his

mother sobbed.

Chris hated Tru.

Tru and Janet continued their talk for nearly a half hour. Tru finally convinced Janet that he wanted Chris to continue with the team after whatever time she felt was a fair punishment.

The scene at Stan Coles' house was similar.

Tru was not sure how long he could hang in, but he was not ready to give up, not yet.

Thank God it was the weekend.

Unfortunately, Monday night's practice took up where Friday's had left off. At first it seemed normal. Arriving Brendon Banks sat in the front seat next to his grandpa, as always. Brendon was a quiet kid also, at least when you first met him, until he felt comfortable. After that, look out! The others had found out about his humor and playfulness, but, according to Coach Bud, they had not seen anything yet. Brendon had become very popular; one reason was that he was one of the best players on the team. Another reason he was popular was that he always used big words and the others were impressed. Words like *proceed*. Once he even said *vicinity*, although no one could remember why. He wore his hair in an Afro, but it was not the buzzed look that most of the others wore. It was not even shaved on the sides—it just tapered down to his ears. It looked kind of like a sixties Afro, only not as large and extremely neat. Most of the kids thought Brendon was pretty cool.

Along with his grandson, Coach Bud always brought as many kids as he could, some of whom would never have gotten there without him. Tonight, however, Tru noticed one of his regulars, Jerrett Thompson, wasn't with him. Jerrett lived on the border of East Hills, Homewood, and

Wilkinsburg. Literally, the three signs could be viewed from Jerrett's tiny porch. Jerrett was a big handsome boy who looked a lot older than he was, and no one quite knew how to talk to him. Kids that didn't know him, with the exception of Big Darryl, were more than a little intimidated by Jerrett. He always flashed a mean look. Tru once asked him about it and Jerrett looked baffled. "I don't got no idea what you're talking about. That's my normal look."

On this bitterly cold evening, only Brendon, Byron, Robbie and Todd were with Coach Bud.

Marcus Haines came with his dad, Ron. From the beginning, Ron was one of the parents who stayed through the entire practice. Lately, he had been filming each practice so Tru and Coach Bud were able to see some problems that escaped them in the heat of the moment.

Bart Hanks brought his son Johnnie for his first regular practice. Bart's eight-year-old son Carl also attended. "Carl is not big enough to compete with the older boys, but what he lacks in size he makes up for in desire," his dad said. Joe Foster and Antonio Williams, cousins living in East Hills near the Wilkinsburg border, also accompanied Bart.

New members had to watch a practice before they were allowed to participate. Tru reasoned that if a kid saw the way the practices were run and still wanted to come back, the boy's chances of sticking with the team would be greatly increased.

As practice began, Tru turned to Bud.

"Where's Jerrett?" Tru asked Bud wondering what the boy's excuse would be this time.

"I'm glad you asked, Tru," Bud said in his typically calm tone, "That boy is in trouble and his dad is ready to throw up his hands."

Bud handed Tru an interim report from Jerrett's school that Jim Thompson had given him. It was from Jerrett's science teacher. It read:

"Disruptive...No regard for classmates and/or authority...constantly being told to stop clowning and instigating roughhousing..."

Tru had seen enough.

"When I got to his house...shoot...you could hear his dad screaming at him from our car!" Bud said shaking his head. "I went up to the door and I heard Jim screaming 'What is your problem, boy...what the hell is your problem?' He opened the door and you could see Jerrett had been crying, but he still had that same 'I don't give a shit look' about him! Jerrett just said, 'I don't know.' I thought Jim was gonna put him through the wall. He just kept saying, ' "You don't know," what the hell kind of answer is that?' "

Bud continued, "After he sent Jerrett up to his room, Jim started telling me how that boy got some strong demons, Tru. Did you know he got busted a couple of weeks ago for shoplifting? I don't know if we'll be seeing Jerrett anymore."

Tru sighed, his heart heavy. How could you save a kid who insisted on making all the wrong moves?

Despite the discouragement he felt, at the next practice Jerrett was back and Tru called him out of the gymnasium to talk to him.

"Jerrett," Tru said supportively, "you and I need a heart to heart. I'm not going to beat your ear in about the trouble you're having at home or in school. It's like this...you're mom and dad asked me to talk to you and I said I would. You know you're about this far from not playing baseball this year?" Tru said as he held his fingers millimeters apart. "I know you want to be thought of as a tough kid and you want to be one...you have to act like you don't care about anything.... That's an old routine...seen it thousands of times. But you know what else I know, you are extremely talented at baseball, and more importantly, you love to play the game. I can see it in your eyes. Use your talent, just use what God gave you!"

Tru paused for a minute. He walked into the gym and yelled something over to Coach Bud before he returned to the hallway with Jerrett. He just wanted the boy to have some time to let things sink in.

"Do you know you're mother and father are special?" he continued.

Jerrett answered with a shrug.

"Oh you still gotta keep that front up, man...that's cool, we can go that way, but I don't know what you mean by that shrug!"

" 'I don't know'...that's what it means!" Jerrett responded.

"Oh, you know all right. You think about it. I have all night, young man!"

Jerrett stared at Tru for nearly thirty seconds. Tru was amazed that Jerrett never looked away. Most kids his age would be intimidated. Not Jerrett.

"Because they care about me," he answered slowly.

"That's right. You know why? You have special talents, Jerrett. You just have to learn the difference between fun and business. You see, if you don't take care of business, you can't have fun. I hope fun to you doesn't mean sellin' drugs, and business isn't blowin' someone away 'cause he was on your turf...but if you don't make the most of your real chances to be somebody. There'll be another kid just like you that will make the right decision and everyone, except for your mother and father will forget about you...it's your move Jerrett! I just want to know one thing, can we depend on you to be shortstop for the entire season." Jerrett nodded.

Though Tru was aware more problems could occur, he felt Jerrett's response was encouraging. When he got home that night, Tru walked into the deserted house on Edgarton and collapsed into his favorite chair. Within minutes, the phone rang.

"What's up Mr. Thompson?" Tru said cordially, "How's Peachy and Jerrett?"

"If you don't mind Tru, Jerrett has something he'd like to ask you," the husky voiced Jim Thompson said handing the phone to his troubled son before ever hearing Tru's response.

"Coach Tru?" Jerrett said in a whisper, "Can I come back?"

"Put your dad on the phone, son," Tru answered.

"We'd love to have your son back, Jim!" Tru said firmly, "Why don't you tell him."

Practices began to improve.

Several nights after, Tru, Manny, and Lance pulled up at Darryl Weston's house but Darryl wasn't waiting. Tru honked the horn several times. When Darryl did not run out, Tru jogged up the short driveway and rang the doorbell.

Chris, Darryl's older brother, opened the door and gave Tru the bad news. "He broke his ankle."

"He broke his ankle?" Tru repeated amazed.

He hung his head in disbelief. As he lifted his head, he noticed Chris smiling. "He broke it while playin' basketball at the Shadyside Boys Club...with a girl!"

He jogged back to the car sending his wishes for a speedy recovery. Manny and Lance thought it was pretty funny.

The following evening, Darryl Weston was back at practice, his leg in a cast.

Bart Hanks and his sons sat in the bleachers watching as the kids ran five laps around the old gym floor. It amounted to no more than three hundred yards and the boys were required to run the entire distance. Manny had even worked himself into good enough shape that he was able to complete the distance without getting lapped. Tru figured the reason was because most of the kids liked Manny and did not want to see him to have to do push-ups for getting lapped. He thought the gesture of compassion and concept of teamwork was well worth the sacrifice of having the leaders not run the laps to their fullest potential. It was also one of the few times during the workouts that Tru and Bud noticed all the boys talking to each other. They wanted to promote communication between the entire team so that these kids from different neighborhoods would become more cohesive.

"You wanna catch with me?" Robbie Elliot puffed at Byron Knight as they rounded the court underneath the antique clock.

"Nah, man, I got someone else in mind," came the strained reply from Byron as he jogged next to Robbie's left shoulder.

Robbie turned to his right and asked Chris Williams with a hint of panic in his voice, "You got anyone to throw with?"

Chris did not respond verbally. He just smiled and continued his jog, picking up the pace slightly.

"Dang!" Robbie said with increasing pain. He knew then he had not started his search for a partner soon enough. All the kids who could catch the best were probably taken by now. This was like the Sweetheart Dance at school, he thought to himself. If you waited too late to ask a girl, all the pretty ones would be gone. Robbie knew he would have to play catch with either Manny or Lance.

In all baseball practices from the beginning of time, playing catch follows the jog. Theirs was unlike most other practices in that, if a ball was missed, both the thrower and receiver had to do two Three D's.

"Catch the dang ball!" Robbie barked at Manny as he flipped him the regulation Little League rawhide. Robbie anticipated he would be doing some push-ups because of Manny's ineptness, but he was comforted by the fact that he did not have to play catch with Lance. Even Manny did not want to play catch with Lance. Manny's catching was not too good, but he looked like an all-star when compared with his best friend. Plus, his throwing was all right, so if he was not partnered with Lance, at least Robbie would not have to do push-ups when he threw the ball. That grief belonged to Joe Foster who was partnering with Lance tonight.

Manny and Robbie ended up doing eighteen push-ups, but that paled to the whopping thirty-three that Lance and Joe Foster had to do before Coach Tru mercifully called an end to the warmup session.

Tru called the boys into the familiar center court area where they received instructions. Meanwhile Joe and Robbie plotted their revenge.

During Tru's speech the rule was simple. Anyone caught talking, laughing, or generally not paying attention was subject to doing pushups until Coach Tru was done talking.

Joe Foster positioned himself carefully behind Lance and Manny. He was chosen for the job because he had the sneakiest look. His face never seemed to change expression. His lack of expression served him well tonight.

Coach Tru began, "All you boys need to concentrate more while playing catch."

Joe seized the moment. He leaned his skinny frame up towards Lance ever so slightly and whispered, "His braids is too tight. They're squeezin' what little sense he had outta that damn melon!"

Lance and Manny fought smiling, but it was futile.

"Let's have the comics up here, front and center," Tru said. "You two think this is funny. You know what I think is funny." Their smiles disappeared immediately but by then it was too late. "I'll try to keep this short so you'll only have to do fifty push-ups."

Surreptitiously, Joe Foster looked over at Robbie Elliot and nodded.

After the lecture, the boys broke into two groups for fielding practice. Coach Tru and Coach Bud took one line each and rolled grounders to each kid. They stressed the proper technique of fielding a ground ball. "If the ball is rolled directly at you," Tru said, "under control, charge the ball and break down into the correct fielding position. Remember the correct position is legs spread about shoulder width and knees bent so your butt is as close to the ground as possible. The glove-side foot slightly in front of the throwing-side foot. Reach your hands out to the ball and gently pull back into the body as the grounder is being fielded. This allows for soft hands, because it takes some of the force away from the baseball. Your face is not to be seen, only the top of your cap. This means you'll be looking at the ball every second until it reaches the glove."

Both coaches began rolling balls to the right and left of each player.

"The only deviation from the rules," Coach Bud called, "will be to use the slide step if the ball is not too far to either side. If the ball is rolled far enough away, like a grounder up the middle, turn your bodies and run so you'll get into the proper fielding position."

Tru added, "Fielding is the most important skill to learn. If you play on teams that don't give away any runs because of poor defense, you'll have a great chance to win the majority of your games."

Listening to the coaches, Johnnie Hanks and his father were watching everything. They moved down from their seats atop the bleachers to court side to see better. These workouts were intense. No minute of the forty-five minutes in the gym was wasted. Next came a drill young Bart Hanks had never seen before—something he heard the kids call "Speedball." Whatever they called it, there were plenty of baseball skills and exercise involved.

Immediately after "Speedball," batting practice began. The coaches gave the boys soft rubber balls or whiffle balls so as not to damage anything inside the gym.

One group of four played soft toss with the balls next to the bleachers under the clock. "Soft toss," Bart explained to his sons, "is when one boy kneels and softly tosses a ball to the hitter. The hitter strides to meet the ball and drills it into the wall. Then he quickly pulls his bat back in order to set for the next swing." He pointed. "Watch them. You'll see each hitter takes four swings before trading places."

In the far corner of the gym, opposite the bleachers, another group of four was hitting off tees, using whiffle balls. They each took five swings, adjusted the height of the tee, then they took five more swings.

The last group of four had traditional batting practice. The pitcher's mound was at center court with the plate under the basket at the far end of the gym. The coaches pitched to the boys. Tru threw the heat while Coach Bud, the junkman threw the slower pitches. Tru threw to half the boys and Bud to the others. Each night they rotated so that the boys would hit off different kinds of pitchers.

Each group spent ten minutes at each station. The coach who was not pitching floated around the gym to provide more specific instruction to each player.

Tru took a few minutes off after he finished his part of batting practice to chat with Bart Hanks. "So, what's up, Bart?" Tru asked, while watching Bud baffle the hitters with trick pitches. "You think Johnnie still wants to come here and work with us?" He thought the constant movement of the practice might have been a little intimidating to Bart's son. He wondered if Johnnie, like some kids who came to watch, would decide this wasn't for him.

The skinny ex-coach of the Wilkinsburg Dodgers did not respond. Tru was uncertain what, if anything, to read into the silence. Perhaps Bart was wondering how to help the kids who were practicing batting, but more likely, Tru thought, Bart was probably looking for the right words to leave without hurting any feelings or making enemies.

The two men stood there without speaking for several minutes while Bart continued to watch Jerrett Thompson with Coach Bud. Jerrett finally "went yard," hitting what would have been a homer on a regular outdoor field.

That brought a smile to Bart's face. No verbal reaction, just a smile. The pair stood side by side and continued to watch. And watch. Tru finally began to realize why Bart had been silently looking for so long. There was something much more exceptional than batting practice going on.

The kids had taken it upon themselves to play every ball hit during batting practice as if it were a game situation. No one was designated umpire, but one of the boys unofficially took on the job, deciding whether a ball was fair or foul, a hit, an error or an out. If it was deemed an error, a Three D was done by the offender. A strikeout called for three Three D's. Since Jerrett was fair but tough, no one dared dispute his calls.

"I've been coachin' Little League for five years, man," Bart said, breaking the silence. "And I never seen anything like that. You got to have a good team with these boys. You, Bud, and me—we'll all coach. Tru, I'd like to see Johnnie get involved with your boys on a full-time basis, but there's got to be a team here for him to do that. I'm ready to get him and myself out of the WBA, but not if he hasn't anywhere else to play."

Tru, keeping his eyes directed on the practice going on out on the floor, replied, "Man, I've been having thoughts of organizing these kids into a team the past few days. I don't know where we'd play. I don't mean what league or anything, I mean, what field would we play on? These kids are from all over the damn place. Some of them aren't allowed to go to East Hills. Some won't go to Homewood, or East Liberty, or Wilkinsburg. You know what it's like. How am I supposed to field a team like that?" The usually talkative man standing next to Tru took a deep breath and shook his head. Tru knew he had no answers either. "On top of that, what league would we play in? You know we couldn't get in Wilkinsburg or East Liberty or any of those places."

Bart did not have the missing pieces to the puzzle that

confronted them both as they watched the practice continue. However, he believed, and was sure Tru did also, that those pieces could be found.

"We have no name either," Tru continued. "These kids are from all over the East End, man. We can't call them Wilkinsburg or East Liberty or anything like that."

Tru stopped when he saw his friend was silent again. He did not know Bart was thinking that there were a myriad of problems to overcome but somehow they could be dealt with.

Tru turned his attention back to the practice and looked over at the modern clock next to the one for the basketball games. It read nine thirty-five. It was time to call the boys over to end practice.

"All right, fellas, listen up," Tru said, shouting to the fourteen boys. Running over, they sat on the hardwood in front of him. "We have a new member as of tomorrow, I assume." He stopped briefly to look at Bart, who was nodding his head. "Okay. Most of you guys know Johnnie Hanks. Give him our welcome!"

When the boys had finished shaking hands and sat back down, Tru resumed. "His dad, Coach Hanks, will be starting to work out with us also. Coach Hanks and I were even talking about starting a team this summer. Think y'all would like that?"

Most of the kids nodded but they seemed subdued. Darryl spoke for the rest. "But this has been our team all along."

"Yeah! Yeah!" the others echoed.

One youngster, however, was not smiling. He was just sitting there like he was at the bank of the Allegheny River, staring at the slow flowing water, contemplating the great meaning of life. Chris Williams had not heard a word.

"Yo, Chris." Tru interrupted the boy's trance. "What's up, buddy? You don't want to play on a team?"

"I . . . ah . . . what was that, Coach?" he responded quietly. "I didn't hear what you said. Sorry."

"That'll be a Three D, man. You might as well do it right now!" Tru thought that would be the end of it and started to turn back to the discussion of the possibility of fielding a team.

Groaning from Chris at his push-ups made that impossible. He was obviously pissed off and mumbling obscenities only half under his breath. After the boy had finished his third pushup, Tru called to him, "Come on up here and sit next to me, man. I'm not done with you yet. I don't care how good you think you are, I'm not toleratin' the 'eat me's' under your breath or the back index finger or any other attitudes while we are at practice." Tru's voice grew to a shout as he pointed to the seated players. "Boy, you'll be off this team before you know it!"

"Yes, sir." Chris sat up.

When he finally was able to talk about the subject of Little League, Tru saw that Bart had walked over to Coach Bud, whose smile outshone the white in his hair. He had never before mentioned trying to organize these kids into an actual team, but Tru knew now that was exactly what he wanted to see happen.

Tru looked over at Bart who was nodding. He walked over to the two men. "We're agreed then." They clapped him on the back.

Then he turned his attention to the parents who had assembled on the out-of-bounds line to the left of the kids.

He felt that the parents would be with them. Tru smiled and continued, "All right. Raise your hands if you want this group to become a team!" he said. All the hands went up before he got the whole sentence out. "I can't promise anything definite, but if we have a team, I promise you it will hustle its butts off and try to win every game. That can never be accomplished unless we all have the same goal and we all are able to put attitudes and problems aside. If you can't do that, you won't be on this team for long. Is that understood?"

Several of the boys responded with exclamations of, "Yes, sir!," but others just nodded their heads.

"What do those nods mean, fellas?" Tru demanded.

In unison they shouted, "Yes, sir!"

"When's our first game?" Antonio Williams asked as the others were getting up and thinking they could go.

"Don't be thinkin' this is already a team, man! We have no idea whether we can pull this off. We have no field to practice on, no league to play in, and we have no team name. Turning us into a team is a dream at this point. Just a possibility. I hope we'll be able to do it, but I don't want you counting on it, understand? Every practice, we practice hard. It don't matter if we have a team or not, we'll still practice with positive attitudes, all right? Oh yeah, that reminds me. Chris, front and center, baby! I think you still owe us. How about a little round of 'Speedball" for your attention lapse earlier."

Chris Williams came to the front of the group and threw his glove onto the floor. The drill of Speedball had evolved from Tru's day when it was just a competition of one kid against another. Now, it was an endurance test. It measured the heart as much as skill. Anyone making an error in Speedball would have to do five Three D's. Chris did his first thirty-second set without errors. Then Tru asked the skinny youngster who was lying on the floor in front of him, "Are you tired?"

For a few seconds, there was no response. Just the sight of a small chest moving up and down looking more like the pistons inside a speeding Porsche, and the heavy sound of labored breathing. "Yeah, I'm tired."

Everyone knew that was the wrong answer.

"I'm sorry to hear that, little man," Tru said. "See, 'cause you're not done just yet!"

The ground balls began again, this time a little further apart and a little quicker between the rolls. Chris was sliding from side to side as fast as his small frame would let him. Tru rolled the balls further and further apart, trying to get one that he might not be able to reach. Chris was so exhausted he began to cry. The only thing that kept him going was the encouragement he heard from the other kids.

"Are you tired now?" Tru asked with eyebrows raised.

"No, sir!" Chris shouted.

The others were smiling, thinking since their friend had given the correct answer this time, maybe the rigors of the usual third round of "Speedball" would be called off.

"Just one more time, baby!" Tru said to the exhausted boy, answering the speculation of all the others. "You can take a minute. Listen up, y'all. If, and I mean if, we get a team, this is the way it'll be. We will tolerate no horseplay. You guys should know that from last summer! You can never be tired on the baseball field. You always have to be ready to meet the challenge, not only in baseball, but in the more important game—that's right—the game of life. If you show someone you're tired, they'll be on you like sharks on blood, man. If you don't have the strength to push yourselves through the obstacles you'll face in your lives, you'll be buried and left for dead. No one will care! You gotta find it within yourself to stand up, to go a little further than you thought you could, to give a little more than you thought you had! Do you understand what I'm tryin' to tell you?" As Tru gazed at the quiet boys, he motioned to little Chris to take his position as he said supportively, "Let's get this one done, baby!"

The balls he rolled this time were further apart than ever before. On the second roll, Chris began crying again. The encouragement from the rest of the group grew to a fevered pitch. Tru rolled one ball so far to his left that he was sure Chris would not be able to reach it. As the ball rolled further from Chris's reach and it seemed he would not be able to catch it, Lance McCoy screamed, *"How far do you wanna go?"*

What happened next was electrifying. Chris went airborne and dove at the ball on the hardwood. As he sailed through the air, he yelled some words that were drowned out by the cheering coming from the parents, kids and coaches witnessing the struggle. Even more inspiring, he came up with the ball and jumped to his feet and as quickly as possible, shoveled it back to Tru. Then Chris assumed proper position to field a grounder, and looked for the next ball to be rolled.

It never came. Tru looked at the young man with a smile and roared, "That's what I'm talkin' about, baby!"

To the others he said, "All right! Better! Okay, fellas, that's about it." Tru rubbed his hands through his braids. "Same time tomorrow. Nine o'clock. All right!"

The boys mobbed Chris. They slapped his butt, patted

his back, and shook his hand. Each tried to give his version of what quickly became known as "The Dive." They simulated his takeoff, how he flew and how he landed. They described to Chris the expression on his face and imitated the look for him, no one even coming close. There was laughter, happiness, friendship, and the beginning of a new history for these boys, most of whom had never played ball before they met Tru.

"Yo, man!" Tru said with pure pleasure as he looked at Chris Williams. "You said somethin' when you decided to make like an eagle but we couldn't hear 'cause of all the noise. It was after Lance yelled *How far do you wanna go?* What was it you said back, man?"

Little Chris Williams who grew greatly in stature that March night, stood up and shouted, "THE NEXT LEVEL!"

In that moment, a team was born. And it even had a name.

Chapter 18

Rain, Rain
Go Away

For those held indoors by the throes of winter, spring-time is when nature begins to fulfill its promises; when the greenness long hidden by the cold and snow begins its much anticipated comeback. Colorful flowers bloom, blades of grass suddenly pop up, and buds emerge on the branches of the trees.

But to a baseball player, spring is nothing but a tease. He is not lured by the robins singing their songs or green leaves returning. He is itching to get back on the diamond. All he wants to do is to play. Despite the promises of spring, the reality is rain. And it seems to come every day, especially in Pittsburgh.

On the rare sunny days, Tru, Bart and Bud religiously checked different fields to see if they were playable. Tru usually drove by Mellon Park and Paulson Field in Larimer. Bart surveyed Turner Field in Wilkinsburg near where he lived, and Bud stopped by Chadwick Park, on the border of Wilkinsburg and Homewood. It did not matter to these coaches that rain had been saturating the ground for days. Though they felt sure the fields would be a quagmire, they still hoped and checked. They knew the chances of keeping the team's interest piqued while they practiced in the cramped gym in East Hills were slim.

"Man, is this damn rain ever gonna stop or do we have to build an arc?" Tru said one evening disgustedly to Bud and Bart. The three coaches had started meeting at Bud's house in Wilkinsburg almost every night after practice in order to decide what steps needed to be taken to make their dreams of a Little League team come true.

"I haven't ever seen anything like this," Bud groaned as he cracked open a cold beer and joined the others at the large round oak table.

"Springtime in the 'Burgh," lamented Bart Hanks.

Each man kicked back his Iron City and settled in, swallowed up in the soft comfortable chairs.

"Practice is not the only thing I'm worried about. The season's coming up fast," Tru lamented. "I've been calling everyone I know. Nothing so far."

"We might not get to play," Bart said as he slid a sheet of crumpled paper over to Tru, "but check this out."

Listed on the paper were the names, phone numbers, and addresses of all the Little League organizations which had participated in the prestigious Shaler Little League Tournament the previous summer. Bart had coached the Wilkinsburg entry in the tournament. "I don't know why but I kept the paperwork given to all the coaches. It might be a start," he said.

"Homewood, Chartiers-Windgap, Ammons—that's on the Hill, right?" Tru asked, pausing as both Bart and Bud nodded. "Swissvale, Manchester, Northside. No one will be there now. I'll start callin' each one tomorrow morning. I'll find some place." He folded the paper into his wallet.

"Well, let's get back to figuring out who's where. Who we got at short?" Tru threw out to the others as if they were going to play tomorrow.

Bud and Bart laughed. "Nothing like an optimist to pick up our spirits," Bart said. Then the two men looked at each other, nodded, and said simultaneously, "Jerrett."

Bart added, "That boy can pick it!"

"How about second? We need to be strong up the middle," Tru continued, glancing hesitantly at Bart Hanks.

Bart's boy had played the infield the previous summer, but Tru felt it was obvious he was not one of the top choices for the two infielders on The Next Level's squad. Tru waited; he didn't want to say something that might cause Bart uneasiness.

"Probably Byron Knight," Bart said with a smile.

"Thanks, man," Tru nodded. "Thanks for being committed to the team's good."

The three continued into the late night putting together a tentative lineup. Marcus Haines and Chris Williams were the two possible third basemen. Neither feared the ball. Robbie Elliot was a pitcher and could probably double as a first baseman. Darryl Weston was behind the plate. Brendon was in left when he did not pitch. Joe Foster was in center and Evin Gales or Lance were in right. Johnnie Hanks was on the mound and in left. Todd Hill, if he would show up consistently, could play anywhere. Antonio Williams, catcher. And Manny, of all people, was the choice for backup catcher.

"We really need to find a field for practices. We need to see what these kids can do outdoors," Tru mused. He rose from the table and got his jacket. "We're not gettin' anything done in that damn gym any more!"

"Be patient, young man," Bud said with the wisdom of

one who had seen many problems. He escorted his coaching colleagues to the door. "I know you'll find it, Tru."

Tru was on the phone by eight o'clock the next morning. Call after call brought answers of "No" and "Sorry." He was about to take a break when he saw Tony Martin's name on Bart's piece of paper. Tony coached the Homewood Little League where Tru had played as a kid. He decided to call Tony before getting some coffee.

"We're signin' kids up right now, Ramon," Tony said. "There's a meeting the eighth of April. Why don't you come up to Willie Stargell Field if its not flooded and we'll see what they say."

"That's great, Tony. All we need is a chance. These kids have been workin' real hard."

"You've been practicin' already? How the hell did you manage that?" Tony asked. "You've been playin' at the stadium?"

"Nah. We have been workin' out at East Hills Elementary a few nights a week. We haven't been outdoors yet."

"I was gonna say, our fields look like lakes. Anyway, be at Stargell the day after tomorrow and we'll see what we can do," Tony said.

There was no rain two days later on the eighth of April, but the sun scarcely shone. Willie Stargell Field did not appear as Tony had described it—a lake. Though the water was slowly drying up, the field was still a pond.

Tru found a dejected Tony amongst the two hundred kids milling around the cement bleachers. "What's wrong Tony, other than the weather?" Tru asked, watching Tony's disturbed demeanor.

"I could live with the weather. It'll clear up, but look at this bullshit!" Tony cried. "You see all these kids around here? You wanna know how many coaches we have? Three! Three damn coaches for two hundred kids. And then these people wonder why their kids get into trouble," he mumbled half wailing to himself. "I'm sorry, Ramon." Then he looked over the disturbing scene.

"Man, you don't have anything to be sorry for," Tru sympathized. "Why are you sorry when you're right?"

"This shit just gets so frustrating. How are we going to have a league with three coaches, man?"

"I wish I knew what to tell you. It's a damn shame."

"It's not your problem, Ramon."

Maybe it was because of the major concern Tony had or perhaps it was because Tru cared enough to come, but the question of whether Tru's team would be allowed to play never came up.

"Here are the rules for Little League and here's the roster form," Tony explained. "All we need is their date of birth for now, but before the season starts you gotta have a copy of their birth certificates. There's also a parent consent form that's gotta be filled out and signed for each kid. If you have brothers or two kids living in the same house, they need separate forms. All the insurance information and fees are on there. Other than that, you'll be ready to play ball. What's your team called?"

"The Next Level. It's just a sayin' we have. That's one we want these kids to try and reach," Tru said proudly.

"I hear you," Tony responded as he looked out over Willie Stargell Field. The three coaches there were waving at him. "I think they're tryin' to get this shit started. Excuse me, Ramon."

Walking away, he called back, "The Next Level. Pretty good name."

Tru looked over the field. Even when the pond

completely dried up, it wasn't perfect. It was a football and two baseball fields combined. The diamonds were placed diagonally to each other on opposite ends of the rectangular space. Behind the backstop of the larger baseball field was a main bus stop where Homewood buses to the other eastern neighborhoods and downtown Pittsburgh congregated. It seemed every minute a large Port Authority Transit bus came roaring down the concrete drag.

The field was enclosed on all sides but one by a fifteen-foot-high chain-link fence. Tru sat down and read over the rules of the Homewood Little League Association.

They were typical Little League rules. Tru told himself, *I'd better not argue with any of them.* He was lucky to have found a place the boys would be allowed to play. The players were required to wear Little League approved protective equipment at all times when on the field of play. All players had to be in uniform. Jewelry was not allowed. It was typical stuff, but some of the rules were difficult for a team which had little money. *Somehow, though,* he told himself, *we'll comply with those.* One of the rules disturbed him. It required all boys to play a minimum of two innings. On the surface it was a reasonable rule, designed to make things fair and promote playing over winning. He didn't have a problem with the intent. He wondered, *does it apply to a kid who shows up at practice every day, whether he is a good player or not, and then has to be taken out for a boy who misses practice but decides to attend the game.* In Tru's mind, that gave a different message than he wanted to give. So despite his intention of not looking a gift horse in the mouth, he went over to Tony and said, "Tony, I have a question about one of these rules. It's not really spelled out, but if a kid misses practice and shows up at the game, does he have to play for two innings?"

"Yeah, man, that's the rule. Any kid on your bench has to play for two innings," Tony said as he handed out forms to the people lined up in front of him.

"Is it at the coach's discretion, at least?" Tru asked.

"Nope."

"So if a kid misses practice for no good reason, I still have to let him play. Does that seem fair to you, man? I mean, I could see it if he was sick or had a family issue or something," Tru said with a puzzled look on his face.

"I know, Ramon, but that's the way the parents want it. They voted for the rule."

"Man, I have a serious problem with that," Tru said. He was upset as he turned away from his busy colleague.

And there were other things that seemed chaotic as he stood there. Boys and adults were wandering about. The field was a mass of confusion in addition to the fact that there were only three coaches. "This is like jumping from the frying pan into the fire," Tru muttered.

Would the association even be able to pull this off, since there looked to be little community involvement? If there were only three coaches at this organizational meeting, how could they assure coaches at games? If the kids never had to be at practice, what incentive was there for them to work hard to make the team or improve for that matter? As Tru watched Tony try to organize the chaos, he made his decision.

"Tony, I'm outta here, man," he said dejectedly. "I have to be honest with you. I don't think the Homewood Little League is right for The Next Level. I just can't get past that rule where all kids gotta play. And then seein' you out here gettin' no help—truthfully, I don't know how you're gonna pull this all together."

"It'll get done, Ramon," he replied. "But you do what you think you gotta do, man. I've no problem with that."

"Maybe we can get some exhibition games in?" Tru asked as he shook Tony's hand.

"Call me if you get your boys a place." Tony smiled as a double-length PAT bus roared by the bleachers, heading downtown. It drowned out his voice.

Tru felt more depressed than before as he walked behind the bleachers. He asked himself, *Have I turned down the team's only chance? Would anyone else want them? Do all Little Leagues have the same problems as Homewood? Why in hell don't parents get involved in the positive activities of their kids instead of just appearing in school or court when their kids get in trouble?* Tru walked from the field to his Jeep, got in, turned on the engine, and headed toward Frankstown.

He drove slowly towards Bud's house where Bud and Bart were waiting word about their new league. Tru sank a little deeper in the seat when he realized that he would have to explain what he'd just done. Tru took the short cut onto East Hills Drive, crossing the shattered parking lot of the East Hills Shopping Center. He needed some air.

Tru slowly exited the Jeep and gazed at the deserted backside of the closed down mall. A huge orange sun began to emerge from behind the clouds that had hung over Pittsburgh for too long. However, what caught Tru's eye was not the sun, nor the graffiti and the broken up concrete.

He stared at the parking lot next to the graffiti-covered wall. "It's almost completely level," he murmured. He began a deliberate walk to the building some two hundred yards away. The closer he got the quicker his heart beat.

"This might be it. This *is* it!" Tru called to the emptiness.

Suddenly a grin came across his face. "Why didn't I ever see it before this way?"

Scanning the area ablaze with light, he envisioned, *Home plate would be there by the bushes in front of the curb.*

They would provide a little backstop to help prevent chasing foul balls, which would save on practice time. Before he knew it, he was walking the sixty-foot distance to first base. He looked out to where right field would be. The chain-link fence was separated from the concrete by perhaps an eight-foot section of grass. *The grass,* he estimated, *is more than two hundred feet from the batter's box.*

He continued walking to second base and saw no broken pavement there either. The only problem was the glittering broken glass around the second base area. "We'll clean it up," he said determinedly. The fence that was over two hundred feet away down the right field line was now approaching major league dimensions, as the rectangular cement moved towards dead center field, where it must be at least four hundred feet away from home plate.

The third base line paralleled the curb separating the concrete playing field from the sidewalk that once carried thousands of shoppers into the now abandoned complex. Third base and home plate were both approximately twenty-five feet, the width of a two-lane road, away from the curb. The home run fence in left was basically nonexistent. It was at a right angle to the right and center field wall, some six hundred feet from home plate.

Everything was perfect, at least in his mind. Tru jumped back into his Jeep, barely able to contain his excitement. He sped through the streets of Wilkinsburg with great anticipation. He must have driven East Hills Drive fifteen times a week and it had not changed in fifteen years. *Why am I only now able to see it?* Tru wondered.

Tru turned on the stereo and shook his head in time to the music. People driving by shot him a look as if to say, *What the hell are you so happy about?* Tru realized then that everything was perception. He had looked at East Hills through dark, indifferent or angry eyes for so many years. It was uplifting to see through compassionate and purposeful eyes.

Bud and Bart heard the loud music before they saw the Jeep pull up in front of Bud's two-story brick home. They watched from the large picture window in the game room as Tru parked at the curb on the secluded wooded street, got out and bounced his way down the sloping driveway whistling. Bart turned to Bud and said, "Who's that? Can't be Tru!"

Tru entered through Bud's garage. He didn't bother to knock but rushed in the unlocked door.

"What happened, to whom, and is it good for us?" Bud cracked, looking at Tru.

"It's not good—it's great!" Tru said excitedly. "We'll be practicin' outdoors from now on, baby!"

Confused, Bart and Bud glanced at each other and then at Tru.

"Tru, you been fantasizin' again?" Bud asked.

"What you talkin' about, man?" Bart said with doubt. "Okay, it didn't rain today, but it has all week. Ain't none of these fields ready to play on!"

"I was just by Chadwick, Tru, and it's a mess," added Bud. "There must be a foot of water at shortstop. That field won't be played on for at least a week, even if we get good weather."

Tru watched the confused looks of his two friends grow. "Where did you practice when you were a kid, man?" Tru asked, beaming at his bewildered friends.

"Mellon," Bart said sarcastically. Even though he did not say it, the message was clear: *so what!*

"Homewood Park," Bud said, mirroring the troubled frowns of his colleague.

"Nah, think about it. Where did you play when it

rained?" Tru exhorted.

Bud looked at Bart. Their eyebrows rose.

"Well, we used to go down to the parking lot behind the house, now that you mention it," Bart recalled.

Bud scratched his head. "The parking lot where Giant Eagle used to be, on Frankstown!"

The three men stood, without speaking, each visualizing himself making a great play on the playing fields of his youth.

Tru snapped them back to the present. "The shopping center in East Hills!" Tru said, breaking the silence. "There's a spot that's level behind where the Hornes used to be. Oh, man, it's perfect! It's even got some bushes behind where we'll put home plate to keep balls from rollin' too far. We gotta teach these kids to roll if they fall and not to try and brace themselves so they don't get hurt. But it's perfect, man! It really is! I thought we'd practice tomorrow at five-thirty. What y'all think?"

"That place is a mess," Bud said.

"The only thing we need to do right away is clean up some broken glass. It's everywhere, but mainly at second," Tru said.

"What happened with Homewood?" Bart asked.

Tru shared his concerns about the ability of Tony Martin to pull the whole thing together by himself, and the rule that everyone must play for two innings. "I just can't see it. How are you supposed to teach kids about responsibility when you don't hold them accountable for their actions? Was Wilkinsburg like this?" Tru asked the ex-coach of the Wilkinsburg Dodgers.

"Sure was," Bart replied. "I think all Little League is like that."

"Are you kidding me? Maybe The Next Level doesn't belong in any league then," Tru said firmly. "I'll be damned if I'm gonna let a kid miss practice and play. We can just play exhibition games if that's the case."

"I think we better get started calling all the kids," Bud suggested.

"Yeah. Let's get started tonight," Tru said.

Tru, Bud and Bart, along with the kids they usually brought, arrived at the parking lot of the East Hills Shopping Center the next day, around two-fifteen. Bart took twenty paces from where he had marked home plate and dropped the third base bag on a line which, at one time, was a boundary separating traffic from parked cars. Bud followed the same procedure, placing first base along lines that separated two rows of cars parked facing each other. They each walked at right angles away from their base and, where they met, Bud dropped the second base bag.

"All right, everyone over here!" Tru called as he stood in front of the bushes that would serve as a backstop on this makeshift field.

The kids sat in front of him and looked around at the concrete diamond. No one said a word, but it was obvious from their expressions that they preferred this (even though it was another gray Pittsburgh afternoon and the place was a mess) to the tiny indoor confines of the East Hills gymnasium.

"All right, listen up," Tru continued. "The first thing we have to do is clean this place up and be careful you don't get cut."

A groan went up, but the boys dutifully got up and took the huge leaf bags Bud was holding. Several hours later the field looked a lot better.

Tru called them together once again. "You gotta be careful out here—that's most important. There will be some cars that cut across the back side," he said, motioning towards the right field fence. "And you gotta give them the right of way. Don't try and be cute and throw a ball over car roofs or anything like that. Practice will be run the same way we did inside the gym. Instead of five laps, you'll only have to do three, but they'll be around the entire back parking lot, which is probably a little over half a mile. Any questions?"

Antonio Williams raised his hand. "We still gotta do the Three D's?"

"You bet!" replied Tru. "Except now you'll say The Next Level. Let me ask y'all something. Anyone know what's the only thing that can stop us from being a really good team?"

No one raised their hand. "This is what it is, fellas. If you can control this," he said, pointing to his head, "and play with lots of this," he said, pointing to his heart, "nobody can beat you! You gotta understand something about baseball. It's one of the few sports that does not require the best player, the one who can jump the highest or run the fastest. What it demands of successful teams is that the team members know the many intricacies of the game: hitting a ball to the right side to move a runner from second to third, the importance of getting ahead in the count if you're a pitcher, the need to put a good swing on the ball if you're the batter and have the count in your favor. Team members also need to know where to throw to the cutoff man and when to try to make an extra base as a runner. They have to throw to the right base; that could mean knowing when to try and throw out a runner at home and when to let the run score and throw to stop another runner from advancing an extra base. There are so many things we need to learn to play a good baseball game. Out of football, basketball, and baseball, baseball by far is the great equalizer for the average athlete, if he knows the game. That is why we're here. Okay, fellas, it's gettin' dark around six forty-five now, so we don't have a lot of time to waste: three laps!"

The three coaches watched as the team ran their three laps around the large parking lot. They heard another example of the comfort level the boys were beginning to feel. Nicknames were being used.

The team passed in front of the coaching staff while into their third and final lap. No one appeared to be tired; in fact, they were all grinning mischievously like they were trying to hide something. One glance at the back of the pack told the coaches why.

"John Doe," the nickname which had been given to Antonio Williams, was running with only one arm. His right arm was tugging at his beltless, five-sizes-too-big blue jeans, trying to pull them up to somewhere near his waist. He was losing the struggle and it was hysterical, even for the coaches, to watch.

"Hey, Doe!" Lance bellowed to Antonio. "You might as well run in them drawers, baby!" Tru couldn't suppress his own smile. Lance thought it was due to his remark, but it really was occasioned by Tru's sense of pride that "his boy," who had never played before, had become an accepted part of the team.

Practices each subsequent day were similar to the indoor practices. Only two things were different: fielding practice could now be done with a full infield and outfield in place and batting practice could be taken with regular base-balls being thrown at regular speeds.

Defensive practice was called CHAOS. It was nothing more than situation drills, a skull session on the field. Whoever was not in one of the fielding positions became a runner.

Coach Bud was usually the designated batter for these drills. Tru and Coach Bart would float around the defense, explaining the reasons each player was given a particular assignment.

Outfield drills were one of the most difficult to perfect. The kids were now introduced to how complex a play from the outfield was. Each outfielder and infielder had to know who was the correct cutoff man for a particular play. They had gone over the situations in classroom skill sessions, but quickly found out what different experiences they were an actual field.

"Remember your jobs!" Tru screamed as the boys prepared to chase the balls Coach Bud was beginning to hit. "If there is a runner on first and someone hits a single to any field, the shortstop is the cutoff man for the throw to third. Third baseman, you line him up so he's on a direct line with the spot where the outfielder gets the ball. Pitchers, back up the throw to third. If the ball is hit in the gap, forget about the throw to third and line up for home and second." He continued explaining each situation that might arise in the course of the game. "Okay. Coach Bud, let's see what these boys can do!"

Coach Bud, with ball and bat in hand and flanked by Darryl Weston, the catcher, cried out, "Nobody on and nobody out!" He flicked the ball in the air and aimed his first swing to be a grounder to short. He missed.

Thinking quickly, he yelled, "Strike three!"

Darryl Weston pounced on the stationary ball, and as Robbie Elliott yelled "Inside!", quickly gunned the ball to first base to retire the batter on a strikeout.

"Good job, Big Baby!" Tru trumpeted from his position just behind second base.

"Way to talk, Robbie!" Coach Bart commended the first baseman.

"All right. One out and nobody on!" Coach Bud bellowed. He was the only one on the field who knew the miss was not on purpose.

He again flicked the ball to eye level and took a slower, more calculated swing.

This time no one moved when the ball dropped to his feet. The fielders stared at each other trying to fight back smiles. The runners lined up behind Coach Bud did the same. Even Coach Tru and Coach Bart were trying not to laugh. No one, not even John Doe, had so much as grinned when the ball flew into the air for the third time. Lovable Coach Bud would be given the benefit of the doubt.

"Aw, shit!" Coach Bud shouted as he tossed the aluminum Easton bat farther than he was able to hit the ball.

It brought down the house. The only three people who were not on the ground buckled over laughing hysterically were the three coaches. Tru and Bart were laughing all right. They just were still standing.

Coach Bud stayed angry for no more than a few seconds. That was how long it took John Doe to pick up the still new rawhide, walk over to Coach Bud, tag him, and say, "You'rrre out!"

The situation served two purposes. One, it permanently ended Coach Bud's hitting career and more importantly, it brought the team that much closer together.

Each day increased the camaraderie. The bonding even included Coach Bart's car, an ugly green compact which the kids called "a hoopty." Lance gave it the name. Lance, because of his affinity for cars, was now being called Motorhead. The boys were at ease with each other and with their coaches.

"We can get on Paulson Field tomorrow, Tru. I was up there earlier and it ain't so bad," Bart said hopefully as he and Tru met back at the shopping center after taking the kids home. "It ain't supposed to rain tomorrow either and if this sun keeps shinin', we're in business."

Tru was looking around and did not hear his friend. The empty shopping center was speaking to him.

"What do you see here?" Tru asked as he stared out to the vast emptiness.

Bart glanced at Tru thinking him a bit daft and scanned the surroundings. "Apathy," he answered, "and what it does to a neighborhood."

"Nah, don't look at it through the eyes of hopelessness. Leave that for the politicians and the news media. Look at it through the eyes of hopefulness," he spoke prophetically. "What do you see?"

Bart studied the nearly empty buildings and broken up pavement. "I guess there is some potential . . . lots of space . . . for something."

"You really can't see it?" Tru asked, observing the puzzled look on Bart's face as he walked around the makeshift diamond.

Bart looked bewildered. He wondered, *Is Tru seeing a mirage?* Being a realist, Bart responded, "You want to know what I really see? Potholes big enough to swallow up a Volkswagen Beetle, the old Mickey D's that used to be right over there, and us gettin' our asses kicked if we don't get the hell outta here soon!"

"No. No. No," Tru said interrupting him. He extended his arms and began to paint his dream. "I see a dormitory for about three hundred kids those who have no homes could live in the complex dormitory and for the others summer and winter academic and athletic camps. Over there," he pointed to the place. "Baseball. Soccer, football and track here. Basketball and tennis courts. Over there, the main building. It will have enough space for a library, computer and audio-video labs, a swimming pool, weight room, an indoor basketball and tennis court, gymnastics area, classrooms, and an indoor batting cage. Over there, maybe the roller and ice skating rink. All the kids have to do is maintain a C average in school. What kid wouldn't want to be part of something like that? Think of the pride that would be generated for this community, to have a youth complex like that here instead of this," he said as his arms swept over the decay.

The last light of the April sun was disappearing behind the rolling hills of western Pennsylvania. Another misty night chilled the two men standing alone under one of the few functional streetlights in this desolate remnant of a shopping center.

Bart Hanks did not catch Tru's fever. He was too much of a realist. "How?" he asked in a bewildered tone.

Tru was undaunted. He turned to Bart and said, "Dedication. Determination. And Desire!"

Chapter 19

Hostile Territory

"Paulson Field?" Janet Williams asked over the phone. "Ain't that Crip territory in Lincoln-Larimer? Tru, I don't know about this! It sounds like trouble."

"The three of us will be there at all times, Janet," Tru soothed. He was sitting with the other two coaches in Bud's game room. "All we'll be doin' up there is playin' some baseball. We'll tell the kids not to speak to any of the gang members who appear. It'll be all right. You'll see."

"You know the first thing they're gonna ask y'all is, where you're from? You know they ain't about to let any kids from East Hills or Homewood up there." She pressed her point. "Those Crips will be there—you can bank on it."

Tru spent a few more minutes calming Janet. After he hung up, Tru turned to Bud and Bart. "I know she's probably right that the gang will find out and come to the field. But I think with three of us there we can handle them. We'll tell them we're from the East End. They don't have to know which neighborhoods exactly."

Bart Hanks and Bud silently finished off a couple of beers as they watched the Chicago Bulls and Detroit Pistons on television.

"Let's hope that's the last complaint, right?"

Tru watched as Bud and Bart nodded their heads, never turning their eyes away from the game.

"Oh yeah," he went on, "I forgot to mention to you that I called a couple more associations from the list you gave me, Bart. You were right. They all have that same bull-shit rule about everyone having to play two innings. They said they would play us some exhibition games, but not after their regular season started. We've got to find a league!"

"Did you try the Hill yet?" Bart asked as the two coaches shut off the television and came over to the oak table. "Clarence is pretty cool."

Clarence Battle was the man in charge of the Little League located in the Hill District. It was called the Papa Dean Little League.

As Bart and Bud discussed their options, Tru dialed the Ammons Recreation Center on the Hill, where Clarence Battle spent most of his waking hours.

"You think we'll have any problems up at Paulson?" the elder Coach Bud asked Bart with concern. "Our kids sure as hell don't need no hassle from any of them gang members!"

"We'll be cool, Bud. We're just goin' up there to play some ball," Bart reassured him. "Plus, more parents are coming and we'll try to increase the numbers at least for the first few practices."

The conversation was interrupted as Tru excitedly hung up the phone. "Guess what! They have an opening. We just have to attend a meeting to pick up our schedule and pay the entrance fee. And Clarence said who plays is up to the coach's discretion. That's all I needed to hear!"

"It's all fallin' into place, ain't it? First, outdoor practice. Then uniforms next week. Exhibition game in a week. League game in a month. These kids are gonna be juiced!" Bud exclaimed.

"Yeah, but that only means we've got much more work to do the next couple of weeks. Papa Dean is a good league, man. I'm not about to go up there and get embarrassed!" Tru added.

"Then I'm gonna go get my rest," Bart said as he tilted his new Next Level teal cap so it fit just right. "I'll see you brothers tomorrow. I should be there by six."

Like the abandoned shopping center in which The Next Level now played, probably the most distinguishing factor about Paulson Field in East Liberty was the graffiti. It blanketed all cement surfaces, from the six-foot-high wall that paralleled the third base line, to the basketball court that was behind the team bench in the dirt shell called the first base dugout. There were no real dugouts. The team benches were enclosed in a twelve-by-eight-foot chain-link rectangle. The only spectator seating was an old wooden six-row bleacher that was awkwardly placed behind the third base coach's box.

Directly behind home plate and adjacent to the base-line of the hoop court was a huge set of steps. There must have been seventy steps which switchbacked their way up the large hill that also paralleled the third base line. Trees and bushes grew out over the walkway making the steps more intimidating. If this had been the Old West, it would have been a great place for an ambush.

The fifteen-foot-high chain-link fence down the right field line, one hundred seventy feet from home plate, was the border between the playing field and Paulson Avenue. It receded to dead center where it met the left field fence that, down the line, was two hundred feet from home. Straightaway center where the two fences met was a formidable two hundred sixty-three feet from the batter's box.

Along the entire distance of the left field fence was an old playground. The decayed swings, spider-webbed climbing apparatus, and a splintery sliding board all looked like they had not been used in years. Beyond the playground lay a group of houses whose paint was peeling.

The field itself was a combination of grass and dirt. Unfortunately, the dirt was sometimes where the grass should have been and vice versa. The infield was made up of the same mixture, mostly dirt with just enough grassy patches to never give an infielder peace of mind that he will get a true hop. Even though it was a city-owned field, it had not been combed to remove the infielder's nightmare of unwanted clumpy grass in years. Bike tire marks from daring runs through the mud when it rained were still visible.

Lights permitted night play. However, there had not been a night game at Paulson for a long time. No one wanted to be there when it was dark, except the gang members who claimed ownership of the place.

The first day for outdoor field practice was a picture book spring day. The sun shone brightly. A slight breeze blew through the branches of the trees which had survived both the winter's savagery and the human kind.

Tru felt optimistic just seeing the signs of spring. The players and some parents of The Next Level began to arrive. Unfortunately, trouble was not far away.

Eight Crips gang members walked in and took seats in the bleachers. Unkempt and tough, they wore blue bandannas either around their foreheads or stuffed in their pockets. On their heads were Los Angeles Dodger baseball caps, further signifying their membership in the Crips street gang. Looking at them, Tru felt suddenly discouraged. They ranged in age from about twelve, the age of many of The Next Level players, to perhaps seventeen. "Already lost," Tru muttered. They did not look particularly happy to have their field invaded by strangers with The Next Level written on their T-shirts. But, for the time being at least, they just sat there watching.

Tru heard the grumbling from the parents. Today he wished for the days of sparsely-seated spectators at the games. He did not have time, nor did he want, to address the group which now came. "Step lightly," he told himself. He ignored the parents' prodding and the gang's distraction and went about the business of practicing baseball.

The lack of reaction from the kids was what surprised him. Of all the people there, the ones who seemed the least concerned about the gang members' presence were the boys of The Next Level.

At the beginning, everything proceeded normally. The boys ran their laps, with Antonio still grabbing at his pants to pull them up and Manny in last place. They loosened up with the same rules as always, although drawing either Lance or Manny was not as big a deal anymore because of the improvement each had made. Infield practice was next.

Looking over at the stands, Tru saw the teenage spectators in blue were getting into their normal routine also. Beer bottles, in the form of the popular forty-ouncers, were being passed amongst them. The aroma of blunts, or marijuana, also was strong in the air. Jibing and joking among themselves, the older boys were also yelling wisecracks "to the little boys playing with their toys."

Midway through practice eight gang members stood up and made their way very slowly past the third base bench

where The Next Level had thrown their gear, onto the basketball court behind the first base line. As previously
instructed by both their parents and coaches, no member of
The Next Level said a word to the group.

Tru kept one eye on the gang, the other eye on his team
and the business at hand. He continued drilling grounders to
his infield as he observed every move of the gang. Even as
they walked, they continued to drink beer and smoke weed.
None of the boys ever removed the heavy winter jackets with
their gang insignias on them. It was comical, almost.

Tru kept his cool, but the parents were visibly
unnerved by the actions of the gang members. They stared
unceasingly at them. They watched intently when the Crips
finally started up the long steps behind the basketball court
to apparently dissipate into the neighborhood above Paulson.
Finally, there was a chance for relief.

It was short-lived. Moments after the gang members
had disappeared into the tree and bush-covered stairway, they
sent a reminder to the uninvited strangers below just whose
neighborhood the players were in. Suddenly, several molotoff
cocktails exploded at center court. The sound was terrifying.

"Cover your heads! Get down on the ground!" Tru
screamed. Laughter could be heard from the mysterious
looking steps. The gang had spoken.

Tru quickly surveyed the situation and saw there were
no injuries. "Let's get back to business," he called firmly, and
began to throw grounders to his team as if nothing had happened. *It would serve no purpose,* Tru thought, *to storm the
stairway and lecture the punks in blue as most of the parents
probably wanted to do. This team is here to practice baseball, nothing more.*

The pack of youths never reemerged from the top of
the steps nor did they reappear on the field. Occasionally

those at the practice could hear laughter, loud talking, hollering, and a strange, high-pitched, almost yelping kind of sound. Throughout the remainder of the practice no one was at ease.

At the end of practice Tru called the team members together. "Tomorrow's practice is at the same time and the same place. I want to commend you on your behavior today. Violence is the kind of thing we have to overcome. Gangs thrive on intimidation, but don't you be intimidated. They want to see fear—don't show any! They want you to talk shit too so they'll have an excuse—you say nothing! You then make them powerless. Always remember why we're here: to learn and practice baseball! Now get all the stuff picked up and let's get outta here. Nice job, y'all! How far do you wanna go?"

"The next level!" the boys shouted in unison.

A nervous group of parents watched as their sons gathered all the baseball equipment and put it in the carrying bags. They also stared at the silent steps, waiting for trouble.

But the boys of The Next Level carried the bags back to the cars. They had settled down and were talking to each other, ripping on Coach Bud about his bald head, and laughing.

The adults, along with Tru, followed perhaps twenty yards behind. There was no laughter in their group. Their collective eyes moved anxiously back and forth between the kids and the imposing steps they had to walk near to get to their cars. They all were worried more violence was going to occur before they were safely in their cars and out onto Paulson Avenue.

"Shit, Tru! What the hell did you get us into?" Evie Oliver, Byron Knight's mom, asserted quietly, her eyes transfixed on the towering, covered passageway to her right. "The Crips are crazy!"

"We'll be all right," Tru reassured her. "All we're doin' is comin' up here to play baseball. And we have every right to play here."

Tru had faced showdowns before and he wasn't about to show fear. As he climbed into his Jeep and pulled away from Paulson Field, he realized he did not have the rage the other adults had. He had a dream.

Practice began at the same time the next day. The temperature was in the mid sixties. The sun shone brightly. The grass seemed a little taller. The boys in blue were waiting.

They were dressed the same. Tru approached part of the field where the teenagers in the bleachers were with the same step he would if they had not been there. He laid the equipment bag up against the chain-link fence along the third base line, turned, and shouted to the team, "Take your laps." Then Tru began to sort the equipment.

"You the coach?" one of the gang members yelled.

Tru jogged to the bleachers where a group of eight sat. "How you brothers doing?" he asked. Not waiting for their answer, he added, "Yes, I'm the coach. What can I do for you?"

"Where y'all from?" incited an older kid, perhaps seventeen. "I ain't never seen none of these kids."

"East End," Tru responded coolly to the provocative question, looking squarely in the boy's eyes.

He stared back.

Tru knew the next ten seconds would probably determine The Next Level's right of passage. The leader of the gang knew the answer was evasive. Tru's answer could have meant a lot of places, some of which would represent warring communities to the Crips. If the gang leaders wanted to create a problem, he could simply not accept Tru's answer and probe until he was given actual names of real places, even the streets if he so chose. He was in his element as the leader. Tru was the intruder and not about to lie. The leader of the Crips gang determined what was acceptable at Paulson Field. However humiliating it might be to have a seventeen-year-old gang member determine the future of something as harmless as Little League baseball, that's exactly what was happening at Paulson Field.

"What league y'all play in?" The boy broke the stare and transferred his gaze to the team running their laps.

"We'll be playin' in the Papa Dean League up on the Hill, but we're gonna play teams from all over: Swissvale, Shadyside, Homewood." Tru's voice was level, steady. "You play on a team? How old are you, if you don't mind?"

"Man, I ain't into no baseball!" The gang leader smirked and looked toward his boys sitting near him on the small bleacher. "We got more important things to do."

"Can I ask you for a favor?" Tru said. The only response from the youth was a slight raising of his eyebrows. "I was wonderin' if it would be possible if you could hold off smokin' blunts in the bleachers while these kids are here. We only practice for about an hour or so. I'd really appreciate it."

Tru took a deep breath and looked toward the others and then back at the boy in front of him trying to judge whether, if necessary, he could handle them all until one of the parents got over to help him.

The Crip stood with his legs far apart and contemplated the question. Tru felt the hard stares from the rest of the group on the bleachers. *If this small group was democratic, I would lose by a landslide*, he thought, but pulled himself to a full stance and stared back. The boy broke the stare first.

"We ain't got no problem with that," the dictator said. "We'll just finish up what we have left."

Tru knew he had played it right and wasn't about to

push any further. "That's cool, man. I really appreciate that. Y'all let me know if I can do somethin' for you, all right?" Tru offered, smiling. "You brothers be safe," he added and then walking away he turned his attention back to The Next Level.

"Word," the boy said.

The parents who had been watching this interaction were relieved to see Tru walking back towards the team. They were further appeased when he came closer and they saw the smile on Tru's face. The adults realized, as Tru did, they had just been given permission to use Paulson Field, not from a directive of the city's permit office, but from the real governing force of the neighborhood.

Practice continued with the gang members watching and occasionally heckling one of the players over a missed ball.They remained fairly calm in the bleachers until batting practice when one of the gang members got hot.

"Ain't no ma-fuckin' way this ma-fucker is twelve damn years old!" the Crip shouted as big Darryl Weston still in his ankle cast came up to take his swings.

"Hey, Coach," he yelled, "what's the age limit for this team?"

Tru called out, "Twelve."

The gang member yelled back, "Get the hell outta here. He can't be twelve."

Another gang member in the bleachers answered him, "He is. My dad knew his dad. He goes to Reizenstein Middle School and he's in seventh grade and smart."

The level of anxiety, that had nearly disappeared from the parents' minds, resurfaced. They stood up in their positions along the first base line across the field from the vocal gang members.

"Believe me, bro. He's only twelve," Tru marveled, equally amazed.

Tru smiled and motioned to Darryl Weston to step into the box. Tru always tried to challenge the hitters. If they had a particular weakness, Tru attempted to help them correct it. Since Darryl's was balls low and away, Tru tried to bring some heat across that part of the plate. His philosophy was that they could always hit the ball thrown to their strength but practice was for working on their deficiencies. Today was different.

He wanted to show these two punks Darryl's real strength.

Two gang members had made their way down and stood against the fence looking at Darryl. They shook their heads in disbelief and one murmured, "Damn, he's big as hell." Then one of the Crips from the bleachers shouted, "I bet he can't hit."

Tru just smiled and said, "Darryl, get in the batter's box." Tru threw a fast ball on the inside part of the plate. Darryl missed it.

Some of the gang members started laughing and the one said, "What did I tell you?"

Tru said to Darryl, "Come on, Big Baaaby! Concentrate. Don't worry about the spectators. All right?"

Darryl just nodded yes. The next two hits were vicious drives up the middle which would have beheaded Tru if not for his quick reflexes. At the age of thirty-five he liked to think he was still quick, but he knew better. "Way to keep your eye on the ball," he said to Darryl. After those hits Darryl sent a blast about three hundred feet out on Paulson Avenue that nearly hit a passing car.

"Whoooo! Did you see how far my man hit that ball?" yelled one of the young men sitting on the bleachers. "I bet you can't do that again. Go ahead. I bet you can't do that again," he continued in an intoxicated cackle. Another gang member just as drunk piped up, "Bet five dollars."

The bet was on. Darryl hit another one into the swimming hole. The next one he sent deep, deep over the left field fence and onto a house's rooftop. The ball was never found, at least not by anyone from The Next Level. Every one of the gang members still sitting on the bleachers rose, came down and lined the fence so that they could watch the man/child launch balls over the fence. They began to buzz like a group of sports writers trying to get the big story.

Darryl drilled the next pitch to the left center gap. Then came a frozen rope down the left field line that hit the base of the fence. After that Darryl hit a pea to center that would have been out of most Little League fields, but fell fifteen feet from the distant fence at Paulson. A laser to shortstop followed that, then a bullet down the line in left. The next hit cleared the fence in right, hitting a swing in the playground. Seven hard hit balls in a row!

"Five bucks this ma-fucker don't hit another homer!" challenged the seventeen-year-old at the other gang members. He had no takers.

Darryl scorched the next pitch into the gap in left center again.

"Bet!" a younger member shouted. "This big ma-fucker is about to go yard again, baby!"

Darryl shot one to right field that fell in the middle of the playground. Half the gang was high-fiving each other, while the other half just shook their heads.

"Double that shit up!" the older one said. Darryl cranked the next pitch well over the fence down the right field line.

"Damn!" the loser said angrily. "Fuck that! Let's do it again!"

It was a monumental blast. The pitch must have traveled three hundred thirty majestic feet before smashing against the aluminum siding of the house on the other side of the playground.

The gang members continued to get high with their boom box blasting, but they were also watching intently. You could see the had-enough look from the gang member who'd lost thirty dollars and the delighted look of relief on Darryl's face when he finished batting. Tru just put his head down and grinned.

Darryl knew Tru had made him look good, because normally Tru would throw a lot of pitches on the inside part of the plate which Darryl had difficulty hitting. The pitches Tru threw Darryl that day were around the waist area and straight down the middle. The amazing part about this episode was Darryl still had a cast on his right ankle from his accident.

As practice continued, the gang members went back to the bleachers and were actually looking on in amazement at the commitment of these kids. Later, when the coaches were discussing what had happened, it was agreed that the team had won the respect of the gang.

After each practice, Tru thanked the Crips for not smoking or drinking. This bit of respect seemed to bring results. Never again did Tru see any gang member smoke a blunt in the bleachers during The Next Level's practices. He never fooled himself, though. He knew after the team left, the carousing began again.

Although Tru never made excuses for the teenage gang, he pitied and understood why they joined. He knew the alienation and anger they felt, the abandonment by parents who had themselves gone under. "I'm not making excuses for them," he said in discussing the gang culture with the boys on The Next Level team. "One of the reasons kids especially in the black community, decide to join gangs, quit school and avoid the athletic fields is because they need something to fill the void in their lives. The majority of them are in so deep over their heads that they'll never rise to the top again. They need a miracle, but maybe for you guys we're the miracle. One thing we want to teach you is something gang members never learned. Don't be afraid to reach for the stars. Don't settle for the bottom of the barrel. No matter who tells you you're not good enough to be a doctor, a lawyer, a jet pilot or a team of champions, you keep reaching and climbing."

He smiled. "Now let's focus on your first exhibition game. We have ten days to prepare for an all-star team from Manchester."

Chapter 20

Another Day, Another Gang

Across the Allegheny River from Pittsburgh's downtown lies Northside. Many different sub-neighborhoods that are known as industrial, social, and historic centers are contained within its borders.

Troy Hill and Spring Garden are home to the narrowest and steepest streets Pittsburgh has to offer, as well as a reminder of Pittsburgh's rich ethnic past.

The H.J. Heinz plant is on the southeastern edge of Northside in a small area known as the East Allegheny. The company boasts its most famous product with a large neon ketchup bottle that empties ever so slowly on its old brick side.

The Andy Warhol Museum opened in 1994 on the North Shore as a tribute to one of Pittsburgh's famous native sons. It is the only museum in the world devoted to the work of only one artist.

Allegheny General, in central Northside, is one of the leading research hospitals in the world. It is best known for its work in transplant and heart medicine.

Also located in Northside is the National Aviary and

the Mexican War Streets, a small tract of land given to soldiers
in lieu of payment after the Revolutionary War. The land was
later named for battles of the Mexican War. The stunning
architecture of the Victorian era is represented throughout the
alleys and narrow streets.

To the west of central Northside lies Three Rivers
Stadium, home of the Pirates and the Steelers. Adjacent to
Three Rivers Stadium and on the shores of the Ohio River is
the sparkling new Carnegie Science Center. The Center's
Omnimax Theater and main attractions include a retired
nuclear submarine, the U.S.S. Requin.

The renaissance that transformed the smoky city's
downtown in the seventies and eighties continues today in
Northside. Renovations and purchases of homes in this historic
district are made easier through lower than normal interest
rates. New developments, such as the proposed river bike route
and a new baseball-only stadium, are targeted for the shores of
the Northside.

This is an area of contrast between rich and poor,
black and white. Manchester, into which no new development funds pour, lies in the central west part of the
Northside. The biggest landmark there is the Western
Pennsylvania State Prison. To people living here and else-
where, it is just another rough Pittsburgh neighborhood to
stay away from.

Two things made Manchester news a few days before
The Next Level was to play their first game there. First, a
pizza delivery man was shot to death for seven dollars in an
abandoned home. Next, an old man, thought to be harmless,
shot and killed a young woman who was causing a distur-
bance on his doorstep after a night at a local tavern.

Those killings, and how his players would react, were on Tru's mind as he rode from Wilkinsburg to Manchester in Ron Haines's van. April twenty-ninth was an abnormally warm spring day, Tru noted, as the sun came through the window and warmed his body.

Their route took the team down Penn to Swissvale Avenue, where the caravan picked up the Parkway East, which passes through the Squirrel Hill tunnels on its way downtown. Passing the Boulevard of the Allies exit, the unique mixture of modern glass skyscrapers and turn-of-the-century high-rises, which define Pittsburgh's skyline jumped into view. The highlight for Tru was the twenty-story red brick building at the corner of Wood Street and Fifth Avenue with its six-story depiction of Pittsburgh's most celebrated athletes. Jack Lambert and Joe Greene of the Steelers, Mario Lemieux of the Penguins, Bill Mazeroski and, of course, Roberto Clemente of the Pirates greeted the visiting team, from the east.

The caravan cruised by Pittsburgh's single most identifiable landmark, the seventy-foot fountain at Point State Park. The Allegheny and Monongehela Rivers meet at Point State Park to form the head waters of the Ohio. Finally, after weaving onto the Fort Duquesne Bridge, the convoy of cars exited onto Ohio River Boulevard and into the heart of Manchester.

Tru noticed that the normally rambunctious, lively kids were rather subdued. Most of the talk was in the form of questions like, when will we be there and where is it? No bantering or gossip. When the van crossed the Fort Duquesne Bridge, Tru said, "We'll be there in a matter of minutes." No one commented. It was the first time that Tru could remember such complete silence.

The van turned left onto Manchester Boulevard and passed in front of Manchester Elementary School. The school's playground abutted the baseball field. The Manchester All-Stars were already on the field and the fans were in their lawn chairs. The team looked big.

An uneasy feeling was almost palpable as Haines's van pulled next to the field and the boys began to unload. Tru did not have to discern why. The boys, Tru knew, felt unwelcome.

Tru was not buying their attempt at coolness as his team headed toward the bench area. They looked unsure about everything. "Yo, fellas!" Tru hollered. "What's up with this equipment? We explained the routine yesterday. Y'all better get your behinds back here and grab this stuff if you want to play some ball today!" They returned still silent, their nervousness evident.

Tru noticed a small congregation forming just outside the cones denoting home run distance in left field. Another gang. There were about eight of them. It was eerily similar to being at Paulson. Their color of choice was red, but their choices of drinking and smoking substances were the same.

The Next Level took the field for their pre-game infield and outfield drills. They knew the routine. Tru started by hitting fly balls to the outfield, left field first. Then he centered his attention on the infield. Each position was hit two grounders in each cycle.

Afterward, Tru turned back to the outfield. The boys had to bring their throws to the plate. First baseman Robbie Elliot was the cutoff man for all throws from center or right. Third baseman Johnnie Hanks was the relay for throws from left.

Tru shifted his attention to the infield to complete the

drill. The last round was identical to the first except that the first grounder was thrown to first and the second one, with the infield up, was thrown home.

At practice, this routine was usually finished in ten minutes with a minimum of errors. Today the gang called out hostilely at each play and the drill seemed to spin out in slow motion.

Each mistake the kids with the fitted teal and black uniforms made was greeted with jeers. The gang and the crowd were malicious. Fights were breaking out in the stands.

"Y'all think you big time, huh? You're a bunch of fruits!"

"Hey, sorry-assed kids, go back where you belong."

"We don't like your kind here. You might just get hurt."

The insults went on and on.

The dejected kids of The Next Level just looked at each other with wide open eyes as they trotted humbly off the field towards Tru. The team had mixed-up emotions. Some were angry, others were scared, but most did not know what to feel.

"How y'all doin'?" Tru asked as the Manchester kids took the field to the cheers of their supporters. His team heard him, but no one looked at him. Some were staring directly into the ground, others watched Manchester take the field, and a few were glancing nervously at the spectators and gang members who had just humiliated them.

"All eyes here!" Tru barked. "We got to come out and play the way we practice and not worry about these people. Getting mocked 'cause of the uniforms and our name and not bein' from here, that's a given. Any error you make, they're gonna rub it in a little! Any strikeout, they're gonna laugh at you! Y'all wanna go home? Wanna quit?" He stopped for a second. "What's the only way to shut these people up?" For the first time there were a few smiles on the faces looking back at Tru. "Yup, that's right. Go out there and beat them! Look at each other. Right now, take a look around. This is who we have to depend on, guys you've been practicin' with for months. Now let's do this, baby! Let's move this season along. Now get your hands in here for the break and let's show these people what's up!"

After everyone's hands touched, Tru said, "You think those kids are all-stars? They already made more errors than you did! Let's get them, baby! How far do you wanna go?"

The boys responded, "The next level!"

The pitcher for Manchester was a kid named Daron Palmer, not quite the size of Darryl Weston, but big nonetheless. It was obvious from his warmup pitches that he was no finesse pitcher. His best pitch was a sneaky fastball. In fact, his only pitch was that fastball. Some fastball pitchers are not intimidating to bat against because a batter can guess where the pitch is going. Other pitchers rear back, cut it loose, and hope it will be somewhere in the vicinity of the plate. These are the guys no one really wants to bat against. This was a good description of Daron. Added to this was the fact that Daron gave the impression he did not really care where the ball went.

Marcus Haines, led off. His stance was an easy one to throw strikes to—far off the plate and tall. The first pitch from Daron nearly hit him. Marcus took the next three pitches and walked. The Next Level had their first base runner.

Instead of hearing the cheers from the bench, Tru and

Bud, coaching in full uniform at third and first, heard nothing but grumbling bellies. Butterflies were swarming inside the kids of The Next Level.

The numbers two-through-four hitters were Evin Gales, Jerrett Thompson, and Brendon Banks. Darryl Weston, the projected cleanup hitter, was still out with his injury. The bat never left Stan Coles's shoulder. He struck out. Jerrett followed Stan's example, but he at least swung at two pitches. Brendon fanned on three. No one had even touched a ball.

Brendon started on the mound for The Next Level. A lanky left-hander with a very fluid motion, Brendon was imposing. His stride to the plate was long and his knees were bent to get every ounce of force on the ball. Still, he did not throw nearly as hard as Daron, but he did have an above average fastball.

In the first inning, Brendon struck out the lead-off man, Daron, and then walked the numbers two and three hitters. He regrouped and finished the first by striking out the next two batters.

Johnnie Hanks and Robbie Elliot became the first Next Level hitters to put the ball in play in the top of the second. Unfortunately, they both grounded out to first. Byron Knight ended the inning by becoming the fourth strikeout victim for the flame-throwing Daron.

The bottom of the second began as the bottom of the first had: Brendon struck out the first man and followed that with two walks. That is where the similarity stopped. He faced Manchester's number seven hitter, a tiny right-hander named Jon. The smallest player on either side did something that nobody else had been able to do. He got a hit. It was not a shot but had just enough steam on it to sneak into center field and get an RBI. Manchester led 1-0 and the vocal fans became louder.

Tru took a time-out and slowly walked to Brendon to try and calm him. It worked like a charm. He snuffed Manchester's rally by again striking out the next two hitters, giving him six for the game.

One of the most important innings in baseball is the inning immediately after the other team scores. If the scoring team shuts their opponent down, they get an additional momentum boost. If, however, the opposition comes back to score, "big mo" is on their side. The pitcher sets the tone.

John Doe led off the top of the third and became a Next Level base runner when Daron walked him. Center fielder Joe Foster was next. He walked on four pitches. Marcus Haines loaded the bases when he walked on five. Stan Coles came up for his second trip to face Daron. It was another free pass, forcing in The Next Level's first run. Daron's fifth walk in a row gave The Next Level their first lead. Quickly, there was life on The Next Level's bench.

They did not score again in the third. Just as suddenly as he lost it, Daron rediscovered the strike zone. He fanned Brendon, and got Johnnie Hanks to ground out. The inning ended with a double play. The pitcher threw to home and the catcher to first base.

The bottom of the third gave Brendon the same challenge Daron had faced in the top of the inning. Namely, how to pitch with a lead. Mirroring Daron, he walked Manchester's lead-off hitter. Brendon induced the next hitter into a grounder to third. Johnnie Hanks fielded the ball flawlessly and threw to Marcus for the force at second. Two consecutive strikeouts ended the bottom of the third, giving Brendon eight strike-outs in three innings. They went to the fourth clinging to a one-run lead at 2-1.

Four walks and an error later, The Next Level had a 5-1 lead on the All-Stars from Manchester. Just as Tru prophesied, they had received some breathing room. Although they were still getting no-hit, they had a four-run lead.

The most dangerous thing about walks in baseball is that they give a team the opportunity to have a big inning without having to produce with their bats. A double to left is harmless if there is no one on base. A double to left with the bases loaded can erase a three-run lead in a hurry. Because of guilt, it is more acceptable to give up that double with the bases loaded if the other runners hit their way on base.

When a team has a lead, it is incumbent on the pitcher to throw strikes and make the batters put the ball in play. The premise is that even if the five best hitters are up, someone will hit the ball at the defense to produce an out.

In the bottom of the fourth, Brendon lost the plate. He walked the first hitter. He lost his confidence when he walked the second batter.

Tru brought in "The Wild Thing," Robbie Elliot, and sent Brendon to first base. Robbie struck out the third batter. He walked the next hitter, loading the bases, before striking out another. Continuing this trend, he walked the next two hitters to force in a run that made the score 5-3 in favor of The Next Level. The bases were still full and there were two outs.

Tru had another decision to make. The only other pitcher he had available was Johnnie Hanks. His next best third baseman was John Doe. That would mean putting in Manny. Tru decided it was Manny's time. The hitters coming up for the All-Stars were Jon, the third baseman, and Stefan, the catcher. Each had struck out in their previous two times at bat.

Jon shot a ball to the left side. It looked destined for left field and, most likely, would score two runs and tie the game. Jerrett Thompson had other ideas. He went airborne and knocked the ball down. There was no possible play, although he almost forced the runner at third. The score was now 5-4 and the bases remained loaded.

Stefan was a big right-handed batter whom Brendon had not only struck out but made look ridiculous in his two at bats. For Stefan, three was a charm. His grand slam flew easily over the cones in left center field. What had been a four-run lead had turned into an 8-5 deficit as seven runs were scored with two hits. Before whiffing the last batter, the Wild Thing lived up to his name and walked another. Out of the twelve possible outs, the Next Level pitchers had struck out eleven, yet gave up eight runs.

"It's time to see what you're made of!" Tru challenged the boys as they came off the field. "You can either pack it in or come out fighting. Only y'all can decide that."

Two walks and two strikeouts later, it was Joe Foster's turn at the plate. Daron had struck him out the previous inning. Joe was one of those kids who looked like he was either sleeping or didn't care about what he was doing. That was deceptive. He seemed to do everything in slow motion but he was the best outfielder on the team. He fell behind in the count one ball and two strikes. That was when the game turned. Joe fouled off seven pitches and finally drew a walk from Daron, loading the bases.

Marcus Haines was next. He took a fastball on the left

shoulder to force in a run, making the score 8-6 Manchester. Stan walked on four pitches to pull The Next Level within a run of tying.

Then Jerrett Thompson broke up the no-hitter and he did it in style. He drove a two-ball, no-strike pitch into the right center gap, plating three runs and giving The Next Level a 10-8 lead. Then he came home on a wild pitch to close the scoring.

Johnnie Hanks came on to throw the fifth and sixth innings. He struck out four, walked two, allowed no hits or runs, and preserved The Next Level's lead.

The teams combined for three hits, with the losers getting two of them, yet were able to score seventeen runs. It was not a pretty game, but The Next Level had won.

Only their cheers and those of their parents could be heard. The gang and the opposite team's spectators were silent.

After shaking hands with the opponents, the boys gathered around their coaches for the postgame talk. "Okay, fellas. Well, the first thing is big congratulations. Remember, a win is a win, no matter how sloppy it was. I was especially proud of how you kept your poise and came right back after they had that big inning. I know y'all know we played like mud, but that's part of this too. Good teams find ways to win when they don't play their best game and we did. But we gotta improve. We don't play again till this Wednesday, if it doesn't rain. That gives us a little time to work on some of our weaknesses. The biggest thing we have to improve is hitting the ball. Daron, their pitcher, was throwin' hard early on, but he was out of gas by the third inning. You have to become aggressive at the plate, even if the pitcher's strugglin' to throw strikes. You can't go up there lookin' for a walk. You

have to want to swing the bat. One hit? C'mon now, that's
not good enough and y'all know it. Our pitchin' was terrible.
What did we walk, something like fifty or so? Man, y'all
throw strikes all day in practice. All day! I don't understand
it! What you're tellin' me is you're scared to throw strikes in
a game!" He paused and turned to Bud and Bart. "Y'all have
anything to say?"

Both coaches shook their heads no as they looked at
the team. "All right, then I hope we come out on Wednesday
in Homewood hungry to win. I know y'all want to play those
boys bad but you better be ready 'cause they're gonna feel
the same way about y'all! By the way, Manny. For your first
game ever in organized ball, that was one helluva game
behind the dish, bro. All right, y'all, practice Monday, five-
thirty at Paulson. Don't be late!"

Tru felt relieved. He was pretty sure the kids felt the
same. He knew their parents did. Their biggest concern had
been getting through the Manchester game without a violent
incident. That being achieved and a win on top of it, made
the adults' day.

The vast orange setting sun sparkled on the flowing
waters of the Ohio River on the silent drive home. Tru wondered how many middle class parents' happiest moments at
their sons' Little League games came when their child did
not get beaten up or shot.

Chapter 21

The Hill

At one time, the Hill was one of the most prosperous and influential black neighborhoods in America. They called the area Little Harlem. For African-Americans it meant society, literature, music, and sports. Wylie Avenue, the road that began with a church and ended with a prison, was the center of that life.

At the top of Wylie Avenue, *The Pittsburgh Courier*, one of the first black newspapers in America, was located. *The Courier* was the only source of news about the black community. National and regional editions were, and still are, published.

August Wilson, Pulitzer Prize winning playwright, called the Hill home. His critically acclaimed plays were set here. Talented performers like George Benson and Lena Horne also lived on the Hill. They refined their talents at places like the Crawford Grill and the Musician's Club, two of the many night spots on lower Wylie Avenue. They were both known for their food by day and for their jazz by night.

The Pittsburgh Crawfords, the first Negro League baseball team, was founded by Gus Greenlee. The Crawfords and
their arch rivals, the Homestead Grays, provided countless
hours of entertainment and major league quality baseball to the
surrounding residents. Stars like Hill native Josh Gibson,
Satchel Paige, and Oscar Chareton displayed their talents for
residents of the Hill for free.

Greenlee Field where they played ball, has disinte-
grated and disappeared. This downward spiral way of the
lower Hill started when the city began its urban push. The
Civic Arena stands where the "Crossroads of the World,"
nicknamed by a local disc jockey, used to be. As this area
vanished, so did a way of life.

The unofficial entrance to the Hill today is the same
church just above the Civic Arena. With black patron saint, St.
Benedict standing atop the steeple with outstretched hands
reaching to the city's downtown, the landmark beckons people
to its steps. It is here at the corner of Center Avenue, Crawford
Street, and Freedom Corner where the people from the Hill
once took a stand and said no to further city development.
Even now when there is civil unrest or protest, it usually starts
at Freedom Corner. The Hill still retains what the wrecking
ball could not destroy—pride.

Ammons Recreation Center is located on Bedford
Avenue. On the downtown side of Ammons lies the Bedford
Square Public Housing Complex. To the west, after Macedonia
Baptist Church, is another public housing area, Crawford
Village. One thing is well known: folks from the Homewood
and Wilkinsburg areas are not welcome. Only a few weeks
before The Next Level was scheduled to play, a basketball team
from Homewood, competing in the prestigious Ozanam

League, dropped out after numerous threats and fights.

The kids of The Next Level didn't pay much attention to possible problems that could arise, but the same could not be said for the coaches and parents.

Most of them knew the Hill. They either grew up there or had family there. But in their youth the Hill was a different, friendly place. They, like most other Pittsburghers of the '90s, watched the six o'clock news and heard of the shootings, gangs, and depression which now pervaded the area. Although they knew the reporters sensationalized the truth, they also knew some buried truths were uncovered by the media. One of these was the hostility toward outsiders.

Despite their early good memories, they now had children to care for; children they didn't want at the wrong place at the wrong time.

"These kids will be all right, Tracie, right?" Evie Oliver asked Robbie Elliot's mom as they sat on the crowded bleachers at Ammons Field. The mothers watched their sons prepare to play their first game in the Papa Dean League.

Evie, a tall and attractive single mother, lived in a neighborhood bordering Homewood, East Hills, and Wilkinsburg. Her sons, Byron, eleven, and his little eight-year-old brother Devin had recently become involved in The Next Level.

Looking past her friend and over at the Bedford Square projects just across the street, Tracie replied, "Tru and Bud ain't gonna take these kids anywhere they think won't be safe, but we'd better keep our eyes on them just to be sure."

However, there were too many unfamiliar faces and too much activity for the women to keep track of it all.

The pool area just behind a fifteen-foot-high chain-link

fence in the right field of the lower baseball field was occupied by rough looking kids in their teens. They were not swimming, but were just hanging out on the concrete wall that separated the Ammons Pool from the one-way street that surrounded the Bedford Square Public Housing complex.

Beyond the pool and across Bedford Avenue was a corner concession stand. As they sat on the bleachers, the women noticed there were more unruly teenagers loafing on Bedford Avenue directly in front of the refreshment stand.

Directly behind them was a small patch of woods that led to the projects. It was yet another area that the women decided had to be closely scrutinized.

"Ron, Marcus's dad, was tellin' me," Evie said as her eyes scanned Ammons Field, "that as long as we ain't inside any project, there ain't nothin' to be worried about. He said he wouldn't be comin' here if it was like that, but I don't know."

"Tru and Bud are real good coaches and now that more parents are coming to these games, I feel better about the kids being safe," Tracie said as she continued her own watch behind dark sunglasses. "Ron and Debbie, Jim and Peachy Thompson, you—if anything starts jumpin' off, we'll have enough people here to take care of our kids."

"And there's Clarence Battle. You couldn't have a better man running the league."

Clarence Battle was a man of punctuality and order. Under his leadership, the Papa Dean League had become recognized as one of the best-run little leagues in the Pittsburgh region. Umpires were always present and unless it was raining at game time or a storm was passing through the area, Clarence saw to it that games began on schedule.

Baseball was taken seriously at Papa Dean. Most of

the players on the Ammons Cubs, The Next Level's opponent, looked at the strange kids with the nice uniforms and
funny club name with curiosity. Usually a team was called by
the name of one of the major league teams or their sponsor's
business; not some silly expression.

Spectators on the Cubs' side took a couple of verbal
shots at the kids of The Next Level. Most of the barbs were
directed either at the size of the man/child, Darryl Weston, or
at the fanciness of the teams' color-coordinated uniforms.

With each spoken assault, Evie looked uneasily at
Tracie and Tracie looked back at Evie. Each bit into her
tongue further. They smiled through the pain, silently com-
municating that the day would come for the defense of their
sons and of the entire Next Level squad if need be.

Tru started Chris Williams on the mound. Chris had
pitched only three innings in the 22-0 shellacking of
Homewood by The Next Level three days prior. It was one of
Tru's personal promises that he would not overwork any
pitcher he had on his team. *Kids ending up having ligament
problems with their arms by age twelve due to a win-at-all-
cost philosophy by some coach is an injustice,* Tru thought.

The lineup changes Tru made were minimal. Darryl
Weston was still out with his ankle injury so Brendon Banks
hit again in fourth position. Unlike Manchester, he followed
Johnnie Hanks, who had moved into the third slot. Marcus
Haines again played second and led off with Chris Williams
moving into the second spot. Jerrett Thompson remained at
short while dropping to fifth. He was followed by catcher
John Doe, right fielder Byron Knight, first baseman Robbie
Elliot, rounded out by the dependable Joe Foster in center
field hitting ninth.

The lineup shift resulted in immediate dividends. Marcus Haines and Johnnie Hanks singled around a walk to Chris Williams. This loaded the bases for Brendon Banks, fresh from a single, double, and triple in the rout of Homewood. The left-handed left fielder drove the first pitch from the diminutive Cub pitcher far past the right field home run cones. Before the top of the first ended, The Next Level added two more runs to take a commanding 6-0 lead.

Chris Williams surrendered two runs back to the Cubs in the bottom of the first to give the Ammons team hope. It was short-lived.

After a scoreless second, The Next Level scored seven more runs in the third. The outburst was highlighted by doubles from Johnnie Hanks, John Doe, and Robbie Elliot. Marcus Haines contributed his second single of the game and Jerrett Thompson added a run-scoring single through the hole at short. Todd Hill sat on the bench recording the statistics. Tru knew it was hard for him, but Todd had to prove himself again.

The Cubs struck back for a pair of runs in their half of the third but now found the only thing it accomplished was not getting ten-run ruled. It only delayed the inevitable.

The Next Level pushed across five more runs in the top of the fourth thanks to doubles by Chris Williams and Brendon Banks, and a triple by Jerrett Thompson.

Chris Williams kept the Cubs off the scoreboard in the bottom of the inning. The final score was 18-4. The Next Level found themselves with a surprising record of all wins and no defeats.

Tru felt good. He had been nervous about how the team would respond to playing in a prestigious league. His fears, he was glad, were unfounded. During the traditional handshake at the end of the game, one of the Cub players was overheard asking his coach, "Why did you schedule these kids so soon?"

Driving Lance home that night, Tru felt the twelve-year-old who had always been wary of affection sleeping contentedly on his shoulder. He didn't have to bust Lance any more about homework. Tru knew from his talks with Lance's teachers he was not only doing it but doing better on his tests.

The Next Level followed their first Papa Dean League win with a 13-0 non-league win over Chartiers-Windgap. Jerrett Thompson led the way on the mound firing a one-hitter and at the plate with a two-run homer. Two doubles by Chris Williams, and a triple each by Johnnie Hanks and Brendon Banks helped spur The Next Level to an easy win.

The Chartiers game marked another first for one of the players on The Next Level. Lance McCoy replaced Brendon in left field in the third inning. It was the first time Lance competed in a regular Little League game. In his first plate appearance, Lance drew a lead-off walk and came around to score the eleventh run of the game on a single by his best friend, Manny.

The team's spirits were high. Everyone on the team except Todd was getting to play and The Next Level thought they would never lose. Their comfort level grew more and more. Each practice found them a little looser than the one before. John Doe handed out more nicknames.

Brendon Banks became Pretty B because of his concern for his personal appearance. Robbie Elliot was Rob-Dawg just because it sounded right. When the team discovered at a

morning car wash Chris Williams' favorite breakfast food, he
was named Bacon. Todd Hill was given the name of Flea
because, as John Doe explained, he was never sure if Todd
would keep coming to practice, but he knew he was around
somewhere. To Todd's credit, Tru thought, his attendance
since his trouble had been regular.

The kids felt good about themselves and their team.
Their confidence was building and multiplying. Parents and
guardians who had concerns about the places their kids were
traveling were being won over by the team's success and a
growing belief in Tru's ability to handle whatever problems
came up.

Summer was approaching. Days were becoming
warmer, darkness came later, and most importantly, school
was ending soon. For young people it was the time of the
year their attention turned to activities like swimming, riding
bikes, going on picnics at Kennywood, the local amusement
park, and hitting Waterworks Mall.

The first indication to Tru that his boys were losing
concentration came at the next practice. They seemed less
serious. *It isn't anything I can pinpoint exactly,* Tru
thought, *I can't say, that poor play or that joke is what I'm
worried about. There's just a change. The kids are less
focused.* Tru worried more as their next wins came rather
easily, too easily.

Finally, right before a game in the Papa Dean circuit,
Tru spoke to them about their attitude. "I know I'm speakin'
for all the coaches and parents when I say that you've done
one helluva job, but you gotta remember, this is gonna be a
long season. Before it's all over, we're gonna play thirty
games or so. We have to stay focused on what we're trying

to accomplish, which is win the championship at Ammons and play at Three Rivers in the Mayor's Cup. If any of you think all we have to do is show up to reach that goal you're sadly mistaken. We're gonna have to double the amount of work we've put in up till now. Remember what this is all about: commitment, teamwork, discipline, sportsmanship, and winning. When other teams play us, I want them to know that if they're not prepared, they will get the piss beat down their legs!"

Robbie Eliot couldn't stifle a deep laugh.

"Son," Tru said as he looked Robbie directly in the eyes, "my remark may have tickled you but that doesn't change the importance of what I'm talkin' about. You see, the moment you let down, somebody will be there to snatch up what you could have had. Don't call that pretty girl across the room for the prom, someone else will. Don't take a job because it might be too hard, someone else will. Don't practice hard, don't strive to be champions, someone else will! Okay, you can go now."

Practice ended and Tru listened as the boys ripped on each other as they carried the equipment through right field to the waiting cars on Paulson Avenue.

He hoped some of what he said had really registered.

Chapter 22

The Pirates

From what Clarence Battle had told Tru, the Pirates were a pretty sharp team. They had won their opener with ease, a 12-3 thumping of the Ammons Giants. They were the Little League's defending champs.

"Y'all better be ready to battle today!" Tru warned his troops as they readied themselves, "These boys are the real deal. They spanked the Giants behinds like they owned them!"

Tru read off The Next Level lineup. "Marcus at second, Johnnie at third, Jerrett at short, 'Pretty B' at first, John Doe behind the dish, Evin in right, Joe in center, 'Wild Thing' on the hill." Then he paused. He looked first at Lance and then at Darryl Weston, who was ready to return today. He held back a smile but he couldn't keep the pride from his voice. "Lance, you're in left! Now let's go get their behinds!"

The boys drew in closer and Darryl Weston, receiving the nod from Tru, shouted, "How far do you wanna go!"

The boys responded, "The next level!" enthusiastically and took the field.

Robbie Elliot was tall for his age and possessed an excellent fastball, but Tru knew that he had not been given his nickname, 'Wild Thing,' for no reason.

There was an electricity in the air that The Next Level had not experienced before. The parents, hearing their Pirate counterparts' vocal support and watching them stride on the field, knew this team was unlike any they had faced before. The women sat in the bleachers where they could keep a much closer eye on their boys. Also, it gave them a chance to hear any derogatory remarks made by parents of the opponents. Evie and Tracie especially liked to be in the middle of the action.

Unlike the jeering fathers whom Tru had seen at games when he'd first watched, the men stood together down the right field line, as far away from the action as possible. They also seemed to have adopted Tru's philosophy. He was glad he'd talked to them about it. Coach Bud said they were in the bullpen. Ron Haines was there, accompanied by Buzzy Elliot, Jim Thompson, and Tyrone King, a friend of Evie's. They had decided they did not want to give the impression they were trying to meddle in any of the decisions that Tru, Bud and Bart had to make during the course of a ball game. Nor did they want in any way to inhibit the coaches from saying whatever it was they felt needed to be said to their sons. Lastly, they did not want to put extra pressure on their sons. Standing down the line as they did, the kids could almost forget they were there.

There was one father, however, who did not care whom he might make nervous. He was a fan first and foremost, and an excited one at that. Antonio Williams, Senior never missed a game and rarely a practice. Most every Little

League teams in America have an Antonio Williams, Senior. He is the person who is just busting with pride over the leaguer he's come to see and who reacts before he thinks. His type are usually obnoxious to fans of the other side and loved by their own. Tru already knew the Pirates were determined. He had watched their skillful pre-game practice. Tru only hoped his team knew it would be in for a challenge.

The Pirates proudly sported the black and gold colors of the team they were named after. Their leadoff hitter was Eric Lee. He ripped Robbie's first pitch into left field for a single.

Pirate third baseman Abdul Nakir was next, and he walked on four pitches. Not four minutes into the game, Robbie was shaken. Tru made his first trip to the mound. He did not want Robbie to lose his composure. "What's up, bro?" he asked, smiling. "I told you these boys are gonna get after you, didn't I? You're ready for this. Now go get them." Tru watched as Robbie looked over at his mom sitting in the bleachers. He listened as she proudly shouted her support, "C'mon now, baby. Relax and throw the pill like you know how. Turn it up a notch!"

"I'm ready." Robbie grinned at Tru.

Robbie responded with a three-pitch strikeout of the Pirate catcher, Montego Johns. The moms of The Next Level exploded, with Tracie Elliot leading the cheers.

The Pirate cleanup hitter was a young man named Chuckie Grant. It was not his size that was imposing, for he was not a large kid. It was not his demeanor—he wasn't cocky. It was his walk, the way he strode to the plate. It shouted confidence. If the walk was not enough, he tapped his spikes as he dug in the batter's box. Then he did something Tru had never seen a hitter do before. He slowly extended his bat with his left arm until it pointed directly at the pitcher, where he held it motionless for a split second, looking directly into Robbie's eyes. The ritual was not done because it was good theater. It was just his way of locking in, but it seemed intimidating.

Cementing his nickname, Robbie's first pitch to Chuckie was wild. Luckily, it bounced back to John Doe who reacted automatically by firing a throw to Johnnie at third. John Doe did not see the runner trying to advance on the overthrow, he just reacted. If he had waited to see if Eric was going or not, he would not have had a play.

When Eric realized he had no chance of making it safely to third, he froze. The problem was that he was halfway between second and third when he realized he was doomed. The ensuing rundown was executed perfectly when Johnnie ran Eric back towards second and flipped the ball to Marcus, who tagged Eric out.

Not having a runner in scoring position relaxed Robbie. He fired a fastball about knee high over the center of the plate on his next pitch to Chuckie. The batter smashed a one hopper to Johnnie Hanks at third, who threw to Marcus covering second for the force-out ending the inning.

Chuckie was also the Pirate hurler. He was not nearly as intimidating on the mound as he was at the plate, but he did possess a pretty good fastball.

Marcus and Johnnie drew walks that put runners on first and second with none out. After a passed ball moved the runners to second and third, Jerrett followed with a bloop single that scored Marcus from third. Johnnie could only advance to third. He had to make sure the ball would drop in front of the left fielder.

Brendon followed with a chopper to third. Johnnie made two mistakes. He broke to the plate when the ball was hit without checking to see that it was not hit at either first, third, or the pitcher. The corners were up to prevent a run from scoring and a runner on third rarely scores on a come-backer to the mound.

His second mistake was stopping when he saw the third baseman make the play. The rule of thumb that Tru preached was to never hesitate once you made a commitment. Instead of forcing the third baseman to make a good throw to the plate while he was barreling down the line, Johnnie froze, and was easily tagged out. Worse, it gave Pirate third baseman Abdul Nakir time to throw to first and complete a double play. Instead of having runners at second and third with one out, there were now two outs and Jerrett on second.

John Doe followed by shooting a single between first and second base. Jerrett was barreling around third and would have scored easily had he not stumbled over the bag.

After a walk to Stan Coles, Chuckie fanned Joe Foster with the bases loaded. That ended the first inning. Two hits and three walks had produced only one run. It was a recipe for disaster. Tru shook his head. He knew it was sometimes the things a team didn't do that cost them the game.

Robbie started the second inning by walking the lead-off hitter. Tru grimaced, another cardinal sin no matter the level of baseball being played. After a strikeout and a wild pitch that moved the runner to second, Pirate shortstop Ricky Allen drove a hard single to left that tied the game at one-all. That ball went under Lance's glove. Then it rolled past the home run cones in left field. The only thing that saved the run was an outstanding relay throw from Lance to Johnnie Hanks to Antonio who applied the tag at the plate.

Robbie followed that bit of good fortune by plucking the number eight hitter, Marlon Phillips, in the ribs. Another wild pitch moved him to second and after striking out the ninth hitter, Raheem Turner, for the second out, Robbie committed another baseball sin.

When a pitcher is ahead of a hitter on the count of no balls and two strikes, two things are not supposed to happen. One is hitting the batter. Robbie had already committed the first and now he committed the second.

Pitchers know that when a hitter is far behind in the count they are willing to swing at nearly anything. The idea is to throw a pitch far enough out of the strike zone that if the hitter wants to chase it, he will unlikely be able to get good wood, aluminum rather, on the ball.

Robbie's fastball was right down the pipe. Eric Lee sent a single screeching into right and the Pirates had the lead. The inning ended with no further damage when Robbie got Abdul Nakir to pop out to right.

It was then that Chuck and Robbie both settled down somewhat.

However, the Pirates were able to push across another run in the third on a walk and two errors.

The Next Level answered with a run of their own in the bottom of the third. In the inning they had three singles and a walk. Again, poor base running took them out of a possible big inning. Jerrett was thrown out at third and Brendon at home. The frustration was growing. The boys on the bench were uneasy. They went to the fifth trailing the Pirates by 3-2.

Good batters eventually hit. Robbie had been able to

get Chuckie to ground out twice, even though both balls were hit extremely hard. After another leadoff walk and a strike-out, Chuckie hit a monstrous drive over the cones in left center. No one for The Next Level ever got to the ball. It was a homer that was thrown back to the lower field by a player on the bench of the other game. The Pirates were able to plate three more runs to take a 6-2 advantage.

Tru challenged the troops as they came off the field for their ups. "Now we're gonna see what y'all are made of. It's only the fifth inning. We've been down before and come back. There's no reason why we can't do it today."

After one out, Jerrett singled to right on a one-ball, one-strike curve. Brendon followed with a homer to right. The boys were answering Tru's call to arms.

The guys on the bench began chanting, "Where we goin'?" to which they, along with Antonio Williams, shouted, "The next level!"

Chuckie Grant regrouped, which was no surprise to Tru. He struck out the next two batters. The Pirates held a 6-4 lead going to the sixth and final inning.

Coming to the plate, the Pirates and their fans were whooping it up right along with the parents of The Next Level. The men who always stood far down the right field line started creeping towards the infield, then moved back and started forward once again.

"C'mon, baby!" Tracie called to her son as the sixth started. "Set these boys down so we can get in here and win this thing!"

"That's what we're talkin' about!" John Doe's dad yelled when Robbie struck out Eric, the Pirates' leadoff hitter. He paced the small area in front of the bleachers so nervously it brought smiles to the faces of Pirate parents. His son and their teammates knew his emotional attention was genuine.

It was also short-lived. Abdul Nakir doubled and Montego singled him home for a quick run that pushed the Pirate advantage to three. Chuck extended that to five on the next pitch when he drove another fastball deep past the cones in center.

Left fielder Bill Barnett followed Chuck with a homer of his own down the line in right. Not a mammoth one; the line drive rolled the whole way to the fence where the men of The Next Level had retreated. Before the inning was over, the Pirates added four more runs. Two walks, two errors, and another homer did the trick. A hopeful 6-4 deficit had turned into a hopeless 14-4 shellacking.

Chuck struck out the side in the sixth.

It was a convincing win for the Pirates. As the teams shook hands after the game, it was the Pirates who appeared surprised; not by the ease of their win, for they were a confident, well-coached group of kids. They were more surprised by the reaction of the boys on The Next Level. It was as if the Pirates had expected a retaliative response. They got handshakes.

Chapter 23

Don't Look Back

The following night Tru and the coaches held a brutal practice at which the boys of The Next Level had to run a quarter mile lap for each run the Pirates had scored against them.

The team's next game was against the Tigers. The Next Level found themselves trailing 7-0 after two innings. They rallied in the third, fourth and fifth to make the score 8-7 Tigers. In the sixth, they had runners at second and third with no one out but could not push across the tying run.

In their next game two days later, their opponents jumped out to a 6-2 lead before Jerrett Thompson led The Next Level rally with a three-run blast to make the score 6-5 in the fifth. However, their old nemesis Chuckie Grant answered Jerrett with a two-run shot of his own to close out the scoring.

The games were well played. In neither loss was there any finger pointing or grumbling. As Tru said, "They're just a couple of games where we came up short. Let's move on to the next level."

They won the next of their games with a 5-2 triumph over the Ammons Giants. The Next Level now had won nine games. During this game, Lance hit two singles. When Tru and Lance returned home to Edgerton that night, Tonya met them at the door.

She held out a manilla envelope that had the return address of the Pittsburgh Board of Education on the upper right-hand corner. Lance's year-end report card had arrived. Though the envelope had been slit open, there was no reading Tonya's face. She handed it to Lance.

Slowly he pulled the paper out and unfolded it. The smile that came over Lance's face was contagious. His mother laughed and cried as she grabbed the happy bespectacled youth in the teal and black uniform that had The Next Level blazed in teal across the white pinstriped shirt. Tonya gripped Lance so tightly he was barely able to hand off the report card to Tru.

Quickly, Tru unfolded the letter. With an emotionless face he studied it. After what seemed like forever to the eager child, Tru looked away from the report card and directly at Lance. It was then he grinned. "Three A's, two B's and four C's! That's one helluva job, Lance! You should be damn proud of yourself! Why don't you go hang that record up in your room, buddy!"

When Lance looked away, Tru knew Lance did not like the suggestion. "What's up, man?" Tru said to him. "You oughta put it up somewhere! It's okay to be proud of yourself!"

Lance asked, "Can I take it to practice tomorrow?"

Tru nodded. He didn't care if hugs were considered weird by twelve-year-olds. He hugged Lance while looking at Tonya. "You're damn right you can! These are the two best pieces of news we've had all week: first the team makes the playoffs and now, Lance, you've shown me you're already a winner!"

The next few days inched by for both Tru and The Next Level team. The playoffs at Ammons began the twenty-seventh of June. The Next Level finished in third place. Both the Pirates and Tigers had records of ten wins with only two losses apiece. The Pirates were the number one seed by virtue of their two regular season wins against the Tigers, but The Next Level had made it to a pinnacle they'd never expected. Tru told them, "I want you to savor each step up you've climbed. You deserve to be proud."

Their first-round opponent was the Ammons Angels, the sixth-place finisher in the eight-team league. It was never a game.

The Next Level jumped on Angel hurler Theo Springer for five runs in the top of the first, highlighted by a bases loaded double by Evin Gales. They never looked back. The boys added two in the second, one in the third, and five more in the fifth, coasting to a 13-3 win. Lance McCoy garnered the win and it was on to the second round. Tru didn't know who he was happier about the team or Lance.

Tru's team eagerly awaited a rematch with the Pirates. Each game against the Pirates they'd played, The Next Level had been missing a key player. The first game they were basically without the services of Darryl Weston. He had just had his cast removed the week before. In the rematch, Brendon Banks missed the game because he severely sprained his ankle playing basketball the day before. The Next Level dreamed and planned to turn the tables in the playoffs.

However, first the Pirates had to win their game against the Cubs. Unfortunately, the Pirates did not show up for their game with the Cubs. Apparently, there was either a lack of communication between the coaches and players, or many were out of town and couldn't be reached since the game was to be played in the school vacation period. Clarence Battle stood strong. League rules said if a team did not have nine players at game time it was an automatic forfeit.

The Next Level never got the chance to play the Pirates again. Because of the forfeiture their opponents would be the Cubs. Before the game on June twenty-ninth, Tru worried that his team would take the Cubs too lightly. Once again, he warned them, "Don't be overconfident. You're going to have to fight your way to the next level."

When the Cubs scored three runs in the top of the first, Tru's fears came to fruition.

However, The Next Level team was still undaunted. Johnnie Hanks started an onslaught when he tripled home Marcus Haines. Chris Williams doubled him in, and, after a single by Darryl Weston and walks to Brendon and Jerrett, John Doe cleared the bases with a double. Six hits later, The Next Level claimed a 7-3 advantage.

Another seven-run outburst ended the game. The final score was 14-4. They had made the World Series Championship of the Papa Dean League.

The only thing left was the game between the Tigers and Giants to see who their opponent would be. The players bet on the Tigers and they were right. The score was 8-0.

The championship series was scheduled to begin on July fifth. Tru was concerned that a week's layoff between games would have a detrimental effect on his team's momentum. Calling around to some of the contacts he had made during the various exhibition games during the season, he arranged to play two games before the final series began.

On July first, The Next Level beat the Uptown All-

Stars by a score of 11-5. The next day, the Wild Thing led them to a 9-1 win over the same group. They were ready.

It was hard to say if the Tigers were a better team than the Pirates. Their records were identical, although the Pirates had beaten the Tigers twice and each had beaten the other once.

Comparing the two teams at their meeting, Tru and Bart decided the only thing the Tigers lacked was a hitter the caliber of the Pirates' Chuckie Grant.

"Melvin Carter is every bit the hitter Chuckie is, y'all!" Coach Bud insisted as he sipped a soda.

It was true that Melvin had two singles and a double in the Tigers 8-7 win back in June, but he did not possess Chuckie's size.

"Mel is good," Tru countered. "It would be a hard call to choose Chuckie or Mel if it came down to picking one hitter you had to face to win the game."

The debate continued into the night. Each coach politicked for a particular lineup, going over each kid's strengths, conferring over the perfect batting order. Around eleven o'clock, as the late news came on, the three men were exhausted. Tru made the final choices and penciled in the starters:

Marcus Haines would lead off as he had done all year, but tomorrow would play third. Lance McCoy would be in right and bat second. All agreed that Stan Coles would be the starter if he had not missed practice that day. Jerrett Thompson would be at short and hit third. Big Baby, Darryl Weston, at first and hitting cleanup. Brendon Banks, "Pretty B," would hit fifth and play left field. Joe Foster would follow and play center. After much debate whether to put him in front of Byron Knight, Manny was given the nod and would bat seventh. He would be catching. Byron Knight would hit eighth and take over the duties at second for Marcus Haines.

The ninth batter and the pitcher was Johnnie Hanks. Robbie Elliot was held out of the starting lineup and he would be the first relief pitcher. The coaches felt it was better to keep him on the bench in case he had to warm up quickly. Todd Hill would keep the book.

It felt like they'd worked on the lineup for the World Series. They went home to get a few hours sleep.

Fans from each team were at the field early. Evie and Tracie took their regular seats, sitting together in the bleachers. Debbie Haines and Peachy Thompson were in the row in front of them. Behind them were Brenda Weston, Roslyn Banks, and Tonya, who had gotten a night off. Antonio Williams, Senior was already pacing and the game was still thirty minutes away.

"Did Byron sleep last night?" Tracie asked her friend.

"Byron?" Evie said as she fidgeted to get herself comfortable. "Look at these rings under my eyes. I didn't sleep a damn wink, girl! I don't know what that boy did. All I know is he talked about this game from the time he got home till the time he went to bed. That's what got me so damned worked up!"

As the rest of the moms related similar stories, the men, in their usual position down the right field line, tried to be cool. Hands were thrust in their pockets and they kicked at the dirt as they walked around in circles waiting for the game to start.

"I hope the boys ain't as nervous as they are!" Tracie said as she motioned to the other women to look at the male scene out in right.

It was a beautiful day. The temperature was about seventy-eight degrees. There was just enough wind to keep the humidity bearable.

The Next Level was the visiting team. Game two

would be their only home game of the three-game championship series. If game three became necessary, the second-place Tigers would have the last at-bats.

"Play ball!" the umpire called.

In the top of the first, The Next Level drew blood. After Tiger pitcher Melvin Carter struck out Marcus on a one-ball, two-strike curve, he walked Lance. Jerrett forced Lance at second when he shot a one hopper to third. After Jerrett took second on a passed ball, Darryl Weston blooped an RBI double down the right field line. Brendon stranded Darryl at second as he struck out on another curve to end the inning.

The Tigers went in order in their half of the first. Jerrett turned a double play. He snared a hard grounder that looked like it was destined for center field, stepped on second to force out Tim Milton who had walked, and fired the ball to first to nip number three hitter Anthony Taylor.

After a scoreless top of the second, Melvin Carter sent a long home run over the cones in left to tie the game at one. Worse than tying the game, it shook Johnnie up. Tru told Robbie to get ready immediately. A walk and a double later, Tru brought him in. With runners at second and third and nobody out, Robbie struck out two and escaped further damage when he retired leadoff hitter Jeff Hardy on a pop-up to Jerrett.

Another walk for Lance led off the third. This time it was followed by a triple from Jerrett. After Darryl struck out, Brendon walked but was thrown out stealing second. Joe Foster singled in Jerrett with the second run of the inning. Byron Knight's fly ball eluded the Tiger left fielder and drove home Joe and Manny who had walked, making the score 5-1 in favor of The Next Level.

The Tigers struck back in the bottom of the third. A leadoff walk to Tim Milton and a fielder's choice by Anthony Taylor put a runner at first. Melvin was next.

When Anthony stole second, Coach Bud looked anxiously at Tru. "First base is open, Coach!" he said, trying to coax Tru to give the dangerous Melvin an intentional pass.

"Nah, it's too early, Bud," he replied confidently. "Let's pitch to him."

After falling behind in the count at two balls and no strikes, Robbie reared back and fired a fastball. Melvin crushed it. No one moved. Even Joe Foster seemed to admire the ball as it sailed high over his head, landing on the infield dirt of the vacant upper field. It halved the lead to 5-3.

Tru said nothing as his team came to the dugout with no further damage being done. He saw in their eyes no dejection. He saw no sign of quitters. This was the kind of spirit he had worked so hard to inculcate.

In their half of the fourth, Jerrett's single plated Marcus after he had gotten on base due to an error by the Tiger third baseman. The score was now 6-3, The Next Level.

The Tigers answered in the bottom of the fourth. A single and two walks chased Robbie from the game. Tru brought in Brendon from left to pitch and sent Robbie to left. Two errors by Darryl Weston, another by Marcus at third, and a single led to four unearned runs. The Tigers claimed a 7-6 lead in the seesaw battle.

Neither Tru, Bud, nor Bart had a speech for the kids as they came off the field. One team member seated on the bench, however, did have something on his mind.

It was Todd Hill. "Pick your damn heads up, y'all!" he pleaded. "You can win this thing! We been through too damn much to come this far and lose, man! Don't nobody here make the last out! Don't worry about nothin'! Just don't make the last damn out!"

Tru and Bud flashed a quick glance between each

other. Never before had a player sworn in front of the coaches without being reprimanded. They both silently agreed and turned back at Todd. This was not swearing. It was emotion.

"Where y'all want to go?" Todd shouted. All the coaches, all the players, and all the fans shouted their reply that had become more than just a name to the team. It had become their identity. "The Next Level!"

Marcus Haines led off the top of the sixth with a walk. Tru looked at Lance on deck and motioned him over to his side.

"I'm gonna let Stan swing for you, bro. That all right with you?"

"Yes, sir, Coach Tru," was his hopeful reply.

Stan drove Melvin's second pitch far past the cones in left. Jubilation came to the bench. They were up 8-7.

Jerrett followed Stan's blast with a sharp single to left, his third hit of the day. Jerrett stole second and went to third on a passed ball. Darryl Weston and Brendon Banks were due up.

Melvin Carter showed his poise. With either batter only needing to make contact to get another run home, he struck them both out. The deep-felt emotion that The Next Level expressed now shifted back to the fans on the home team.

Joe Foster, one for two today, was up next. He had struck out his last time up. Now he worked the count to two balls and two strikes. The next pitch from Melvin was a fastball, and it was probably a pitch Joe should not have taken. Tru breathed a huge sigh of relief when it was called ball three.

Melvin fired the full count pitch with all his might, right down the middle, as if saying, "Here, what you gonna do with that?"

Ping!

It was not a very solid ping. It was, however, solid enough to drop behind the second baseman and in front of the right fielder. The insurance run The Next Level wanted, dashed home.

The Tigers had one last chance in the bottom of the sixth. They had the meat of the team coming up: Anthony Taylor, Melvin Carter, and George Pilson.

Anthony Taylor led off with his second single of the game. Melvin Carter was up and, sure enough, the run came home in his at-bat.

However, Melvin did not drive him in with a blistering double or towering homer. What brought Anthony home was a wild pitch after he had stolen second and third. Three pitches, no swing, and a run crossed the plate. It was devastating because it brought the Tigers to within a run of The Next Level's score, there were no outs, and Brendon still had to finish pitching to Melvin.

It was Brendon's turn to show some poise.

He struck out the side.

The Next Level had taken a one game to nothing lead in the best of three series.

Brendon was mobbed by his teammates.

After perhaps two minutes of on-field celebration, the teams met at home for an emotional handshake. There was respect on both parts.

When the formalities were over, the parents of The Next Level ran onto the field and swarmed their sons. Tru waited awhile to address his team. He wanted to soak in the exultation.

Finally he said, "Fellas, I know this is wonderful and I, like your parents, am very proud. But listen up! Two days from now, we have to do this again, what do you think?" he asked emotionally. "One more win and we've got out first goal. Then it's on to Three Rivers, baby! Where y'all want to go?"

"The Next Level!" the team cried in unison.

As picture perfect a day as it was for game one of the

series, it was that dreary and stormy when game two was scheduled to be played. The game had to be called off. Clarence informed Tru, "The game will be rescheduled for July eighth."

Tru called the kids as soon as he found out. There was a major problem.

"That's the day we planned for our outing at Sandcastle, Tru!" Evie protested over the phone. "He can't make the kids play that day! They've been looking forward to this for too long."

Sandcastle is a popular water slide amusement park some fifteen minutes upstream on the Monongehela River.

"Hold on, Evie," Tru countered. "Our boys are goin' to Sandcastle! They deserve it. These kids worked too long and hard to cancel that celebration. We'll just have to leave there around five. That should be plenty of time to get over to Ammons since we'll be goin' opposite rush hour traffic."

"These kids'll be dead, Tru. They'll be sittin' out in the sun all day ridin' them water slides. Ain't no way they'll be ready to play that game!"

"Shoot, Evie. These kids got more energy than you know. Adrenaline will get them through the game. Besides, even if we lose, we get another chance."

"Why don't we go to Sandcastle another day? That ain't that big a deal. People would understand."

"Tracie worked too damn hard puttin' this all together and some of these kids are visiting relatives later this summer. I'd sure hate anyone to miss it. Nah, it's supposed to be fun for them. Let's let the kids enjoy themselves and we'll see what happens. It's only a game, remember!"

The kids enjoyed themselves and then some. The only thing that was unenjoyable was the rush to get to Ammons Field by six o'clock. By the time the parents coaxed their kids off all the rides, it was nearly five. By the time all the kids had put on their uniforms in the restrooms, it was five-ten. The single file, full uniform march through the pool and slide areas began at five-fifteen. They finally pulled out of the Sandcastle parking lot at five-twenty.

The twelve car convoy—all the parents were there—arrived at Ammons at a quarter to six. The kids sprinted from the cars to get in some loosening up before the game. They would have no time for the usual pre-game infield ritual.

Tracie walked down to her familiar seat with Evie and Debbie Haines. They watched proudly as their sons threw on their spikes and warmed up. "How many coaches do you think would've let today happen this way?" Tracie day-dreamed, unaware she was talking aloud.

"One," Debbie and Evie responded together, never breaking stride. By the time they got comfortable, the game was beginning.

Anthony Taylor was the starting Tiger pitcher. He and game one starter Melvin Carter had reversed roles. Anthony was diminutive, but he was tricky. His off-speed pitches made his fastball appear a little faster than it was, but it was pretty good anyway. Melvin was an excellent catcher. The rest of the Tiger lineup, which had come so heartbreakingly close to being up one game to nothing, remained intact.

The Next Level countered with their game one starter Johnnie Hanks. He had only pitched a little more than one inning three days before. Tru was hoping to get at least three or four out of Johnnie today. His breaking pitch, a curve, had been improving with each outing, and Tru was hopeful he would be on today. The only change in The Next Level's lineup was that Darryl Weston took over the catching duties and Robbie Elliot was at first.

The Next Level team could not do a thing with

Anthony Taylor. He kept them off balance all day with an assortment of off speed pitches to go along with his fastball. Every time they expected a fastball, he threw a curve. Every time they thought curve, he came with the heat.

Meanwhile, in their game, the Tigers were not faring much better against Johnnie Hanks. Johnnie had overcome the butterflies he had after his stint in game one. Through the forth inning he had only given up two unearned runs in the third.

In the fifth, the Tigers plated three more runs to take a commanding 5-0 lead. Jeff Hardy chased Johnnie Hanks with a one-out two-run single. Tru called on Brendon, the game one pitching hero, to put out the rally. He was successful but not before Jeff scored the third run of the inning on an infield error.

Back at The Next Level's bench, it was Jerrett Thompson's turn to give an emotional plea to rally his team. "Let's go, man!" he challenged. "I ain't gonna quit. How 'bout y'all? We ain't losin' this game, man! We can do it!"

Tru and Bud stood back and watched. "These kids are doin' it by themselves, Bud," Tru said quietly as he folded his arms in front of him.

"That's what it's all about," the soft-spoken Bud said proudly.

The quiet Next Level bats woke up.

Johnnie Hanks and Chris Williams led off with back-to-back home runs. Lance was up next and this time Tru let him bat instead of pinch hitting with Stan. The noise coming from The Next Level bench got louder when Anthony threw ball one to Lance. It grew when ball two whistled just outside. At ball three, the bench stood up and hugged the chain-link fence in front of them. Lance walked on the fourth pitch. Jerrett followed with another walk. That brought Darryl Weston to the plate.

The first pitch to Darryl got to the backstop and both

Lance and Jerrett moved up. Darryl sent Anthony's first strike in nine pitches screaming into right. Lance scored easily. Jerrett rounded third as the ball was gathered by right fielder Andre Clayton. He came up firing but could not get the speedy shortstop. Darryl took second on the throw.

Pandemonium broke loose on The Next Level bench and in the bleachers behind them. There were even some high fives being exchanged down the right field line.

Melvin Carter took a slow walk to the mound. He draped his arm around gutsy Anthony Taylor. No one could hear the words being exchanged, but all the parents, even those from The Next Level, wanted to help comfort the stricken pitcher. Melvin finally turned away and walked the forty-six feet to his catching position as Anthony wiped his eyes.

Showing the poise many major leaguers lack, the twelve-year-old regrouped and struck out the side, stranding Darryl at second.

The Tigers took the field tentatively in the bottom of the sixth, precariously nursing their one run lead.

Lance stepped up as The Next Level came off the field for the bottom of the sixth. Barely in the dugout, he began their trademark chant.

"It's time to go where?" Lance shouted.

"To the next level!" the team answered back.

"It's time to go *where*?"

Tru watched silently. Intense feelings of pride made him unable to speak.

"To the next level!"

"It's time to go WHERE?"

"To the next level!"

Unfortunately, Anthony Taylor had other ideas.

He retired the first two batters with ease. Chris

Williams popped up, and Stan Coles, this time pinch-hitting for Lance, grounded out.

Jerrett Thompson was their last hope. He deposited Anthony's next pitch two hundred twenty feet into left center. That quickly, it was 5-5.

Darryl Weston was next and he reached base. It was one of those balls that official scorers would argue over many times whether it should be scored as a hit or an error.

It was a "tweener," an incredible dilemma for an infielder, and it chopped at second baseman Jeff Hardy. If this kind of ball is charged, it will almost certainly result in a nearly impossible in-between hop to try and field. On the other hand, if the ball is not charged and it is permitted to take that extra bounce to make it easier to field, there will almost certainly be no chance to throw the runner out at first.

Jeff chose the first option. He very nearly made the play.

That brought Brendon Banks to the plate.

It also brought the sheer joy and utter sadness that Little League baseball can produce. Brendon belted a two-run homer to bring the Tigers' season to a heartbreaking end and The Next Level's to an ultimate high.

The final score was 7-5. The Next Level had swept the Tigers en route to the championship of the Papa Dean League.

The team went crazy with joy. The scene in the infield was sheer madness. It was a sea of bodies entangled, jumping in the air and on each other.

After all the emotion was spent, the two teams met at home for their last handshake.

One champion was congratulated and another champion was consoled.

Chapter 24

The Mayor's Cup

Who would have thought, Tru mused, *that in our first year of existence we would be in line to play for the Mayor's Cup.*

The major league All-Star Game had been held at Three Rivers Stadium the previous season and now government officials decided to hold other festivities there hoping to hype Pittsburgh. Having kids involved, they believed, would make baseball and the city look good.

Teams from all over the city, forty-eight of them, became involved. To earn the honor of playing at the stadium would take four wins. To actually win the tournament, five.

In the first round, The Next Level drew a team from the Ninth Ward of Pittsburgh encompassing an area consisting of the neighborhoods of Garfield, Lawrenceville, and Bloomfield as their opponent.

The morning of the game in which Brendon Banks would be on the hill, he was hot. When a pitcher throws a no-hitter, he does not need much help. Brendon only allowed four walks and never permitted a runner to get beyond second base in posting the shutout.

Darryl Weston drove home the only runs Brendon would need when he tripled in the fourth with the bases loaded. The icing on the cake was provided by Johnnie Hanks, with a two-run shot in the sixth. Darryl closed the scoring with a two-run homer of his own later in the sixth. Their 8-0 win propelled the team into the second round. It also propelled them into a collision with an old nemesis.

Morningside.

Some of the kids had been on the precursor to The Next Level team the year before, when they lost the heart-breaker to Morningside in the first round. They remembered. The parents who were there also remembered.

"Oh, I just can't believe we're playin' them again!" Evie said to Ron Haines and Tracie Elliott as they watched the boys practice on Paulson Field. "Remember how they cheated us and how rude them parents was?"

"They sure did squeeze the plate on us," Ron said matter-of-factly.

"That was the worst game I've ever been to," Tracie added. "Those parents put so much pressure on their kids to win; it was terrible. I don't know how kids are able to play when their parents act like that. Or how those white kids can practice tolerance when their parents act like bigots. It sure would be sweet to beat them!"

"Oh yeah, with all their attitude? I'd love to see us beat Morningside," Evie said.

After practice, Tru gathered the boys for a short talk. "I know you kids that played last year remember the bitter taste we all got when we lost to Morningside; so I won't go over that. I know you feel we got cheated. But all that's over," Tru said calmly. "Put aside your bad feeling and think only about now. If you think it was tough last year, if you think winnin' up at Ammons was tough, listen up! Morningside will be even more difficult. Believe me when I tell you, you're up against not only a good team, but history. Morningside has a reputation. Somewhere along the line, you're gonna have to beat that rep also. It will show itself in one form or another. Guaranteed. Remember, it's gonna be tough out there. But if you beat them, it will be the best feeling you have had yet. So, Desire, Determination, and Dedication and on to the Next Level! See you tomorrow! Get some rest!"

The place they were to play Morningside was the same as the previous year, Mellon Park. That was where the similarities ended. The Next Level team wasn't wet behind the ears anymore. The team now had a name. And the boys had been through some tough times together. They weren't just going to field a team from the so-called ghettos. They were there to win. They had a goal: Three Rivers Stadium.

"Morningside's pitcher Timm Sibetto's technique is nearly flawless, and he possesses a pretty good fastball," Tru observed. He told his kids, "Be aggressive. This boy will always be around the plate."

The Next Level lost the coin toss and would be the visitors. After a one-out single by Byron Knight, Sibetto struck out the next two batters, Chris Williams and Darryl Weston.

Johnnie Hanks was the starting pitcher for The Next Level. He ran into trouble immediately by walking the first two hitters.

"Look at this bullshit!" Antonio Senior yelled to no one in particular. "They're squeezin' him again, just like last year! They just gonna take it away from these kids! Ain't this a bunch of shit!" he said, alluding to the fact that the plate for The Next Level was different than the one Morningside's pitcher was throwing to. "Open your damn eyes!" he screamed at the ump.

The scene got worse. Tru, who usually kept his cool, was almost ejected for arguing balls and strikes. Five walks and two hits later, Morningside had scored six runs. For The Next Level the best that could be said about the game was that Morningside had not scored more.

As his boys came off the field, Tru met them at the third base line. "So they think they have you beat," he said waiting to see their reaction. In their eyes, he did not see frustration, disgust, defeat. He saw anger. *That's good*, he told himself.

When they got back on the field, Jerrett led off depositing a two-ball one-strike fastball about twenty feet past the cones in left field. Joe Foster tripled on the next pitch and Stan Coles brought him home with a single. The comeback stalled, at least momentarily, when Brendon, Lance, and John Doe fanned to end the inning.

Morningside picked up another run in their half of the second on a two-out singled by left fielder Michael Mazzata.

Johnnie Hanks got that run back when he led off the third with a solo home run to bring Morningside's lead down to 7-3.

After holding the opponents scoreless for the first time that day, Darryl Weston led off The Next Level's fourth with a single. Momentum built when Jerrett drilled a Sibetto curve ball and began running hard. Seeing the ball sail majestically over the fence, he slowed his sprint to a slow jog and thrust his right arm up in the air, fist clenched. He was going to savor every second of his homer. As he came to the last few feet of circling the bases, he walked. Then he stomped his right foot down on home plate as if saying to Morningside, *Here, take that!* Turning his head, Jerrett looked at the Morningside coaches for a couple of seconds as his foot rested on the plate and his hands on his hips. Finally, like a stallion, he threw his head back and trotted towards The Next Level bench.

Johnnie Hanks had found his groove. He struck out eight of the nine Morningside hitters during the next three innings. As the sixth inning began, The Next Level had cut Morningside's lead to 7-5.

Four pitches later, the game was tied. Marcus Haines took a strike-one fastball on the outside corner before roping a shot in the right center gap. The relay throw from Morningside's shortstop was good, but not good enough to prevent Marcus from being safe on his headfirst slide into third. Byron Knight took ball one before crushing a fastball well past the cones in dead center.

For The Next Level spectators the jubilation was immediate. Parents were hugging and the players yelled their identifying chant, led by Lance.

"It's time to go where?"

"To The Next Level!"

"Where?"

"To The Next Level!"

Morningside's team, coaches and parents, on the other hand, were not in a celebratory mood. They threw insults at The Next Level team and pleaded with the ump to "do something" about the cheering.

When the parents of Tru's team heard the attack, they joined Lance's cheer. The men moved from their position down the left field line behind their wives and John Doe's pacing father. They joined him in his nervous walk.

Sibetto settled down and retired Chris Williams on a strikeout. Darryl Weston followed Chris and singled through the infield to right. That bought up Jerrett.

It also brought out Morningside's coach. A new pitcher, Jeff Selcio, was brought in and Timm Sibetto switched positions, with the left-handed Selcio coming on to face Jerrett.

Morningside's fans now yelled support to their own team while still stabbing at The Next Level. "He was lucky before!" one called out. "Just throw it over, Jeff. He ain't no hitter!"

Now it was not Jerrett who was angry; he probably did not even hear the fan.

Jim and Peachy Thompson did. "Well, that boy ain't no pitcher!" Peachy retaliated. Tru watched them. This was not good-natured competition. It was getting ugly.

The first pitch to Jerrett was a ball. It nearly hit the plate but it did not stop Morningside parents from challenging the umpire's eyesight. On the second pitch, strike one was called when it split the center of the plate. The Next Level parents thought it had almost beaned Jerrett.

The third pitch would have been called a ball had Jerrett not swung, and it would still have been a tie game had the ball not cleared the home run fence by thirty feet. There was no debating this one.

Utterly exhilarated, Jerrett rounded the bases. The anger, like his smash, was gone. His third home run put The Next Level in position to have very sweet revenge. Three outs were all that separated them from round three of the Mayor's Cup.

For a few moments there was silence from Morningside's spectators. Then it started.

"Call the game, ump!" a Morningside fan hollered from the stands, speaking directly to the umpire. "It's dark out there. Someone will get hurt!"

"You got any lights?" cried another.

Minutes after the first words about darkness, the umpire stepped from behind the plate. He looked up at the still sunlit sky and rubbed his hand through his hair as if he was having a hard time making a decision.

Then the umpire made his way from behind the plate towards the city official required to be at every game of the Mayor's Cup Tournament.

Tru knew what was going on. He went ballistic. His eyes seemed to double in size, sweat poured from under his cap, and his muscles tensed as his body sprang from the bench and followed the umpire. "Don't stop this game, man!" Tru was incredulous as he tried to keep Coach Bart, who was right behind him, from physically challenging the ump.

"Everybody out here can see just fine! Let's play ball!" Bart said menacingly over Tru's shoulder, anger contorting his face.

"I can't," the umpire said quietly.

"You gotta be kiddin' me! If it was so dark, why the hell didn't you call the game at the top of the inning? You made the decision to start the inning—you can't stop it now. This is bullshit, man! C'mon!" Tru argued.

"The game goes back to the inning before, right?" suggested Morningside's coach who had followed the others out to the field. "The rule says if an inning can't be completed, the score reverts back to the previous inning and the game is over!"

"That's a bunch of bullshit! You can't call a playoff game in the middle of an inning 'cause of darkness! The ump's gotta call it before the inning is started if he feels it will be dark before the inning can be completed. Once you start an inning, you have to finish it. C'mon now, we've all known that rule since we were little kids. It isn't the same as if it got rained out. Don't tell me you want to win so damn bad that you'd resort to this bullshit! That's pathetic, man!"

Jen, the official scorer and city representative, was confused. She was unfamiliar with the exact rule. Therefore, she did not want to say on record which way the ruling might go. She took the phone numbers of both coaches, "Someone from the city will call with the decision," she said leaving.

By this time, the parents were irate. There were seven or eight brothers playing basketball on the courts next to the field who had become interested in the game as it progressed. They knew none of the kids on The Next Level, nor their parents, but when the game was called they became extremely upset. The situation looked to Tru like it could escalate into a serious physical confrontation between these bystanders and some of the parents of Morningside.

Some people, when they are losing, will do or say damn near anything to win. To Tru, it was just a group of kids being treated unfairly, because another group of parents did not want their kids to lose. To Tru, it was not because the kids were black: they just happened to be black. To the brothers who were playing ball on the nearby court and to the parents, it was *racial* and the ump's decision was *racist*.

Looking around and moving quickly, Tru intervened. "Let's get moving!" he said to Bart and Bud. "Some of these people are gonna start doin' some crazy shit if we stay here and continue to argue. Get the kids in the cars and let's go to Plum. Tell the parents we'll talk to them out there."

Everyone moved fast; Tru succeeded in preventing an ugly situation from occurring but he was unsure whether or not the scene would influence the city's decision about the game.

With the Next Level players and their parents in cars, the caravan drove to Plum Borough, ten miles east of Pittsburgh. They still had a night tournament game to compete in. After arriving at the field, Tru talked to the parents about what was going on. "The city has no choice, I think, but to rule in our favor. Which means the game will start again from where we left off. Byron will be on third with two outs and

The Next Level up nine to seven." He also informed them that the Morningside coach had argued the score should revert back to the previous inning and they should be declared the winners.

During the tournament game at Plum, Tru telephoned city officials, but he received no clarification. That bothered him. The more they delayed the decision, the more he figured it favored Morningside. If the officials were going to rule that the game should be completed, he reasoned, they would want to do that as quickly as possible. That way the tournament could continue and finish on schedule. The one definite commitment was the final game at Three Rivers Stadium. That could not be rescheduled.

In the bargain, the dejected Next Level team now got shellacked in the tournament game. The score was 12-0 in three innings. No one on the bench or in the stands cared. Their minds and conversations were completely on Morningside.

After the game, Tru met with the parents on hand. "Here is the situation as I know it. The game will either be picked up where we left off, with us ahead nine to seven in the top of the sixth, or the score will revert back to the fifth, with us losin' seven to five, and be called 'cause of darkness, which means we lose," he said as the group of eight adults sat together in the bleachers.

"How the hell can they call that game? That can't be right!" Evie was nearly in tears.

"I'll tell you one thing, they won't get away with it!" Tracie said emotionally. "I don't know exactly what we'll do or who we got to talk to but there is no way they're gonna do our kids like this. It's ridiculous!"

"You can't call a game because of darkness after the inning has started," Jim Thompson said calmly. "That's the rule. How are they gonna try and justify it?"

"I know, I know, I know," Tru responded gently but firmly. "All we can do right now is go home and wait. I think we'll be okay, because they can't blatantly cheat like that. Just sit tight until I hear from someone with the Mayor's Cup. I'll call y'all as soon as they tell me something, anything. Tell the kids everything should be all right. Tell them we'll have practice tomorrow at six at Mellon. I'm sure by then we'll know what's up."

As they all walked away to the darkened parking lot at Plum Field, Ron Haines was not optimistic. "Mark my words, baby," he said quietly to his wife, Debbie, "they're gonna take that game away from our kids, as sure as I'm black!"

Throughout the night and early morning, Tru received no word from any Mayor's Cup official. Around noon, as Tru was picking up Byron Knight and his younger brother Devin from day camp, he received a call on his cellular phone from Linda Brown, an official with the Mayor's Cup.

"I'm sorry, Tru, but the ruling went to Morningside," the soft voice said amid the honking horns and roaring buses of a humid downtown Pittsburgh lunch hour.

To Tru, everything stopped. There were no cars, no commotion, no people rushing all around him. The only thing he heard was Linda's voice and his own blood pounding.

Tru went off. He began a verbal assault on Linda. The volume of his booming voice attracted the attention of pedestrians as well as motorists. What stopped Tru from continuing his shouting was a Pittsburgh police officer, motioning him to move his car or else.

To Linda's credit, she took the abuse and let him vent. Finally, Tru said:

"How the hell am I gonna tell these kids they lost, Linda? You tell me that! How do I face them? How do I tell a bunch of kids we lost when we were winning?"

"Tru, I'm really sorry."

"Sorry doesn't cut it, Linda. You've got a serious problem y'all have to deal with. Here we have an all-white team from Morningside, an association established for fifty years or so, being given a win when they were losing to an all-black team from Homewood, Wilkinsburg, and East Hills in their first year of existence. The umpire, or the city official, gave no indication, no warning that the game might be called due to darkness. Nothing! Only as soon as the black team takes the lead, the game is called. I don't want this to become a racial issue, but the parents and others. . . ."

Linda broke in. "Do you think it is, Tru?"

Tru paused, his voice steel-edged. "You know I don't play that card, but I can't help what others will believe or do."

"I hope you don't incite that type of thinking, Tru!"

"I can't stop them, especially with what this looks like. It would've been different if the umpire had said before the inning started that the game was canceled. Instead, he waits for us to take the lead. Then some parent from Morningside begins to yell out to call the game for darkness when the damn streetlights haven't even come on yet. What would you think, Linda?"

There was only silence from the black female on the other side of the conversation.

"You'll never know how hard and how long these kids worked for this," Tru told her. "For you or anyone else to take their dream away from them unfairly is unbelievable. It's an injustice and you know it. I will not be a part of it. We're practicing today at six at Mellon. You send some officials down there. Better yet, tell the mayor to come and tell these kids they lost. I will not!"

"Okay, Tru. I'll ask them to be there."

Tru phoned all the parents one by one. They were irate. Each one said he or she planned to be at practice that night to let the city officials know precisely what they thought of the ruling.

By six the tension easily cut through the haze and the humidity that saturated the obscenely hot summer air. It was an easy day to be angry.

Tru saw the official car pull up. Linda Brown was accompanied by Lou Polito and Gus Martinelli, the other administrators of the Mayor's Cup. Tru approached the trio in one last-ditch effort to get them to change their minds and, if he couldn't, to warn them of the anger the parents were feeling.

As he approached the group, he noticed they were all smiling. Without saying a word, Tru knew the ruling had been reversed.

"Why?" he asked, overjoyed but confused.

"Thank Linda," Gus replied. "We had you on conference call this morning. We heard everything you said to her."

"I don't know if we'd call it eloquent," chuckled Lou. "But it sure was convincing!"

The three heads of the Mayor's Cup walked slowly over to the parents and players of The Next Level. After a quick explanation of who they were, Gus told the group why they were here.

"How does tomorrow morning at ten sound to resume the game?" he asked.

"Right where you left off!" Lou added.

For the kids and parents frowns turned to smiles, anger to excitement.

The tournament officials left and wished the team good luck. The coaches congratulated Tru. Coach Bud turned to the players and parents and said softly, "Three Rivers Stadium!"

The next morning at ten The Next Level took the field for the bottom of the sixth in their game against Morningside with the score 9-7 in their favor. It was another excruciatingly hot and humid day. Three outs separated them from advancing to the quarter finals of the Mayor's Cup. Brendon was on the mound for The Next Level and somehow, despite the excitement, he looked like he'd gotten some sleep.

The game began again. Brendon walked the first two batters before striking out the third. Another walk loaded the bases with only one out and brought up Morningside's cleanup hitter, Denny Russell, who had doubled in the first two runs of the ball game.

Tru went to talk to Brendon and called the infield to the mound. "Beatin' pretty fast, huh?" he smiled as he placed his hand over Brendon's heart. "There's nothing to worry about, man. These guys got your back! Am I right?" He looked at the infield nodding in agreement. They might have been unsure but it did not show. "I'll tell you what. Let's bring the infield up, get a grounder, turn two, and we're outta here!" Tru said confidently, flipping the ball back to Brendon. "Just concentrate on making good throws!"

Brendon's first pitch to Russel, a big righthander, was a fastball on the outside corner. Russel hit it hard all right, but he tried to pull to the left. What results when a righty tries to pull an outside pitch is usually a grounder to short, or maybe to the pitcher.

Brendon fielded the ball cleanly and fired to Darryl Weston to force the run out at the plate. Darryl had the option of throwing the ball to any base to complete the double play. Thinking quickly, he chose his easiest throw, to third.

From the angle along the first base line where Tru sat on the bench, the throw was offline. Chris Williams was at third and Tru saw that he was already waiting for the throw.

Stan Coles was in left and he reacted perfectly and was in good position to back up the play. Tru did not think two runs would score unless the ball got by Stan, so what happened next was amazing.

Chris Williams contorted his ten-year-old frame. Not only did he shorthop the offline throw, he miraculously kept his right foot on the bag.

The game was over.

The Next Level had won!

The Morningside coach was stunned. He did not say a word as The Next Level's players, coaches, and parents swarmed the field.

Chapter 25

Moving On Up

After Morningside, The Next Level knocked off Sacred Heart by an 11-4 count. Then they jumped on Sheridan for six runs in the first. The Next Level could taste victory by the sixth inning.

"Steeerike one!" yelled the ump as the ball popped into Darryl Weston's glove.

"That had to be eighty miles an hour!" Bart said to Coach Bud. "C'mon, Robbie! Three more outs, baby, and we're at Three Rivers!"

The next pitch peppered Darryl's glove again as the hitter helplessly flailed away. "Attaboy, Robbie!" Tru jumped off the bench. "Now you're smokin', baby! That's what we're talkin' about!"

Robbie's next pitch was what baseball players call the radio ball. It could be heard, but not seen.

"Steeerike three!" bellowed the umpire under the misty lights of Banksville Field. "Batter's out!"

Two outs and the trip to the stadium was theirs.

"You gotta want it. . . ."

"To win it. . . ."

"But we want it more!"

The Sheridan rooters became louder as the game neared its end. Even though The Next Level was only two outs away from eliminating Sheridan and had an 8-3 lead, Sheridan would not quit.

Their attitude began to affect Robbie. He walked three straight hitters. With each pitch, the chants became louder. He struck out the next batter, momentarily regaining his poise, but the incessant chant continued.

Two more straight walks made the score 8-5 in favor of The Next Level. Tru knew Robbie was out of gas. He went to the mound and made his last move.

The only pitcher left with any experience was Jerrett. Tru sent Byron to short, Marcus to second, Robbie to first, and Brendon to left.

"Just throw strikes, baby!" Tru winked confidently. "Keep the ball down and let's get out of here!"

His next pitches seemed to be right on the corner but Jerrett never seemed to get a call from the ump. He walked the first two batters to make the score 8-7 with the bases still loaded and two outs.

"C'mon, ump!" Tru pleaded as he went out to the mound for the last time. "You can't give them both sides of the plate!" Turning to Jerrett, his voice became calm. "Son, you're in it for the ride. You're the best pitcher we're using." Very slowly, Tru said, "G-e-t h-i-m!"

The first two pitches to the next hitter were right down the pipe. The Sheridan hitter fouled the next pitch, then Jerrett threw two consecutive balls. The roar of the crowd was incredible. No one could hear anything.

As Jerrett delivered the two-ball, two-strike pitch, Tru buried his head between his hands as they rested on his knees. He only listened.

"Ball!" bellowed the ump.

Behind the bleachers, Ron Haines, Jim Thompson and Buzzy Elliott, all with hands in their pockets, were the epitome of cool. Their wives, Debbie, Peachy, and Tracie, were wrecks. Their fingernails were bitten to the quick and they were now resorting to biting their lips. Evie, who had been in the stands, knelt in the grass next to the bleachers, unwittingly pulling out big clumps of grass and placing them on her lap.

Looking around, Tru observed everything: the beautiful summer night, the temperature in the seventies, the brilliant stars in the cloudless sky, and, through the mist, lightning bugs lighting up the woods behind the bleachers. It was a night made for baseball.

It was a moment frozen in time.

Then he looked at the parents and saw the contrast of nature's beauty and their frayed emotions. He turned his attention to Jerrett and wondered what he would say to him if they lost. How could he let him know that it was only a game?

The tension rose.

Suddenly, Jerrett knelt down. Right there on the mound. Tru knew what he was doing. Jerrett was taking himself to the next level.

He stood up, turned, and walked slowly to the mound, never taking his eyes off the hitter. The decibel level of the noise from the spectators grew even higher. Tru said nothing. Did nothing. He waited.

Jerrett was set to deliver the full count pitch. Ball four, and it would be tied. Strike three and it would be over.

The pitcher went into his windup.

That is when everything seemed to go into slow motion.

The fastball slowed as it moved towards the plate.

Tru watched the hitter. He saw the panic in his eyes when the boy realized it was a strike.

There was complete silence as he swung.

Too late.

Darryl Weston reached Jerrett first.

Then Coach Bart. He hoisted Jerrett on his shoulders as the rest of The Next Level team danced, hugged each other, threw their hats into the air, and shouted how unbelievable it was, over and over again.

Jerrett sat on top of Coach Bart's tall shoulders, with his fists clenched skyward. On his face was the largest smile ever seen, and tears of joy flooded his cheeks.

Parents took turns waving the team's black and teal The Next Level flag, as if they were passing the Stanley Cup around. United, standing in the bleachers, they proudly watched the accomplishment of their sons being recognized.

The Sheridan fans, and players, were gracious in defeat. There were smiles on their faces, too. They embraced The Next Level players and parents, celebrating with them.

Tru stood alone. The emotion of the season and the emotion of what had just unfolded before his eyes staggered him.

"They have no idea the joy they've given me," he said out loud. "I am blessed. I am truly blessed."

The tailgate party began at Three Rivers Stadium

around ten in the morning. Luckily, the Mayor's Cup championship game with Brookline was not until one-thirty.

"The Sheridan game was the best!" Evie said proudly as she put her hot dog in a bun and slapped on ketchup and relish. "I thought I was goin' to die!"

"Jerrett's face," Peach agreed, "said it all. To see the emotion of the whole season explode on that one pitch was somethin' I'll never forget!"

"Even he would have loved that!" Antonio Williams, Senior said as he gazed over at the bronze statue of Roberto Clemente outside Gate A of Three Rivers Stadium. "I wouldn't have believed it if I wasn't there!"

When the party was over, the parents who stayed to clean up were still talking about the game.

"A full count on that kid, too!" Brenda Weston exclaimed as she put dirty paper plates in the garbage cans. "It was either gonna be a tie game or a big win!"

"I'm still nervous!" Tracie Elliot added as she held up her trembling hands. She shook her head and tears welled in her brown eyes. "But to see those kids run out there, and to see Jerrett, who hardly smiled all year, with that, excuse my French, big-ass grin on his beautiful face, I've never felt anything like that in my whole life!"

"I don't know, the Morningside game was it for us," Ron Haines said as he and Debbie sat back on lawn chairs. "When the Mayor's Cup people came over to Mellon and told our kids they were going to be able to continue the game, that meant a lot."

"I gotta go with the Sheridan game," Joyce Harvey said wistfully. "Remember how gracious the Sheridan fans were? I think that added to the whole enjoyment of the game.

It was so different from the tension we had with Morningside. It was plain fun. They were cheering, we were cheering. And after it was over, they were happy for our kids. And we were sad for theirs. That is one of my best memories."

"How about the games up at Ammons?" Tracie suggested. "Those were pretty intense, too."

"I don't care what y'all say," Evie said standing, "Sheridan was the game. Jerrett just rose to the occasion when he had that full count. If that were me, I would've been so scared I couldn't have moved. I'll never forget how he stood so tall when all their fans were screamin' and all us was screamin'. How he was able to pitch the ball, let alone strike out that boy is beyond me. I was so proud of him and all our kids." She began to sob.

She looked over at the players scattered over the immense parking lot outside Gate A. Celebrating.

"It's their day. One of the best."

John Doe floated around everywhere. He visited the parents for a while and then the players, always finding something to kid about. Always smiling.

Darryl Weston could barely hold back his tears as he stared at the statue of the most famous Pirate who'd ever played—his father had been a big Roberto Clemente fan.

Brendon and Marcus were acting out the last play of the Sheridan game. Brendon was pretending to be Jerrett and Marcus was playing the role of Darryl Weston. Brendon threw his glove thirty feet in the air and shot both fists skyward as Marcus threw off his catcher's mask and rushed him.

Joe Foster, Jerrett Thompson, Johnnie Hanks, and Chris Williams were playing catch while each pretended to be his favorite major leaguer.

Todd Hill and Byron Knight raced around the paper-plate bases they'd put on the level concrete at the bottom of the ramp leading to Gate A.

Tru's thoughts turned to the game that afternoon. Robbie Elliot would be pitching today. He was resting in the shade provided by the towering obelisk that marked the Gate A entrance to Three Rivers.

Manny and Lance were jumping off the three-foot-high wall, seeing who could perform the most death-defying twists and turns, while still landing on his feet.

Tru glanced at Lance whose success not only as a team player but at school meant so much to him. Then, with pride, he looked at the others. The smiles the boys had on their faces gave him the warmest feeling he ever had in his life. These kids, especially Lance, had changed his life forever. The outcome of today's game was meaningless. They had already attained their goal.

He called the boys over to the statue of Roberto Clemente and looking at it and then at them, said, "You're all real champions. Thanks for a great year, fellas. And onto the next level!"

Darryl Weston hoisted the flag of The Next Level. It was black satin with the face of the Tasmanian Devil in the center. To the left, printed in large teal letters bordered in white, was *The Next Level*. To the right were the words, *The Beast From The East*, signifying the neighborhoods they came from. He waved the flag proudly.

Then they all marched into the stadium together.

Epilogue

After being dropped off by Joe, the truck driver who had been so kind, Tru continued walking. He crossed many small boroughs and villages in his home state of Pennsylvania, meeting all kinds of strangers who helped him. Sometimes it was a cup of coffee, sometimes it was a firm handshake, sometimes it was a wish of good luck. Others gave money to his cause.

He saw firsthand the untapped goodness in people. He gained strength and it propelled him onward through the bitterness of inclement weather, rain, and sleet, and snow.

Whenever he needed an extra push, he telephoned one of the kids. "Dang, Coach Tru, you in Philadelphia?" Then he heard a yell, "He's in Philadelphia, Mom!" They all wanted to know the same thing. "Where are you, Coach Tru? Is it cold? How far you got to go?"

Tru had given each team member a map to keep so that when he told them where he was, the boy could find the spot and, in a sense, as they all traced the route of his trip, be with him. Just seeing the name on the map made them feel closer to this man who had done so much for them and was now making this trek to gain publicity and funds from national urban and children's organizations so that the Next Level could expand from a little league team into a sports/learning complex for thousands of inner city kids.

Day after day passed. Tru walked on.

One Thursday night in December Tru phoned Coach Bud.

"I'm in New Jersey, Bud!" Tru's frozen voice called out.

Bud couldn't speak.

"What's up, Bud?" Tru asked. "Didn't you hear me? I'm in Jersey, baby! New York's next!"

"I never thought you could make it. Not with this weather and you on foot."

"I had to make it, Bud. This is for the kids."

Words never came easy for Bud, but this time he spoke from the heart. "Tru, you'll probably never know how much what you're doing means to them. They come up here all the time: Jerrett, Darryl, Marcus. This is all they talk about. Sometimes they laugh and say you must be crazy, but, boy oh boy, you can just see the pride in them, how important it makes them feel. God bless you, Tru."

"Tell them knuckleheads it would've been a much easier walk if we would have won the Mayor's Cup, Bud!" he said, not caring in the least that in the end they had fallen to Brookline in the finals that summer day at Three Rivers Stadium, by a 7-3 score.

Bud chuckled and said, "Yeah, but a thirty-three and seven won-lost record ain't all that bad now, Tru!"

"Not bad. We were and are some great team."

"It was a heckuva year, wasn't it? And now this, Bud. See if you can get a few of the kids together Saturday. I should be pulling into the Big Apple about then. I'll call them then."

Tru and Bud talked for a short while longer and then Tru was back on the road.

Tru spent Christmas Day in Princeton. There were less than fifty miles to go.

His pace became slower and more reflective. His dream of The Next Level Youth Complex was so vivid in his mind he felt it already existed.

He kept alive his picture of where the baseball field would be: in the south part of the parking lot up in the East Hills Shopping Center. He visualized once again the dormitories and computer classrooms right where the old Giant Eagle was. The swimming pool where Horne's was. Audio/video labs, a library, the ice and roller rinks, as always he could see it all.

On December twenty-seventh, Ramon "Tru" Dixon looked across the Upper Bay Inlet, gazing at the Statue of Liberty.

Then Tru continued walking toward the New York line. When he reached the city line he found a telephone booth and called Bud. "All the kids are here," Bud said proudly.

Tru talked to each one. The last boy to whom he spoke was Lance.

"Thanks, Coach, for walkin' there for us," the young man said passionately. "We wish we was there with you."

Tru said his voice breaking. "Hey, baby, y'all been with me every step of the way!"

Then Bud got on the phone.

"I've reached the city!" Tru cried.

"Congratulations, Tru!" Bud replied emotionally. "How's it feel to be done?"

"Done? Oh no, Bud, we're not done. We're only starting!" Tru said definitively. "It's time to go to The Next Level."

Expressions

My experience with The Next Level little league baseball team was great. It gave me the chance to meet a lot of new friends from all different communities like East Hills, Wilkinsburg, Penn Hills, and Homewood. This team brought us together as a unit. Our practices were hard but I hung in there. We had to do three push-ups every time we dropped or missed a ball. When I first started out I probably did at least 100 push-ups a day. It was hard but it improves your skills and made me think harder. There are drills that have you working a lot and make you tired and there were times when I wanted to quit, but I didn't give up because it kept me off the streets and out of trouble. All that work paid off when we won a championship in the Popa Dean's Little League baseball league and had our awards banquet at Sandcastle. And last but not least we entered in the B.I.G. League little league baseball tournament, also called the Mayor's Cup. We went undefeated to the championship at Three Rivers Stadium but unfortunately we lost 7-3 to Brookline.

Darrell 'Manny' Wright
11 years old
Homewood

In this league we learned more. They took more time to teach us. In the other league they just wanted to win. We learned not to give up. We never had a home field or home game. We were always playing on someone else's field. In some games they would talk about us. We also had fun and we always got along. In this league it was not just about winning, it was for us to learn not to give up and that you mostly would be on some one else's turf and we learned to play good solid baseball. When I was in the other league I played with people who were not as good as me so I was not really getting any better. But in this league there were lots of kids who were better than me so I would always learn more.
Chris Williams
10 years old
Wilkinsburg

One day the door bell rang and there were two men standing on my front porch. One I recognized as Bart Hanks and the other was introduced to me as Tru. They wanted to know if my son, Darryl could play baseball for this new team they were trying to form. I knew Darryl had a love for baseball and would stop at nothing to play or practice the game. So I said, "Yes, sure, why not?" All winter long this young man whose name I knew only as Tru would come and pick up my son in this little red Jeep full of kids to practice in the East Hills School gym. Sometimes they wouldn't come home until 10:30 p.m. I would worry because it was on a school night. But when I thought it out they were doing something positive with the kids instead of selling drugs or robbing people. As time rolled on I watched Darryl's attitude mellow out, taking more pride in himself, reasoning with difficult situations, and just growing up right in front of my eyes. I thought to myself, "Who is this man and just what is he saying to my twelve year old child to bring about this change? Every time I said something to him his response would be coach Tru said that. He even has his younger brother brainwashed with the coach Tru syndrome. As a mother I began to ask around town about coach Tru. I couldn't find one person that had anything negative to say. When a friend of mine told me that on his lunch breaks years ago he would sit under a tree and read the dictionary I knew he was different. In early January I lost my husband. This had a tremendous impact on our family. First I had to find counseling for my three sons and I did. But Darryl Jr. refused. He told the psychologist there was nothing they could do to bring his dad back (sign of depression). When he was asked if there was someone who he could confide in, his response was coach Tru. I really knew then that this man would become the light of his life. I continued to pray and hope that God would give Coach Tru the right words to say to Darryl and whatever he needed to hear in time of his sorrow. He knew coach Tru wasn't his dad, but he became a great replica for him. Through all the pain and hurt my child experienced he has learned to hold his head high, speak his mind, and barrel his chest out with pride. And most of all to step to The Next Level when times get hard. Not only I but our whole family thanks Coach Tru for saving little Darryl mentally. Coach Tru, just remember every time you take a step and raise your foot up there's a little boy stepping in your prints that you leave behind. So continue to be strong and walk diligent in your works and as always I will continue to pray for you and the team as you move to The Next Level.

Brenda Weston

This past summer was the best I've ever had because I got to meet new friends from other communities. My best friend over the summer was Coach Tru because whenever we were together we had fun. Even in serious practices he made it fun. I don't know how, but he did. I also had fun with my teammates. Well, I've really been having fun with some of my teammates such as Jerrett, Brendon, Johnny, Marcus, Joe, Antonio, Byron, and Evan and a few others, since I was eight when I played for Wilkinsburg. I had two memorable highlights this season. The first was our tournament game against Wilkinsburg who I played for last year. I hit the game winning homer off Jermaine Stewart who I've been playing with since I was eight. The second highlight was playing at Three Rivers Stadium like the pros. That was all coach Tru was talking about back in February. We had to practice at least 100 times this year. Some were serious, some weren't but they were all fun. That's what coach Tru always said "It's all about fun." And fun it was. Now that I really think about it, it was all worth the hot practices, coming home from school doing homework, and going to practice even when I didn't feel like going. Oh yeah it was all worth it and the saying I'll never forget, "How far do you wanna go?" The coaches would ask us that and we would say, "The Next Level", which was our name and that meant trying to be the very best we could to me. So I'll never forget that saying, never.

I personally would like to say thanks to all the coaches, parents, and players of The Next Level for a great summer.
Darryl (Sponge) Weston
12 years old
Homewood

I enjoyed playing for The Next Level. It made my attitude change. It showed me to give 110% in whatever I do. We had good coaches. It made my baseball skills good.

Byron Knight
Age 11
Penn Hills

This season was fun. It was superb! Before The Next Level started I called Coach Tru and asked him if I could be on the team and Coach Tru said "Okay." I called some of my friends and told them I was going to play for The Next Level. Oh yeah, our school grades were always on Coach Tru's agenda. "How are you doing in school?" would be his first question every time he met you. We started practicing in February. The first rule was, be on time. Later on we found out what to be on time meant. I told my parents I have to be on time because Coach Tru takes no excuses. One day I was late and got to see the consequences of it. Laps, laps, and more laps around the field before I got to practice that day. Every day we did push-ups and we got used to it. The first game we played was against the Northside All-Stars and we beat them. The field was in gang territory. There were gang members watching the game. The best game we played was against the Tigers in the championship game. We were losing 5 to 0 through four innings. Then we scored 4 runs in the fifth inning, with 2 homers by Chuckie Jr. and Chris Williams. Then in the sixth I was up with 2 outs, nobody on, losing 5 to 4 and the count was 2 and 2. I looked down the third base line and Coach Tru said, "This one isn't over with yet." I hit a homer to deep left field. That tied the game, 5 to 5. Then Brendon got up to bat and he hit a homer to win the game. We won the Championship.

When we played Wilkinsburg in the Swissvale Tournament, we beat them after they were talking all that mess. This was another close game. Then we got in The Big League Little League Tournament. The rules were if you beat four teams, you get to play at Three Rivers Stadium. We had a tailgate party before the championship game against Brookline. We lost, but it was fun getting the pleasure and experience of playing ball in a stadium where the professionals play.

Jerrett Jamil Thompson
12 years old
East Hills

The Next Level has been a very rewarding experience for my family this summer. When I think of the group I put them into three categories. The players, the team, and the coaches.

The players were there for a reason, they wanted to play ball. My son Robbie told me he was doing his job and played ball the way coach Tru wanted him to play. Not only did our team look professional, they played professionally and acted accordingly on and off the field. Because I love children I took the time to talk and know the kids. They were impressed with what they were involved in with The Next Level.

The team acted as one; they were very together and caring for one another. They took the practices very serious and their skills came to the games. They came to the games wanting to win and feeling they were the better team. The few games they lost were not upsetting because most of the kids thought they had tried their best and did their jobs so 'attitude' was not a real problem.

The coaches were very involved with all of the players. They went way beyond what any parent would expect.

There's a right way and a wrong way to do things and this year they were taught the correct way to participate in sports. A personal thanks has to be given from my heart to Coach Tru, Coach Bart, and Coach Bud for there sincere involvement with the baseball team. I look forward anxiously to next year's involvement with the team, coaches, and parents.
        Tracy Elliott

        What do I think about the 1995 baseball season? This is the best baseball I have seen a group of young kids ever play. The discipline of those kids was unbelievable. This was because of a remarkable coach by the name of Tru Dixon. He was a father-like figure for the team and all he wanted was the kids to know good baseball. He always told them that as long as you played your best you did all you could do. That's called good baseball. There were two other remarkable men who helped keep The Next Level on top. They were coach Bart Hanks and Glenn (Bud) Harvey. The sometimes long hard practices showing the kids how to play good baseball was run by these three men. The Next Level was like a family. Not only did they play baseball together, but they also did other activities together. At times after practice they would go to the movies or went over to coach Bud's house for video and computer game entertainment. The one thing I loved about The Next Level coaches was no matter what the weather may have been there was still practice. If it rained we were inside a gym, if the gym was occupied the team went to a room, pulled out a baseball scenario board and went over game situations. That is called dedication, loyalty, and the love of baseball. For that reason that is why the 1995 Next Level baseball season was the greatest!
        Evelyn Oliver

Congratulations To My Eighteen Sons!

I am grateful and thankful to all of you, The Next Level. I was very fortunate to have been chosen as part of the coaching staff. Coach Tru and Bart are two wonderful people who have quietly made a difference in the lives of all of us who dared to go against the odds and win. They reached out, gave back and became our dedicated, understanding, exciting and inspiring teachers. We became richer people because of their presence. Together my son and I thank you for allowing us to experience a new game of baseball, The Next Level. I applaud the achievement of a dream many would never have sought to reach. On February 1, 1995 I remember coming home from practice at East Hills Elementary School. I searched to get in touch with my feelings and realized that the last time I felt that excited was years ago. What I wanted to offer to the program was to end those nightmarish rumors that we couldn't play the game of baseball on the next level and as you can see we have broken barriers, shattered obstacles, and emerged victorious. There are many moments about our inaugural season that I can write about but the one I remember most is one cold February night at the gym. Coach Tru had a drill called side to side. After performing this drill four or five times Coach Tru would ask the player, "Are you tired yet?" The player would say "yes" but the answer should have been "no." Tru would make him stay and do some more. I didn't know if they were trying to test or challenge him, but they never gave up. These young warriors were so tough within I couldn't believe it. It is no secret that to get where you are going you have to first set sights and when excellence is the goal there are no limits to what can be accomplished. I saw that night the molding of a great team that would win games

every way possible. It is with great pride to say that I have
been part of The Next Level... How Far Do You Want To Go?
Glenn 'Bud' Harvey

For those of you who thought this organization
wouldn't get off the ground, well how do you like us NOW!!
I remember the summer of 1994 when Coach Tru approached
me about my son, Brendon Banks, playing for his team after
his season was over with. I thought who is this man? Why my
son? Well he explained to me who he was, "My name is Tru
Dixon, and you may know me as the umpire for Wilkinsburg.
I'm trying to form my own team and we'll be practicing at
Mellon Park every morning to participate in the Mayor's Cup
Tournament in which the winner will play at Three Rivers
Stadium." As I listened to him explain himself he then
answered my second question. "I've watched all the kids that
signed up for the team, and they are kids with a positive attitude which I will only deal with," he said. So he let me know
in so many words that my son Brendon Banks was that kind of
kid in his eyes. Something that I already had known, but for a
stranger to notice this about my child made me feel blessed. So
son would go to practice my every morning. I was still in
doubt about this team, even though Tru tried his best to assure
me that this was going to be a positive experience for my son.
Although baseball is my son's first love and something he
never failed at, there still was something missing, and that was
fundamentals. Every thing he learned was from watching professional ball on TV. When Coach Tru said he would like my
son to play for him next year, I was ecstatic because he already
had taught these kids fundamentals about baseball in the little
time he had the summer of 1994. Spring 1995 rolled around

and Coach Tru already had his team and it consisted of thirteen boys as well as my son and two other coaches. Coach Tru made a pamphlet up which described in plain words what his goal was with this team. Everything Tru stands for came true before our eyes with the help of Coach Bud and Coach Bart. Practice started, they learned how to catch a ball, throw a ball, pitch a ball, bat a ball. etc. The boys learned the real fundamentals about how to play baseball, which looked good to me. These boys learned how to stick together when they were away from home. They were brothers for each other, whether it be big or little brothers they were there for each other. They played, lost, won, laughed, and cried together. The boys came from every neighborhood in the East End and they all bonded. If you ever thought your son couldn't speak, learn or hear, well I think we all saw something in our children that we never saw before and that was how to reach a goal or help reach a goal. I've never seen a team with such discipline.

Three cheers for Tru, Bud and Bart for sticking together and making this a great season for our kids!

Roslyn Banks

This is the best experience of my life playing with The Next Level. I was so glad when I heard coach Tru wanted me to play for the team. It was an honor to play for The Next Level. Coach Tru, Coach Bart, and Coach Bud taught me discipline, determination, desire, dedication and unity, playing for The Next Level. The next couple of years I look forward to playing for The Next Level. With Coach Tru and the rest of the coaching staff. I will always take another step. I will always take it to "The Next Level".

Brendon Banks
12 years old
Wilkinsburg

Playing for The Next Level was a great experience for me. While playing for The Next Level I learned to keep my body in front of the ball. I learned how to snap-throw a ball. A snap throw ball is when you throw the ball immediately after you catch the ball. I learned that 90% of baseball is mental, like keeping my eye on the ball so I can hit better. This summer I had fun with my friends and teammates. With each win and loss we gained a greater understanding of the game. I got a new nickname, "John Doe". I finally got to play with my cousin and best friend. I liked playing in the catcher position, but most of all I liked just playing good baseball.

Antonio "John Doe" Williams
12 years old
East Hills

The Next Level was a new experience for me. I really liked the team because we were organized and we stuck together. We always played together and never gave up. I really liked Coach Tru, Coach Bart, and Coach Bud. They always helped us and never put us down. When we put our heads down, they helped us pick them up. If it wasn't for them we never would have won the Championship or went to Three Rivers Stadium to play for the Mayor's Cup Championship. I just thank you all for a good season.

Stan Coles
12 years old
Wilkinsburg

I feel the season was good because we had fun, we were a good team because we were taught to never put our heads down.

Devon Knight
8 years old
Penn Hills

This summer I did a lot of growing up. With the help of Coach Tru, I learned responsibility. Responsibility to your teammates and friends. Team spirit and team-work was what 'The Next Level' taught me. I became a better person over the past summer, learning to control my temper and get rid of my attitude. There were many times when Coach Tru made me mad. Doing drills and practicing all the time was not the most fun I ever had, but when the time came to play, I knew all that hard work on the field was paying off. Winning was not everything, but it felt darn good to get to Three Rivers Stadium and play like the pros. Having your name called when you got to bat was such a thrill. It definitely was an experience I shall never forget. Coach Bart and Coach Bud were also very helpful to me over the summer. Every time Coach Bart hit to us, he hit most of the balls over the fence and Coach Bud helped me with my swing, part of their job was to get us hyped and with that they did very well. Coach Tru, Coach Bart, and Coach Bud are the nicest men I know and I would just like to thank them for the opportunity to play on their team. "THANK YOU ! !"

> *Lance McCoy*
> *11 years old*
> *Homewood*

The Next Level was a team that I believe was very productive for their first year. The team stands out more than all the others in the league. The first thing is that it has a standard. That's very important when you have a bunch of kids coming together from different neighborhoods. Not only that but the organization's primary goal is reaching youth who are concerned with more than playing sports. The coaching staff cares not just for winning but for the kids and that's very important to me. They took care of our kids like they were their own. They gave 100%. That's what makes The Next Level.

Jim Coles

When I first played for The Next Level Coach Tru said, "You're with the big boys now." I like doing push-ups. It's fun playing with The Next Level because they buy you things and lots of other stuff. In the tournament we made it to the championship game at Three Rivers Stadium, but before we played we celebrated. We lost in the Three Rivers Stadium championship game. The score was 7-3. It was a fun season though. Oh, I almost forgot, we won the championship when we played in the Popa Dean's League on the Hill. That was the best game I ever saw. It was a fun season.

Bart Hanks, Jr.
8 years old
Wilkinsburg

This year I learned the most I have ever learned in my whole life. We started practice in February inside the gym of East Hills Elementary school. We had some hard practices and if we made a mistake we had to do a Next Level three push-ups for each mistake. In the beginning we made a lot of mistakes but we improved every practice. We didn't just learn a lot of things. We had fun too, like when we had car washes to raise money. We made it to two championships and won one of them. We made it all the way to Three Rivers Stadium by beating 9th Ward, Morningside, Sacred Heart, and Sheridan. In the Morningside game they tried to stop it in the 6th inning for darkness but it wasn't even dark. I could still see even though I wear glasses. We continued the game and won anyway. Nobody could sleep the night before we played at the stadium because we were so excited. We had our awards banquet at Sandcastle which was as fun as Kennywood Park and this was the best year of baseball I can ever remember.

Johnny Hanks
12 years old
Wilkinsburg

I thought playing for The Next Level was a great experience. One of the things I liked most about playing with The Next Level was playing at Three Rivers Stadium. I also thought it was a great experience when we played in the semi-finals against Sheridan. The crowd was loud and it was hard to concentrate. I heard our mothers cheering loud and clear which made us want to win even more. The thing I enjoyed the most was that I learned to play good baseball and was able to have fun with my teammates. We became really good friends and we met people from other areas. Thanks to all.

Marcus Haines
12 years old
Homewood

What I enjoyed most about The Next Level is how great the coaches and teammates got along. There was always laughter when we were all together. Coach Bart, Coach Tru, and Coach Bud are some of the best people you can meet. They taught us things such as discipline and accomplishment. The baseball team was a lot of hard work and determination. The three trophies we earned were worth every bit of it. I learned that sometimes you have to take a bigger step up. As Coach Tru would say, "Let's take it to The Next Level." I plan

on stepping higher with The Next Level.
   Joseph Foster
   12 years old
   East Hills

   Destiny is the word I believe best sums up The Next
Level. I remember times when it seemed as if we were going
to lose a game or take on a task that seemed too hard, Coach
Bud would calmly comment, "I'm not worried about nothing.
We're supposed to win, it's our destiny." When we were
behind in the championship series against the Tigers it was
destiny that brought us back to win what I believe were the
best little league games I ever saw. It was destiny that helped
us come back and score four runs against Morningside in the
last inning of the Mayor's Cup quarter final game. 'It is our
destiny,' became our rallying call whenever we needed that
extra effort to rise above astronomical odds and put together a
successful program such as The Next Level in just one year.
Sure we had our critics, but now that we've achieved success
we can go on and continue to organize the best youth organization on the East Coast and maybe in the U.S. The average
thinking folk think I have gone off the deep end when I tell
them what The Next Level is striving to do in Pittsburgh's
inner city. I am completely sane. We are just fed up with people telling us that we can't accomplish this or that for the
improvement of our communities. I say "Yes, we can!" Within
the next couple of years, this city and perhaps the nation will
know that The Next Level has made their presence known. We
are planning to put together something that the average person
would have looked at and said, "No, too big a hill to climb."
Our goals may seem as big as a mountain now, but The Next

Level already has a running start and our momentum will take
us to the pinnacle of our dreams. We know how far we want to
go. Do you?

Coach Bart Hanks